HOUDINI

HOUDINI

The Life and Times of The World's Greatest Magician

CHARLOTTE MONTAGUE

CHARTWELL
BOOKS

Look at
this life—all
mystery and
magic.

HARRY HOUDINI
(1874 – 1926)

CONTENTS

Introduction

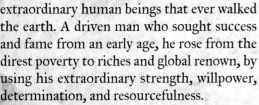

Harry Houdini was one of the most extraordinary human beings that ever walked the earth. A driven man who sought success and fame from an early age, he rose from the direst poverty to riches and global renown, by using his extraordinary strength, willpower, determination, and resourcefulness.

Houdini struggled for many years in the lower echelons of show-business. He worked his way across America in "dime museums," circuses, medicine shows, and burlesques,

Houdini in chains, 1899.

honing his act, learning from others, and scratching a living.

Throughout, he had the support of the love of his life, his wife Bess, who became part of his act, and for whom his love never wavered during the thirty-two years they were together. His family, too, were hugely important to him, especially his beloved mother who was never far from his thoughts.

As his father lay on his deathbed, he made Harry swear that he would always look after his mother, and he did. He sent her money for the remainder of her life, and installed her in his grand house in New York. When she finally passed away, Harry was devastated and it took some time for him to recover from it, if, indeed, he ever did.

Erik Weisz, as he was then known, was born into humble circumstances in Pest in Hungary, but his family's migration to the United States, along with millions of other immigrants, opened up undreamed of opportunities. The United States was a young country, recovering from a catastrophic civil war, but was about to become a world power.

Economic and technological development with the introduction of the motor car and the beginnings of mass media made it a land in which people could progress, regardless of class, ethnicity, or origins. Harry Houdini, a brash individual with complete confidence in his own abilities, embraced this shiny new world and used it to his own advantage.

Houdini was a consummate salesman, and manipulated the press in a way no one before him had ever done, using newspaper reports of his staged escape stunts in police stations as free advertising for the shows in which he performed. Houdini also had an innate understanding of how to market himself. This self-awareness, coupled with his ability to overcome pain, fear, and exhaustion, allowed him to transform himself from a second-rate turn on the vaudeville circuit into one of the most famous people on the planet.

He also seized on the new technology of aviation for publicity stunts. People were fascinated by the few dozen airmen of the early 1900s who took to the sky in flimsy craft. Houdini became one of this select band of heroes, learning to fly in Germany, before becoming the first person to make a powered flight in Australia. Aviation became a brief passion of Houdini's because once he had achieved that record, he rarely flew again. As usual, it was all about his ego, and about filling the theaters where he was performing.

History also favored Houdini. In the First World War millions of young men lost their lives, and the world was devastated by their loss. This led many ordinary people to reach out to the new "religion" of spiritualism to contact their deceased loved ones. It gave them a kind of solace. But, as séances and mediums proliferated, it became evident that many fakers were making considerable sums of money from other people's grief.

Houdini, who initially had retained an open mind about these attempts to contact the spirit world—he would have loved to have spoken to his mother, after all—was quickly disillusioned. He could see through the tricks of the mediums and he resolved to expose them as fraudulent. In his last years, he devoted his life to such exposés, using his stage shows, and writing books on the subject.

En route, he made enemies of just about everyone in spiritualist circles, including, most notably, his erstwhile friend, Sir Arthur Conan Doyle, the creator of the great detective, Sherlock Holmes. The feud between Houdini and Conan Doyle became poisonous—Conan Doyle believed implicitly and often very naively in spiritualism, and Houdini exposed fraudulent mediums wherever he went, splashing it all over the newspapers.

Houdini died tragically when he was only in his fifties, but this man with a huge ego and a relentless desire for success would be gratified to know that his name is still widely known—indeed, it is synonymous with

magic. His fame is undiminished, and his life and achievements still fascinate many around the world. He captured the imagination of the public like no other similar performer, and created a template for the modern magician. We still see it in the stunts of contemporary illusionists, and magicians, such as Dynamo, and David Blaine.

This book takes the reader through the highs and lows of Harry Houdini's life and career, describes his major illusions, and explains the secrets behind how they were done. It also features the lives of many people he encountered along the way. Above all, it is the story of Houdini's own courage and resolve to succeed as the world's greatest magician.

The World-Famed Mystifier poster, advertising Houdini's anti-spiritualist lecture tour in the early 1920s.

PART ONE

CAPTURING THE IMAGINATION

My brain is the key
that sets me free.

HARRY HOUDINI

THE LAND OF GOLDEN OPPORTUNITY

The world's most famous escape artist, Harry Houdini, was born Erik Weisz in a small apartment in the Jewish section of Pest, part of the newly united city of Budapest in Hungary. Although his actual birth date was March 24, 1874, Houdini would later always say April 6 was his date of birth, and he used it on official forms.

Ever the great dissembler, Houdini claimed sometimes to have been born in Appleton, Wisconsin, and not Budapest. This lie was particularly useful during the First World War, when the magician was trying to play the role of the great American patriot.

Houdini's parents, Mayer Samuel Weisz and Cecilia Steiner Weisz, had seven children. Apart from Erik, who was the third oldest, there was Armin (1863 – 85), who was a half-brother, by Rabbi Weisz's first marriage; Natan J. (1870 – 1927); Gottfried Vilmos (1872 – 1925); Ferencz Dezso (1876 – 1945); Leopold D. (1879 – 1962); and Carrie Gladys (1882 – 1959).

THE NEW WORLD

Like millions of other Europeans searching for a better life, Mayer Samuel Weisz decided to chance his luck in the United States. Cecilia's mother and her two sisters also emigrated to America. The pregnant Cecilia, and the four children they had at this point followed later, arriving in New York City on July 3, 1878, having traveled on the steamship, the SS *Frisia*.

Cecilia paid thirty dollars for her steerage class ticket, where they huddled together like cattle, with around 620 other hope-filled émigrés. Fortunately, however, the voyage was not as bad as it could have been. The ship was less than half full.

At the Castle Garden immigration building, Battery Park, Manhattan, they were not only welcomed to their new country, they were also allocated new names—English versions of their existing ones. Thus, Armin was re-named Herman, the 8-year-old Natan became Nathan, 6-year-old Gottfried Vilmos became William, and Ferencz Dezso became Theodore, later nicknamed "Dash." As for Erik, he became Ehrich, known at home as "Ehrie." The family name of Weisz was translated to Weiss.

APPLETON, WISCONSIN

After a brief stay in New York, the family relocated to the open spaces of Appleton, Wisconsin, which had only been incorporated as a village twenty-five years previously in 1853. Things were still fairly backward there. Livestock roamed the few streets, it would be several years before a proper sewage system was installed, and longer still before there was a municipal water supply. But it was a town on the up.

Lawrence University, only the second co-educational college in the United States, had been founded there in 1847, and an opera house was planned. The town was a very different proposition to New York, with its crowded and cramped streets. Appleton had parks, woods, and lots of open spaces for children to roam in.

MAYER SAMUEL AND CECILIA WEISZ

Mayer Samuel Weisz (1829 – 92) was a former soap-maker who had studied and gained several degrees. A scholar and a poet, he practiced German Reform Judaism, a Jewish denomination that had its origins in nineteenth-century Germany.

He spoke German and Hebrew, as well as his native Hungarian, and had been married before meeting Houdini's mother. When Mayer Samuel met Cecilia Steiner (1841 – 1913), he was a widower. His first wife died giving birth to their son Armin.

Following his first wife's death, he moved from the countryside into the city. It is said that a friend of his was in love with Cecilia Steiner but, too shy to declare his love, he asked Mayer Samuel to intercede for him. Mayer Samuel already knew Cecilia's mother Hannah (c. 1821 – 87) and her three daughters, and agreed to visit the girl's family in their small apartment on his friend's behalf.

Unfortunately for the friend, however, as Mayer Samuel made an impassioned plea on his behalf, he realized that he had fallen in love with this pretty young girl, twelve years his junior. Cecilia felt the same way, and marriage ensued in 1863, after he had sent her a written proposal of marriage.

DAVID HAMMEL

David Hammel (1838 – 1928) was born in Prussia, in modern-day Germany, and emigrated, at the age of 14, to the United States along with many other Germans in 1852. Settling first in Syracuse, New York, he moved to Hamilton, Ontario in Canada, where he established a business manufacturing and selling staves for flour barrels.

Moving to Wisconsin, he became a horse and cattle trader and was proprietor of a stable in Appleton. He became a Democratic politician and won election to the Wisconsin State Assembly where he served in 1876 and 1877. He also owned a lumberyard, a mill, and a wheat farm.

He served two terms as mayor of Appleton in 1900 – 03 and 1906 – 07. But with his health beginning to fail, he moved to Chicago, where he had family. He died there of a stroke in 1928, at the age of 89.

David Hammel, mayor of Appleton.

RABBI WEISS

One of the reasons they settled in Appleton, was Mayer Samuel's acquaintance with one of the town's most successful business people, David Hammel. When the Weiss family arrived in Appleton, Mayer Samuel was told by Hammel that Appleton needed a rabbi. Deciding it was just the role for him, the ever-resourceful Mayer Samuel accepted the job.

He conducted his services in a makeshift temple, earning $750 a year. The local Jewish population was delighted to have a new rabbi. They hoped that he would stay on in the position, even though Rabbi Weiss was still unable to speak English, and conducted all his services in German.

THE CIRCUS COMES TO TOWN

When Ehrich was 7 years old, he enjoyed the first glimpse of his future life when a circus came to Appleton. The performance of a tightrope walker made a deep and lasting impression upon the boy.

The man in bright red tights, whose name was Jean Weitzman, climbed to a small platform about twenty feet above the floor of the circus tent, and walked across a wire drawn taut between two poles. He used another long pole to maintain his balance while keeping his center of gravity low. Working without the luxury of a safety net, a fall would have resulted in certain death.

Young Ehrich was enthralled by the spectacle and the idea of someone risking his life for entertainment. His excitement was all the greater when Weitzman concluded his act by hanging from the high wire by his teeth, a phenomenal feat of strength and bravery.

STAYING ONE STEP AHEAD

In 1879, Cecilia gave birth to yet another boy, Leopold, but finally a daughter, Carrie Gladys, arrived in 1882. She would be rendered virtually blind by a childhood accident. That same year, the Weiss family officially became American citizens, but trouble was looming.

Mayer's congregation became dissatisfied with his Old World services conducted in German. They wanted the services to be in English, and more up-to-date. He was fired, as Houdini later explained:

One morning my father awoke to find himself thrown upon the world, his long locks of hair having silvered in service, with seven children to feed, without a position, and without any visible means of support. We thereon moved to Milwaukee, Wis., where such hardships and hunger so became our lot that the less said on the subject the better.

It was an unsettled time for the Weiss family. Having arrived in Milwaukee in 1882, they moved address four times in four years, perhaps staying one step ahead of the rent collector. To bring in the money to feed the family the boys all found work. Ehrich and Theo were shoe-shine boys, and sold newspapers.

BENDING OVER BACKWARD

A friend back in Appleton decided to put on a circus in a field in Appleton's 6th Ward, charging five cents entry. Determined to perform, Ehrich cajoled his mother into knitting long red stockings for him, mimicking the tights that his hero, Jean Weitzman, had worn as he made his way across the high wire.

On October 28, 1883, 9-year-old trapeze artist, "Ehrich the Prince of the Air," swung from ropes and performed acrobatics at the Appleton circus. It was a date marked by Houdini as his public debut in show business. He was paid thirty-five cents for his performance and later said:

My training as a contortionist was, of course, the first step toward my present occupation of escaping from strait-jackets and chains, for it is chiefly through my ability to twist my body and dislocate my joints, together with abnormal expansion and contraction powers, which renders me independent of the tightest bonds. Thus, to any young man who has in

mind a career similar to mine, I would say: First try bending over backward and picking up a pin with your teeth from the floor ... That was my first stunt.

Meanwhile, he was absorbed by all the books that he found in his father's library, anything from Bible tales to Talmudic legends. In Appleton, he had developed an interest in magic when he bought a ten-cent pamphlet on the subject by a magician named Hoffman. In Milwaukee he became a habitué of the public library.

THE WAY AHEAD

Ehrich had also been fascinated with locks since he was very young. In Appleton, he had spent a lot of his free time at Hanauer's Hardware Store, playing with the locks the store sold. He also practiced on locks at home, using a small buttonhook to open the drawers, cabinets, and closets. Locally he had been notorious as the boy who had unlocked

Ehrich Weiss in 1882.

all the shop doors on College Avenue in Appleton.

While the family were enduring particularly hard times in Milwaukee, he was sent back to Appleton, at age 11, to start an apprenticeship with Mr. Hanauer. On one occasion, using a piece of piano wire, he unpicked a lock on a pair of handcuffs for the sheriff whose key had broken. This was an incident that pointed the way ahead to the path he would later choose, as he explained:

> *The very manner in which I then picked the lock of the handcuff contained the basic principle which I employed in opening handcuffs all over the world. Not with a duplicate key, which seems to have been the only way others had of duplicating my performance.*

Unfortunately, Ehrich missed home, and soon gave up his apprenticeship in Appleton, returning to his family in Milwaukee.

MAGICAL CONNECTIONS

Mayer Samuel sometimes took Ehrich to watch magic performances. When "Dr. Lynn" came to Milwaukee during his US tour, they went to see him. Needless to say, Ehrich, who spent all his spare time reading about magic, was entranced by the sight of a real live stage magician cutting off his assistant's head and limbs, and then restoring them.

Mayer Samuel had some other magical connections too. His first wife was the cousin of the greatest magician of his time, Compars Herrmann (1816 – 87). Such experiences and stories must have left a deep impression on young Ehrich, who started performing simple magic tricks at the Litt Museum in Milwaukee.

Meanwhile, the family continued to struggle. Unable to secure another position, Mayer Samuel tried to earn money teaching Hebrew, but it never brought in much in the way of funds. The Hebrew Relief Society bailed the family out on a number of occasions, providing much-needed cash for essentials such as coal and food.

DR. LYNN

"Dr. Lynn" was born Hugh Washington Simmons (1831 – 99) in either England or Australia. He joined the British Navy but left in 1861, to launch a career as a professional magician in Australia, billing himself as "Professor Simmons, the Great Basilicothaumaturgist."

He performed in the Far East and Europe before arriving in San Francisco in 1863, where he changed his name to "Dr. Lynn." He was the first person in the west to perform a famous trick known as the "Japanese Butterfly." He claimed to have encountered the trick while traveling in Japan prior to arriving in the United States. The Japanese Butterfly is an illusion in which butterflies hover over and flutter at the end of a fan.

In the 1870s, he created a puppet illusion called "Living Marionettes," in which he used the magic technique of Black Art, whereby a black background is used to conceal anything black that is in front of it. He also created a trick he named "Palingenesia," which involved the apparent cutting-off of limbs and the head. It was this trick that so impressed young Ehrich Weiss.

A skilful and innovative performer, his catchphrase was "That's how it's done!" Dr. Lynn was loved for his wonderful on-stage patter. He cracked jokes, told stories, and made fools of the audience members who volunteered to help him in his tricks. He retired in 1895 but when it was learned that he had fallen on hard times, other performers staged benefit concerts for him. He died in 1899, at the age of 68. Houdini later purchased his props from his son, J. Wellesley Lynn, who was a conjurer and ventriloquist between 1900 and 1920.

Dr. Lynn was a man who liked to keep on the move, and used many different names during his travels. He was also known as John Simmons, a.k.a. Washington Blythe, a.k.a. Washington Simmons, a.k.a. Hugh Washington Lynn, a.k.a Hugh Simmons Lynn, a.k.a Dr. H.S. Lynn. The decapitation trick (above) was just one of many illusions he pioneered.

COMPARS HERRMANN

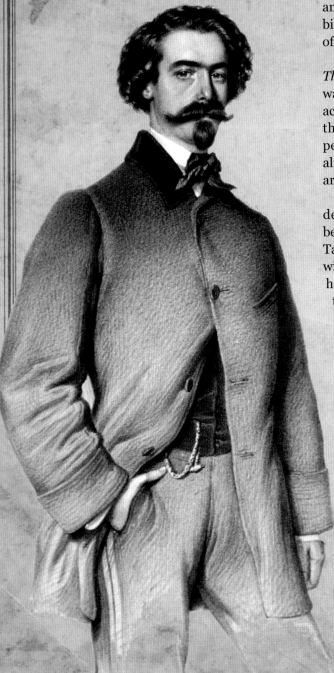

The German magician Carl "Compars" Herrmann (1816 – 87) was a member of a magic-loving family. His father Samuel was a doctor, but magic is said to have been his hobby. Legend has it that Samuel was a favorite performer of the Sultan of Turkey who often paid for him to entertain at his court. He taught Carl his magic tricks, and he went on to become a professional magician.

Carl spent much of his time at the theater of the great French magician, Jean Eugène Robert-Houdin (1805 – 71), the man from whom Houdini would later take his name. He quietly bought a number of Robert-Houdin's tricks and illusions from the magician's assistant, and set out on a tour, starting in England. He billed himself as "The Premier Prestidigitateur of France and the First Professor of Magic."

In 1848, his performances were praised in *The Illustrated London News*. The periodical was unaware, of course, that the tricks were actually the creations of Robert-Houdin. When the great man himself came to London to perform, he was fuming that his tricks had already been debuted in the city before he even arrived.

Herrmann performed across Europe, developing striking sleight-of-hand skills, before returning to his parents' house in Paris. Taking his eight-year-old brother Alexander with him, he next left for St. Petersburg, where he performed before Czar Nicholas I. The two traveled to America several times, and began to earn good money from the full houses they attracted.

When the brothers went their separate ways, Carl continued touring the capitals of Europe before retiring in the early 1870s, but the financial panic of 1873 forced him to return to performing. He died in June 1887 at the age of 71. Alexander continued performing until his own death in 1896. However, that was not quite the end of the Herrmanns. Alexander's wife Adelaide Herrmann (1853 – 1932) became the first well-known woman magician, performing in vaudeville under the name "The Queen of Magic."

CHAPTER 2

METAMORPHOSIS

In December 1885, tragedy struck when Herman, Mayer Samuel's 22-year-old son from his first marriage, died in New York of tuberculosis. It hit him very badly, and he became ill and took to his bed. He was touched, however, by Ehrich offering him all the money he had saved—the princely sum of ten dollars—to help pay for his half-brother's funeral.

For months, Mayer Samuel was depressed by the death of his son, but he called Ehrich to his bedside on his twelfth birthday. He took his copy of the Torah and made Ehrich promise on it that he would look after his mother in her old age. He solemnly promised, and it was an oath he would keep until his mother's death.

Ehrich realized that the only way he could be of help was to run away and seek his fortune. It would be one less mouth for his parents to feed, after all. He packed a small bag with some books, his trusty lock-pick, and a deck of cards, before joining up with a column of the United States Cavalry heading westward. He aimed to earn money by shining the troopers' boots.

THE SCRUFFY URCHIN

At Delavan, Wisconsin, the column stopped for the night at the town's armory where Ehrich bumped into a local boy named Al Flitcroft. Ehrich, calling himself Harry White ("Harry" being an evolution of his pet name "Ehrie"), told Al his story and when he mentioned he was hungry, the other boy suggested that he come back to his house to eat. Al's mother Hannah immediately took a liking to the scruffy urchin her son brought home.

He was fed and washed, and his clothes were mended, and when the cavalry set off the next day, Mrs. Flitcroft and her husband insisted that Harry should remain with them. He began a search for work, jumping on a freight train and traveling to the nearby city of Beloit, Wisconsin.

The effort was all hopeless, though. A few days after he left, he was forced to walk the twenty-five miles back again to Delavan. Harry never forgot the kindness shown him by the Flitcrofts. Later in life, he often sent Al's mother presents from wherever he was in the world, and made a point of visiting her in her final days as she lay dying.

UNPAID RENT AND NO COAL

Meanwhile, back home things were no better. Mayer Samuel decided to see if his prospects would be improved in New York. Leaving Cecilia and the children behind, he headed east. At some point in 1887, Ehrich joined him there. The two found lodgings at Mrs. Loffler's boarding house at 244 East 79th Street in Manhattan.

Mayer Samuel was still trying to make ends meet by teaching Hebrew, but he would never earn enough money from that to enable him to pay for Cecilia and the children to travel to New York. Ehrich, however, found work as a messenger boy.

The following year, he was able to welcome his mother and siblings to the second-story, cold-water apartment that he and his father were now renting, at 227 East 75th Street. Things remained tough, however, and their first winter in New York was worrying, with unpaid rent, and no coal to heat the apartment.

RICHTER'S NECKTIE COMPANY

Ehrich's resourcefulness shone through when

Ehrich Weiss in 1890, wearing medals he won as a member of the Pastime Athletic Club track team in New York.

he lost his messenger-boy job. He applied for a position at Richter's Necktie Company, situated on Broadway. When Ehrich turned up at the company's headquarters, he found a long line of men who were also responding to the sign that said "Assistant necktie cutter wanted."

Ehrich removed the sign and announced to the waiting hopefuls that the position had already been filled. The waiting men walked off, and Ehrich strode into the building and got the job.

Now age 17, Ehrich was taking part in gymnastics and boxing, fighting on one occasion in the Amateur Athletic Union's championship. But he fell ill and failed to make the finals, although he had already beaten the eventual winner of the championship. Long-distance running was another passion. At the age of 18, he set a new record for the Central Park run. He was supremely fit and exceptionally strong.

ERIC THE GREAT

The money that Ehrich and his brothers were bringing in from their various jobs brought a slight improvement in the Weiss family fortunes. In 1890 they moved to a larger apartment at 305 East 69th Street. Ehrich, meanwhile, was honing his magic skills although his lack of money meant that he was limited to card or coin tricks.

He had found a friend who shared his interest in magic, however. Jacob Hyman also worked at Richter's, and he and Ehrich practiced together, sharing knowledge and tips. When Ehrich went to see a magic performance with friends, he always insisted that he knew exactly how the person on stage had done his tricks.

They became irritated with him and suggested that if he knew so much, perhaps he should go on stage himself. Thus, he began to perform his card and coin tricks at various venues, sometimes billing himself as "Eric the Great."

THE ART OF MAGIC

Around this time, he made one of the most important discoveries of his life. He bought a book—*Memoirs of Robert-Houdin, Ambassador, Author and Conjurer, Written by Himself*. Ehrich devoured the book in one sitting, and it had a profound impact upon him:

> *My interest in conjuring and magic and my enthusiasm for Robert-Houdin came into existence simultaneously. From the moment that I began to study the art, he became my guide and hero. I accepted his writings as my text-book and my gospel ... To my unsophisticated mind, his Memoirs gave to the profession a dignity worth attaining at the cost of earnest, life-long effort.*

To Robert-Houdin, a magician was an actor, playing the part of someone with extraordinary, supernatural powers. It is probably no coincidence, therefore, that Ehrich began studying acting at the Edwin Forrest Amateur Dramatic Association on Columbia Street in New York.

BECOMING HARRY HOUDINI

It was from Robert-Houdin's name that Ehrich devised his stage-name. His friend Jacob Hyman with whom he sometimes performed in magical acts, insisted that if he added "I" to the Houdin part of the great magician's name, it would mean "like Houdin" in French. He was wrong, of course, but the idea appealed to Ehrich. Thus, "Ehrie" was once again transformed into "Harry," and "Harry Houdini" was born.

HUBER'S DIME MUSEUM

On April 3, 1891—a momentous day—Ehrich resigned his position at Richter's, and became Harry Houdini on a full-time basis. He and Hyman launched their new act, The Brothers Houdini, in the fall of 1891, performing fairly simple tricks. It was hard to find bookings, though, forcing Harry to sometimes go out on his own.

Eventually, in the spring of 1892, he landed an engagement at Huber's Dime Museum which was situated on 14th Street. Several circus sideshow acts performed there, and Harry Houdini did card tricks for people visiting the museum.

INSIDE KNOWLEDGE

The best thing about this job was that he was introduced to George Dexter who was the museum's manager and also acted as master of ceremonies at performances. With his talent for talking, it was a role he was made for. He directed visitors around the dime museum introducing each sideshow performer in serious rhetorical tones. More importantly, however, George Dexter was an expert at rope-tie escapes. He passed on to Harry some invaluable inside knowledge in the secret art of escaping.

By mid 1892, Harry and Jacob Hyman had fallen out. Hyman was replaced in the partnership by Harry's younger brother Theo, who brought to the act the twenty-six dollars he had earned while working. It was still hard to get bookings, however, and in the meantime Harry did anything to earn money. Working at Huber's Dime Museum he was giving some twenty performances a day.

THE FREAK SHOW

Dime museums were about as low as you could go in show business. They were usually large open rooms in which long stages had been erected. The "curio halls," as they were known, were partitioned off so that several acts could perform at any one time.

The "freak show" was the main attraction of most dime museums. All physically unusual human life was here. The performers were mainly biological rarities, and people came to stare, and be shocked by the large, the small, the fat, the thin, the armless, the legless, the "pinheads," the albinos, the tattooed, the hairy, and the downright scary. Harry Houdini fell under the category of "novelty acts," which included snake charmers,

JEAN EUGÈNE ROBERT-HOUDIN

Justifiably, Jean Eugène Robert-Houdin (1805 – 71) is known as "the father of modern magic." His achievements in the art of magic are legion and his influence on the magicians of the twentieth century is inestimable. From a French clock-making family, he practiced magic initially as a hobby, entertaining friends with sleight-of-hand tricks.

His father had been a watchmaker and, at 24 years old, Robert-Houdin started his own clock-making business in Paris. He spent his spare time watching magic performances and became friends with a number of amateur and professional magicians. He was particular friends with Louis Comte (1788 – 1859), who owned his own theater and performed for three French kings, and a magician named Philippe who used electricity in his act.

He began to build mechanical figures as well as clocks, and a small automaton, constructed for the Universal Exposition in Paris, 1839, was bought for several thousand francs by the great American impresario, P.T. Barnum (1810 – 91). This money enabled him to complete work on a magical theater he was building at the 200-seater Palais Royal.

Robert-Houdin launched theatrical performances entitled *Soirées Fantastiques* at the theater in July 1845. The shows did not catapult him immediately to riches and fame, but they did allow him to hone his magic craft, develop his gift for presentation, and introduce weird contraptions that brought people flooding in.

He performed mind-reading tricks such as "Second Sight" and used a device that appeared to make his son float in mid-air in an illusion named "Suspension by Ether." His most famous illusion was "The Marvelous Orange Tree" in which fruit magically grow on a tree on the stage. He used electricity in his act and, instead of the customary wizard's garb, he dressed in evening attire, setting a trend that many magicians follow to this day.

As his fame spread, he performed throughout Europe in front of packed houses. He eventually retired in 1855. He moved to a farm outside Blois, the town of his birth, and devoted the remainder of his life to publishing the *Memoirs of Robert-Houdin*, and writing books on magic. He died in 1871, at the age of 65.

jugglers, sword-swallowers, hypnotists, and mesmerists. All the performers were collectively bracketed together as "freaks of nature."

Times were very hard, and at home, Mayer Samuel was very ill, having recently been operated on for cancer. He returned from hospital, faded away, and finally died. Harry was now the head of the family, and he felt the pressure of having to keep the promise he had made to his father about taking good care of his mother.

CHICAGO WORLD'S FAIR

The World's Columbian Exposition was a world's fair held in Chicago in 1893 to celebrate the 400th anniversary of the arrival of Christopher Columbus in the New World in 1492. The Houdini brothers performed at the fair. Harry played the part of a dark-skinned yogi with copious amounts of sales patter, and Theo—now known to the Weiss family as "Dash"—took on the role of eastern musician. One of the illusions they performed was based on Robert-Houdin's "Marvelous Orange Tree."

They were in Chicago because of a 23-year-old man named Sol Bloom (1870 – 1949). An entertainment impresario and sheet music publisher from Chicago, Bloom had an imagination as vivid as P.T. Barnum's. He was in charge of developing the mile-long Midway Plaisance at the fair.

FIRE-EATERS AND BELLY DANCERS

The Midway Plaisance was a fringe show far removed from the grandeur of the more conservative official exposition. With Sol Bloom's vision and entertainment skills, he scrapped the original plans for an educational journey through the evolution of humankind. Instead he transformed the show into a street-wise spectacle offering enticing games and exhibitions featuring fire-eaters, belly dancers, and acts like the Houdini Brothers.

Bloom was a songwriter and theater manager who became known for penning the

song that became the anthem of the Hoochy-Koochy dance craze that swept America. He was also a magician. Practitioners of the magic arts made a beeline to Chicago when they found out he had been put in charge.

THE KEY TO SUCCESS

The Houdinis played the fairgrounds for around a month, after which Theo went back to New York and Harry found an engagement at another dime museum, Kohl and Middleton's in Chicago. He had played there before and had been very impressed by one particular sideshow act—Mattie Lee Price.

Miss Price was a woman who, despite being a mere 90 pounds in weight, was seemingly able to perform feats of strength and endurance way beyond her capabilities. Houdini knew how she did them, of course, but what was of particular interest to him was the way her husband and manager presented her act. The man was a phenomenal salesman with a silver tongue, and a real talent for showmanship. He was an integral part of the act.

When Houdini caught up with Mattie Lee Price for the second time, however, her husband had moved on. He had been replaced as presenter by Mattie's new lover, who was not possessed of the same verbal marketing skills. Mattie's star had fallen, and she was nowhere near as popular. Houdini learned from this that good presentation and communication with the audience was key to the success of any entertainment show. He later wrote:

> *This was one of the most positive demonstrations I have ever seen of the fact that showmanship is the largest factor in putting an act over. Miss Price was a marvelous performer, but without her husband-lecturer she was no longer a drawing card and ... her act was no longer even entertaining.*

The Secrets of Houdini
Metamorphosis

Metamorphosis is a trick invented by the English stage magician John Nevil Maskelyne (1839 – 1917), and first performed as early as 1865. Other magicians performed it too, but in Houdini's act a man and a woman were featured—once Houdini's wife Bess had joined the show. This made it very special, and absolutely amazing.

In the trick, Houdini's hands were fastened behind his back and he was placed in a large bag that was knotted closed at the top. He was then helped to step into a large trunk which was not only locked but also strapped shut. This box was then placed inside a cabinet.

Bess then stepped forward, closed the curtain around the cabinet and herself, and clapped her hands three times. As she clapped the third time, Houdini himself pulled back the curtain and Bess was gone. The box was then flung open and there, inside the bag—knots and ties unbroken—was Bess, her hands bound in exactly the same way as Houdini's had been. It was quick, it was sharp, and it was masterful.

HOW DID HE DO IT?

The restraints on Houdini's wrists hold the answer to the whole escape. The knots were slip-knots that could be loosened easily, and tightened again later. He freed himself from the slip-knots quickly, as soon as the bag was being pulled over his head. Inside the sack, the rope ran through a series of eyelets around the upper edge of the bag. The rope securing the sack was, therefore, both inside and outside the bag.

All Houdini had to do was pull on the rope from inside the sack to undo it. The trunk itself had a fake rear panel, with a secret release on the inside. When the curtain closed, Houdini quickly triggered the release mechanism, and got out of the box. In fact, the handclaps the audience heard were not from Bess, but from Houdini himself.

During the clapping, Bess was busy climbing into the sack, and pulling the rope tight again from the inside. She got into the trunk through the open panel, pulled it closed, and tightened up the loosened wrist restraints with the slip-knots.

Houdini, at this point, had already appeared from behind the curtain. The audience were still gasping with surprise, as he undid the fake rope bindings that apparently held the outside of the trunk firmly closed. He then dramatically flung open the lid of the trunk to reveal his trussed-up wife. It was an astounding trick that was the sensational centerpiece of the show.

(Facing page) The Houdinis with the trunk and curtained cabinet used in the Metamorphosis escape. The picture is probably taken in 1895 at the same time as the photos used to create the Houdinis' first Metamorphosis poster (above).

CHAPTER 3

The Value of Staging a Stunt

Houdini was learning all the time at this early point of his career. Another valuable lesson came from an incident involving an experienced old showman called Risey. He had been publicly insulting the Houdini Brothers' performances at the Vacca Theater, particularly their signature stunt "Metamorphosis."

Risey claimed that an act called the Davenport Brothers had performed the trick far better twenty years previously. The argument between Risey and Houdini became acrimonious, and the theater owner suggested that Risey should be locked in the box to show how the trick was done. Houdini offered to give him $100 if he could replicate it.

On the night of the test the theater was packed. Houdini and Theo were so confident that Risey would not get out of the trunk that they did not even bother to tie his hands behind his back. He climbed into the sack and was locked in the trunk, before the curtain was pulled around it.

Five minutes later, muffled shouts of "Help!" could be heard from inside the trunk behind the curtain. Harry and Theo leapt to the box, opening it and cutting the binding ropes. A breathless Risey emerged from the sack, perspiring.

A Profit in Collusion

It is almost certain that Houdini and Risey colluded together in the whole caper to provide publicity for the act. Houdini now fully appreciated the value of staging a stunt. The drama and controversy along with the financial inducement all added to the excitement generated by such a challenge. Publicity stunts became the stuff of Houdini's act for the rest of his career, and were a major contributory factor in his future fame and celebrity.

The following day Harry Houdini married Wilhelmina Beatrice (Bess) Rahner. She replaced Theo on stage in the magic show, making Metamorphosis an even more astounding transformation.

Playing the Circuit

On the road, Houdini and his new partner Bess played all kinds of small venues, sharing the bill with such acts as Unthan, the Legless Wonder; Big Alice, the Fat Lady; and Blue Eagle, a native American who demonstrated how strong his skull was by smashing wooden boards on it.

It was tough being a performer in those days. If an act was going down badly with the audience, the performer was dragged offstage with a long hook that grabbed him or her by the neck. Bess was not exactly what an audience wanted to see. She later explained that her slimline figure did not help. It was a time when fuller figures were fashionable. Managers of theaters, she said, "looked askance at my uncompromising flatness."

But they got on with it, Harry rarely sleeping little more than four hours a night, rising at five and going shopping for food. He would spend the day raising a little extra cash by doing card tricks and playing cards in bars. It was a depressing existence, and Bess often despaired of them ever being successful.

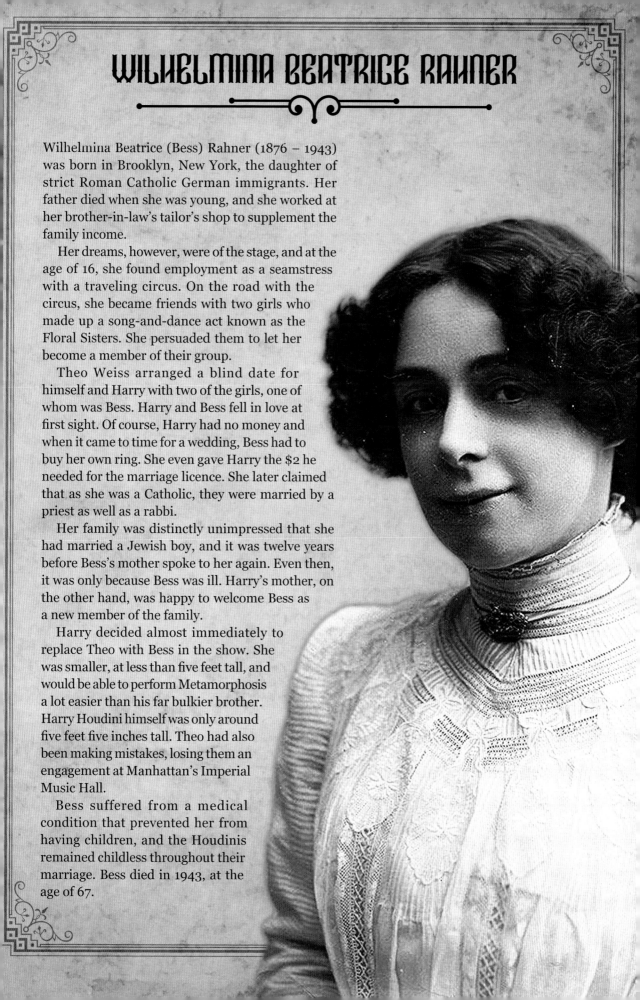

WILHELMINA BEATRICE RAHNER

Wilhelmina Beatrice (Bess) Rahner (1876 – 1943) was born in Brooklyn, New York, the daughter of strict Roman Catholic German immigrants. Her father died when she was young, and she worked at her brother-in-law's tailor's shop to supplement the family income.

Her dreams, however, were of the stage, and at the age of 16, she found employment as a seamstress with a traveling circus. On the road with the circus, she became friends with two girls who made up a song-and-dance act known as the Floral Sisters. She persuaded them to let her become a member of their group.

Theo Weiss arranged a blind date for himself and Harry with two of the girls, one of whom was Bess. Harry and Bess fell in love at first sight. Of course, Harry had no money and when it came to time for a wedding, Bess had to buy her own ring. She even gave Harry the $2 he needed for the marriage licence. She later claimed that as she was a Catholic, they were married by a priest as well as a rabbi.

Her family was distinctly unimpressed that she had married a Jewish boy, and it was twelve years before Bess's mother spoke to her again. Even then, it was only because Bess was ill. Harry's mother, on the other hand, was happy to welcome Bess as a new member of the family.

Harry decided almost immediately to replace Theo with Bess in the show. She was smaller, at less than five feet tall, and would be able to perform Metamorphosis a lot easier than his far bulkier brother. Harry Houdini himself was only around five feet five inches tall. Theo had also been making mistakes, losing them an engagement at Manhattan's Imperial Music Hall.

Bess suffered from a medical condition that prevented her from having children, and the Houdinis remained childless throughout their marriage. Bess died in 1943, at the age of 67.

The East Indian Needle Trick

A member of a Japanese balancing act taught Houdini how to pull off the trick of appearing to swallow things and then regurgitate them. It must have been around this time that he devised or learned "The East Indian Needle Trick."

It had been performed since at least 1820, when a Hindu magician named Ramo Samee (? – 1850) used it in his act. Houdini always asked a member of the audience to come up onstage to act as witness. They were asked to inspect fifty to a hundred loose needles and a separate six-foot length of thread. The witness was also instructed to examine the magician's mouth, to ensure nothing was hidden there.

Houdini began to swallow the needles and the thread, washing them down with a glass of water. He then regurgitated them, pulling the thread from his mouth with all the needles attached one by one at intervals along its length. He amazed audiences with this trick for the entirety of his career.

HOW DID HE DO IT?

The secret of the needle trick was revealed by Houdini's prop-maker, R.D. Adams. Houdini placed a second unrevealed length of thread with the needles already threaded on it, between his cheek and his teeth. Knots on the thread kept the needles in place on the thread. The thread was then rolled up into a flattened packet shape.

When Houdini opened his mouth for the inspection, he used his fingers to spread his upper and lower lips away from his gums. As he pulled his cheeks apart, he hid the packet under one of his fingers. If the audience member was particularly diligent and insisted on him removing his fingers, Houdini simply slipped the packet under his tongue.

He then placed the unthreaded needles and the thread on his tongue and pretended to swallow them as he drank the water. But he was really spitting them out into the glass, leaving enough water in the glass, so that they were obscured by the reflection.

If the volunteer got too close to him, he merely put the loose needles under his tongue. At the end of the trick, he would take another drink, spit the needles into the glass and hand it to an assistant.

Houdini performing The East Indian Needle Trick.

At one point she even quit the act, leaving Harry to complete the dates they had agreed to on his own. But she returned and they were engaged for twenty-six weeks by the Welsh Brothers Circus, living in cramped conditions in a tiny partitioned section of a train carriage.

SIDESHOW MULTITASKING

Working with the circus, however, they were expected not only to perform their own act, but to fill-in and multitask around the sideshows. Harry manned the Punch and Judy stall and anything else that was short-staffed, while Bess did mind-reading.

At one point, Houdini acted as a stand-in for "Projea, the Wild Man of Mexico." He messed up his hair, painted his face, donned a caveman outfit, and rattled the bars of his cage to frighten the circus-goers. Bess employed her skills as a singer and a dancer in their own act, the high point of which was the sensational Metamorphosis.

THE ARMLESS MAN

All the time Houdini was learning, even from the circus freaks. From an armless man, he learned how to use his toes, instead of his fingers. It was a skill that later stood him in good stead in escape stunts when his hands were bound or cuffed.

The circus engagement was a profitable one for the Houdinis. They were able to bank everything they earned, all except the $12 they sent to Houdini's mother every week.

Houdini also had enough money to invest in "The American Gaiety Girls Burlesque Co.," a traveling troupe of chorus girls and entertainers of whom Harry Newman, one of Houdini's cousins, was the owner. Houdini and another partner, Fred Harvey of Paterson, New Jersey, paid $400 to become co-owners of the show itself and all its theatrical clothing, according to the bill of sale registered with the authorities.

THE AMERICAN GAIETY GIRLS BURLESQUE CO.

When the circus engagement ended, the Houdinis toured the north-east until the end of January 1896, and then moved into New England. In February, Houdini improvised when they briefly teamed up with a burlesque company, billing himself as "Professor Morat," purportedly a hypnotist from Europe.

"Professor Morat" hypnotized members of the audience to believe they could feel no pain, and then invited other spectators to stick needles in them. It was a fairly run-of-the-mill hypnotist act, people were put into trances, and then performed ridiculous tasks.

In March 1896, Houdini joined financial forces with the American Gaiety Girls, and his fellow investors. Keen to attract bigger crowds, they introduced a show-stopping lady wrestler, May Morgan, to the show. May was prepared to take on all-comers from the local male volunteers, up to 122 pounds. She was also Fred Harvey's wife.

Disaster struck when the troupe was playing Woonsocket, Rhode Island, in April 1896. Although the show played to packed houses, according to the reviews, Houdini and Harry Newman discovered that Fred Harvey and his wife were draining the money from the box office to such an extent that the group could not be paid. It was front page news in Woonsocket.

MARCO THE MAGICIAN

The American Gaiety Girls venture ended in disarray. The show disbanded, and both Fred and May Harvey were jailed for fraud. Harry Newman continued as a show business manager, but Houdini gave up being an entrepreneur. Having lost all their money and feeling betrayed by the world, he and Bess decided to focus on performing.

They traveled to Boston at the end of May 1896, where they joined another entertainment show, to work with "Marco the Magician." In reality, Marco was

BURLESQUE

The word burlesque derives from the Italian *burlesco* which is derived in turn from the Italian word for a joke or mockery—*burla*. In the theater it tends to mean extravaganza, and was particularly in use in English theaters between the 1830s and 1890s.

It was normally musical theater parody in which a well-known opera, play, or ballet, was adapted into a comic play often rendered slightly risqué. Burlesque in the United States began about 1840 and was an offshoot of the English version. Burlesque shows staged in New York featured songs and bawdy comic sketches performed by comedians, singers, magicians and/or acrobats, and chorus numbers often in the style of the English burlesque, parodying a play or satirizing current politics. The entertainment usually concluded with an exotic dancer or occasionally a boxing or wrestling match. English burlesque died out at the end of the nineteenth century, but the American version continued to draw audiences.

As time passed, however, the shows featured increasingly titillating content, focusing most often on female nudity. Gradually, burlesque evolved into striptease, and by 1932, strippers such as Gypsy Rose Lee (1911 – 70), and Blaze Starr (1932 – 2015), had supplanted the singers and magicians.

By the end of the 1930s, a burlesque show featured as many as half a dozen strippers, a couple of comedians, and a master of ceremonies. It finally faded away in the 1970s, but has made something of a comeback in recent years with performers such as Dita Von Teese (a.k.a. Heather Renée Sweet, born 1972), an American burlesque dancer, vedette, model, costume designer, entrepreneur, and occasional actress.

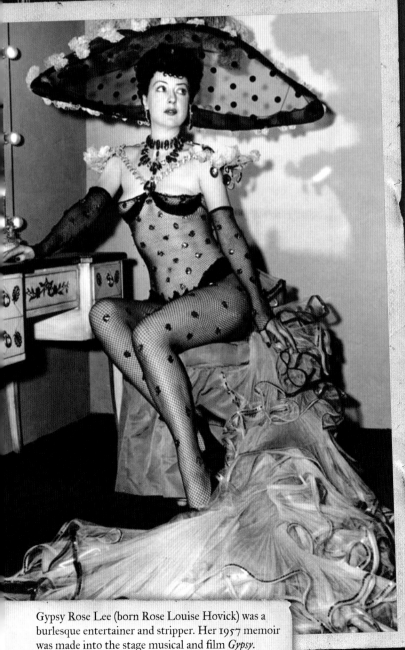

Gypsy Rose Lee (born Rose Louise Hovick) was a burlesque entertainer and stripper. Her 1957 memoir was made into the stage musical and film *Gypsy*.

Edward J. Dooley, a church organist from Connecticut, whose performances were based on those of his idol, Alexander Herrmann, the most famous living magician at the time.

Houdini looked on him as a father figure, and Marco introduced Houdini as his son-in-law, and his successor. It all ended badly again, however, when Marco ran out of money while they were touring in the Canadian Maritime Provinces.

HANDCUFF ESCAPES

Around this time, Houdini became intensely interested in a type of escape that would become a major part of his act—the handcuff escape. It began as an added complication to the Metamorphosis stunt, but evolved into a means of advance marketing for his performances.

In September 1895, Houdini had purchased a handcuff escape act from a Boston magician, W.D. LeRoy (1862 – 1919), who had become a merchant of magicians' tricks. Devised by a man named B.B. Keyes, it was not really a complete escape act. Instead, what Houdini bought was a bunch of keys that would unlock all sorts of handcuffs.

During Metamorphosis he always got someone to handcuff him before entering the trunk. Another development of the act was asking to borrow a jacket from the audience. Houdini would put on the jacket, before getting into the trunk. When Bess emerged from the trunk, amazingly, she would be wearing the same jacket.

THROWING DOWN THE GAUNTLET

Houdini's genius for salesmanship also began to come to the fore. In Gloucester, Massachusetts, he had a brainwave. To generate free publicity in advance of the show, he challenged the city police force to lock him up in handcuffs.

With all the local reporters in attendance, he then proceeded to amaze everyone by breaking free of any cuffs the cops put on him. The next day, the newspapers were full

Houdini in 1896 when he was working with Marco the Magician during the tour of Canada.

of Houdini, and the show ended up being a sell-out.

The Gloucester handcuff stunt was such a success, providing so much free advance advertising, that Houdini did the same thing on every stop of the tour—throwing down the gauntlet in all the local police stations he walked into.

ANY CUFFS ANYTIME

Houdini next announced that he would escape from any handcuffs that were brought to any of his shows. In June 1896, in St. John, New Brunswick, Canada, he took only a few minutes to escape from a complex array of heavy chains, handcuffs, and leg irons, that had been brought to the theater by two members of the audience.

A police sergeant came forward in Halifax, Nova Scotia, a few weeks later with police handcuffs. Despite his body having been contorted by an audience member and a helper, Houdini was free in under a minute.

W.D. LEROY

William Davis LeRoy (1862 – 1919) was a Boston-based illusionist and manufacturer of magic tricks. He had made his first performance as a magician at the Fountain Theater, San Francisco, where he was living. He moved to Boston in 1887 and began to manufacture props for magic shows. A few years later he opened a magic shop and what he described as a "School of Magic." At the time there were few magic shops as large as his. He wrote about magic as a correspondent for the magic periodical, *Mahatma*, and was later correspondent for another magic magazine, *The Wizard*.

He founded The Magic Mystics Fraternity in 1895, the first official society for magicians in the United States. Their objective was "... to unite, fraternally acceptable men who are recognized performers of ability in the art of magic or sleight-of-hand, or who possess some skill in legerdemain, and the establishment and maintenance of a place for social meetings."

Unfortunately, however, membership of the Fraternity never managed to stretch beyond its seven founder members. He was also the first president of the Boston Conjurers' Club and was an early member of the Society of American Magicians (SAM) which was founded in 1902. It was said that in the organization's first fifteen years, LeRoy was responsible for the recruitment of about sixteen percent of its members.

In 1906, he altered the spelling of his name from LeRoy to Leroy, no one knows quite why. He died in 1919, at age 56.

The Secrets of Houdini
How to Escape from Handcuffs

As handcuffs are intended only as temporary restraints, managing a criminal while in transit or before he enters a prison cell, their locks are not overly complicated. Magicians latched onto this fact and that is why they were so often used in escape acts.

The ways to escape are: slipping the hands out when the restrainee's hands are smaller than the handcuffs; picking the lock; releasing the ratchet or pawl inside with a thin wedge of metal, or shim; or, simplest of all, using a duplicate key that is often hidden about the person of a stage performer.

Unfortunately, adjustable handcuffs were invented. They could be adapted to any size of wrists, reducing the chances of slipping the hands out. By contorting the body, handcuffs that fasten the wrists behind the back can be brought round to the front. This obviously requires a huge amount of suppleness in the body and can be very painful.

The first magician to effect an escape from handcuffs is thought to have been the American magician, and mentalist, Samri Baldwin (1848 – 1924), who was known as "The White Mahatma."

HE GETS OUT OF THESE IN TWENTY SECONDS   AND FREES HIMSELF FROM THESE IN HALF A MINUTE

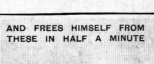

Page from *The Tatler*, February 17, 1903, featuring Houdini The Amateur Prison-breaker and Handcuff King.

CHAPTER 4

Dr. Hill's California Concert Company

After Marco the Magician went bust, Houdini borrowed his props and staged a purely magic show in Canada. It was very well received but, unfortunately, it did not pay enough. Times were tough again. The Houdinis stayed in show business by the skin of their teeth, traveling between summer 1896 and fall 1897 to wherever there was a chance of a booking.

Houdini became "Cardo, the King of Cards," and they worked up a comedy routine and even appeared in melodramas. They tried to find work as assistants to a number of magicians such as Alexander Herrmann, and Harry Kellar (1849 – 1922), but to no avail.

MAKING ENDS MEET

Hard though it was to find work, it was equally hard to actually get paid when you found it. Houdini sat in the box office on one occasion, in Toledo, Ohio, until enough money had come in to pay him what he was owed. Sometimes, he would be forced to negotiate a lower fee just to bring in something.

Back in New York in July 1897, with Bess dispirited and intermittently unwell, Houdini went to the newspapers and unsuccessfully offered them the secrets of his tricks for $25. He tried opening a school of magic, but no one wanted to learn. He even tried to sell his props, but there were few takers.

Things only got worse when they hit the road again. They were defrauded of their wages at a hall in Milwaukee by the manager and in Chicago Houdini lost $60 in a game of craps.

CALIFORNIA CONCERT COMPANY

Suddenly, things began to look up. In December 1897, Houdini landed a fifteen-week booking with an old-fashioned medicine show, Dr. Hill's California Concert Company. The main problem was the logistics of getting there, as the Houdinis always journeyed with four large, heavy, traveling trunks. At one point, on their way by rail to join the company, they had to change trains.

The four heavy trunks were hard to move at the best of times, but, with an absence of porters at the station, it was even more challenging. As they were dragging the trunks over to their next train, the guard shouted "All aboard!" By that time, they had only managed to transfer two of their four trunks. Houdini immediately went to the front of the train and lay on the tracks, preventing departure.

The station staff and train crew tried to shift him, but Houdini was a very strong man and could not be budged. Only when he was told that his luggage was finally aboard the train did he get up, brush himself down and climb on board. He later described it as a very illuminating incident, claiming that:

> [it] has always seemed to me to be the turning point in my career. That was the first time I realized the public wanted drama. Give 'em a hint of danger, perhaps of death—and you'll have them packing in to see you!

THE TRAVELING MEDICINE SHOW

Dr. Hill's California Concert Company was a typical traveling medicine show of the era. Dr.

HARRY KELLAR

Born Heinrich Kellar to German immigrants in Erie, Pennsylvania, Harry Kellar (1849 – 1922) has been described as the predecessor of Harry Houdini. Often referred to as the "Dean of American Magicians," he staged large shows during the late 1880s and early 1900s.

His career was launched after he stowed away on a train, fleeing his home town after blowing a hole in the floor of the drugstore where he was working while experimenting with explosive compounds. While on the road, he answered an advertisement placed by the English magician, Isaiah Hughes (1810 – 91) who performed under the name of "The Fakir of Ava." Hughes was looking for an assistant and Kellar landed the job. He went on to become one of the most meticulous magic performers of his time.

Kellar retired in May 1908, but Houdini enticed him back in 1917 to perform at a benefit for men who had died when a troop carrier had been sunk by a German U-boat. Houdini saw to it that Kellar was carried off the stage after this final performance in triumph as the 6,000-strong audience sang "Auld Lang Syne."

An 1894 poster depicting Harry Kellar performing levitation.

Hill was a young man with good oratory skills. He worked in partnership with Dr. Pratt, who played the organ from a large carriage, accompanying Bess who sang, and Houdini who banged on a tambourine. The whole purpose behind the "Concert Company," however, was not the music, it was to peddle large quantities of Dr. Hill's "miracle cure" medicines and remedies, between the various entertainments.

When the music had attracted a big enough crowd, Dr. Hill would start his sales pitch patter. He assured his audience that there was not an illness, not an ailment, not a disease, sickness, infection, nor affliction, that could not be cured by his marvelous, miraculous medicine. Cajoling and enticing customers with the usual medicine show exhortation: "Step right up, ladies and gentlemen. Get your 'miracle cure' right here, right now!"

After he had finished his hogwash and double-talk, Dr. Hill went on stirring up the crowd some more, reminding them that that very evening, for their enlightenment, edification, and amusement, The Californian Concert Company would be putting on a sensational, entertainment extravaganza at the local hall. The townspeople all went along to the show that night and soon, to excited tumultuous applause across the country, Houdini's magical act became the number one attraction of the tour.

REVELATIONS OF A SPIRIT MEDIUM

Toward the end of the nineteenth century, a fascination with spiritualism spread like wildfire across America. Spirit mediums began to talk to the dead everywhere, and were pulling in big audiences doing it. Old-style medicine shows like Dr. Hill's were losing out.

Despite their enterprising entertainment value, attendances at medicine shows were dwindling. The paying public wanted more melodrama, so Dr. Hill moved with the times, and asked the Houdinis to come up with a fake spiritualist act to help bring the crowds back.

HOUDINI'S BRUSH WITH ETHEREAL VOICES

Houdini, the son of a rabbi, with a belief in God and the afterlife, became very interested in spiritualism when he was young. He attended a number of séances run by a tailor at his home in Beloit, Wisconsin, and was mesmerized by the man's connection to the spirits of the dead. The tailor used a small trumpet to contact great historical figures such as George Washington and Christopher Columbus. Ethereal voices would emanate from the trumpet as it lay in the middle of a table.

Houdini eventually became uneasy, however, when the medium moved on to converse with Abraham Lincoln. Houdini knew a lot about Lincoln, and the disembodied spirit voice gave out wrong answers to the questions. He confronted the medium who confessed that his contact with the dead was all a complete hoax. Furthermore, the tailor admitted that all mediums were shysters and tricksters. Houdini was intensely disappointed:

It came as a complete shock to me, that one whom I had trusted and believed in completely should so readily confess himself a fraud.

Houdini was so shattered that he been fooled, he refused after that to have anything more to do with mediums and their fake spirit world. During his travels, however, he would later come into contact with the Davenport Brothers—crossover escape-artist magicians from Buffalo, New York, who performed spiritualist illusions, while tied up in a cabinet.

SPIRITUALISM

The modern spiritualist movement began in 1848 when the Fox sisters of Hydesville, New York, produced knocking sounds that were said to be spirit messages from the dead. The sisters' story led to an explosion of interest in spiritualism in the United States and beyond.

Margaret and Kate Fox had begun to "communicate" with the dead soon after moving to a new home. In reply to the claps and snapping of their fingers came knocking sounds, assumed to be responses from beyond the grave.

They devised a simple code to communicate with a spirit that was presumed to live in their home. They established that the spirit had been a peddler and that his body was buried in the cellar of the house. Within months the sisters became major celebrities.

Unfortunately, however, tests undertaken in 1851 suggested that they were actually producing the knocking sounds themselves. All the same, their popularity continued unabated until 1889, when Margaret confessed that the sprit sounds were fake:

> *My sister Katie was the first to observe that by swishing her fingers she could produce certain noises with her knuckles and joints, and that the same effect could be made with the toes. Finding that we could make raps with our feet—first with one foot and then with both— we practiced until we could do this easily when the room was dark ...*

The religion of spiritualism became highly fashionable with both men and women across all classes of society. In the late 1920s and early 1930s, the movement gained credibility with the support of notable people such as Sir Arthur Conan Doyle (1859 – 1930), creator of Sherlock Holmes, and the physicist Sir Oliver Lodge (1851 – 1940).

Daguerreotype of spiritual mediums Margaret (left) and Kate Fox (right).

Houdini was well qualified for the job, he knew all the tricks the mediums used. A few years previously, in 1891, he had discovered a book entitled, *The Revelations of a Spirit Medium*, written by A. Medium. This publication went into great detail about how mediums did it.

The book also explained how mediums could be trussed up, escape from their ties, do their spooky tricks, and tie themselves up again. In fact, Houdini and his childhood friend, Joseph Rinn (1868 – 1962), learned how to escape from bound ropes using that very book.

SOMETHING OF THE SUPERNATURAL

Disgusted though he may have been by spirit medium fakery, Houdini was not averse to making a dollar or two by incorporating spiritualism into his act. So when Dr. Hill asked the Houdinis to become mediums, they obliged, and came up with an act that would capture the audience's imagination.

In Garnett, Texas, Houdini and Bess began their careers as mediums, contacting the spirit of a young woman who had been murdered in the town. By the end of the evening, the crowd were quivering with fear in their seats.

On January 9, 1898, at the Opera House in Galena, Kansas, Houdini was getting top billing as "Houdini, The Great." Their spiritualist séance act went from strength to strength, and they were getting rave reviews. Some even suggested there was something of the supernatural about Houdini.

A FINE RED DRESS

Dr. Hill's show went on to feature regular spiritualist séances, Houdini and Bess alternating in the role of communicator with the dead. They drew large audiences, astonished by the details that emerged. Little did they know, Houdini had usually done his homework with a tour of the neighborhood graveyards in the company of a local expert, gleaning names and family histories to use in the show.

At this time, Houdini and Bess were earning decent money with Dr. Hill's show—sufficient to allow them to replenish their wardrobe with a good coat for him and a "fine red dress" for Bess. They were living well.

RISKING THEIR SAVINGS

In February 1898, he had enough spare cash to leave $100 with the mayor of St. Joseph, Missouri, with instructions:

> [*give the money*] *to any person who can furnish or place upon him handcuffs from which he is unable to extricate himself or to fasten him to a chair that he cannot release himself there from.*

Naturally, Bess was concerned that Houdini was risking their savings again. However, he reassured her there was nothing to worry about—the $100 was as good as back in his pocket. In the end, as in most matters when it came to escapology, he was proved right, and the money was never claimed.

BORDERING ON CRIME

Spiritualism was where the money was at, and Houdini decided they would seriously enter the business of communicating with spirits. He learned about "The Blue Book," which was a directory of clients' details available to mediums. He threw himself into this work, networking among the spirit-world workers. Before turning up in a town, Houdini made sure he was fully armed with information about the local people who were séance regulars.

Another valuable trick he learned from other mediums was that there was a huge amount of treasured, personal information to be gleaned from family Bibles. He and Bess, therefore, posed as door-to-door sales personnel for a musical Bibles company. This involved checking out the family Bible and making comparisons between it and the one they were hawking. As they did this they sucked up information from the old one.

As the son of a rabbi, however, Houdini began to anguish about the vulnerable people to whom their messages from dead relatives gave hope. He finally brought the curtain down on the fake medium act after a prediction about a child breaking his arm came true. He later wrote:

> *When it was all over I saw and felt that the audience believed in me ... they believed that my tricks were true communications from the dead. The beautiful simplicity of their faith—it appealed to me as a religion—suddenly gripped me ... from that day to this I have never posed as a genuine medium. I was brought to a realization of the seriousness of trifling with the hallowed reverence which the average human being bestows on the departed ... I was chagrined that I should ever have been guilty of such frivolity and for the first time realized that it bordered on crime.*

RETURN TO THE CIRCUS

They gave up traveling with the medicine show, and during a brief interval of acting in theatrical melodramas, Houdini tried to disguise himself so no one would know the depths to which he had stooped. Eventually, he and Bess signed on for a second tour with the Welsh Brothers Circus. This time they refused the part of the contract that obliged them to work sideshows.

The Welsh Brothers had worked hard, and their show was now the largest and the best in America. As the "King of Cards," Houdini earned $25 a week, and he and Bess also performed Metamorphosis. They soon made it to the top of the bill.

King of Cards is one of Houdini's very first posters, printed in 1895.

NO MEAN FEAT

Houdini also took the opportunity while with the circus to learn acrobatics from another act on the bill. He developed a piece of the routine in which he would throw a card out over the audience so that it would come flying back to him. But before the card had returned to his fingers he had executed a perfect back somersault—no mean feat!

Nonetheless, by the end of the circus engagement, the Houdinis were struggling to make ends meet. Once again they found themselves strapped for cash. Houdini was offered a steady job, appropriately enough, in the Yale lock factory, but he turned it down, even though he must have been seriously tempted by the prospects of a regular income. He was still convinced that some day they were going to make it to the big time—it was just a matter of when ...

HARRY HOUDINI

KING OF CARDS

NATIONAL PR. G. ENG. CO. CHICAGO

PART TWO

THE SECRET OF SHOWMANSHIP

The secret of showmanship
consists not of what you really do,
but what the mystery-loving
public thinks you do.

Harry Houdini

CHAPTER 5

HITTING THE BIG TIME

At the start of 1899, the Houdinis were in Chicago. The end of the previous year had been full of foreboding. They had played Toledo, Ohio, where they were poorly received, and the booking was terminated halfway through.

Moving on to Grand Rapids, Michigan, things were little better. But next on their tour was Middleton's in Chicago, where their act had always gone down well. Hopefully, they would make enough there to buy some free-time back in New York. Houdini needed to ponder on whether there was any future for them in the illusion business.

MIRACLE IN THE ROLL-CALL ROOM

In Chicago, however, something happened that would change everything. Houdini met up with a local detective, Lieutenant Andrew Rohan, who organized a demonstration of his escape prowess in Chicago's Central Police

Station. On the day, around two hundred curious people gathered in the station's roll-call room.

Police officers along with a large number of press representatives watched Houdini being locked into leg-irons, wearing handcuffs of the latest model that were locked to the leg-irons. He was secured in such an awkward position that he had to be helped to his escape cabinet.

Two minutes later, Houdini stepped from behind the curtain, leg-irons and handcuffs held aloft. That night, he escaped from every device they tried on him. Rohan and the other officers were in awe of his ability. A bemused Rohan said to the reporters:

I cannot explain how that fellow got out of those handcuffs. It was simply impossible to either pick the lock or slip them off. I would have banked my life that a prisoner bound as he was, could never have regained his freedom. It is miraculous. These cuffs are the

Walls and chains do not make a prison for Houdini.
Movie still from *The Grim Game* (1919).

best made, and the prisoner they will not hold cannot be kept in custody by the strongest bars or the best locks.

The next day, Houdini's name was splashed all over the newspapers. The *Chicago Journal* trumpeted the headline *"Amazes the Detectives."* It looked like Houdini had finally gained the recognition he had craved so much.

THE WINNING FORMULA

For the next eighteen months he toured America. As soon as he arrived in a town, he headed for the local police station, where he staged escapes from every type of restraint that the police officers could put on him.

To the assembled press, the local chief of police would express a desire never to encounter a prisoner like Harry Houdini. He would add that Houdini had helped them improve their security and a letter of commendation would be handed over to Houdini.

It was all organized by Lieutenant Rohan in Chicago. Houdini began to appear everywhere, using the newspapers to expose card chicanery, and revealing how confidence tricks such as the Three-card Monte were performed.

Houdini had discovered the winning formula. He was certain it would make him famous.

BULLET IN THE HAND

The inside knowledge of lock breaking that Houdini possessed could sometimes cause major problems. One night after he came offstage, he was approached by two men who offered him $100 if he would get them into a gambling house in the middle of the night. They wanted to mark some decks of cards to help them win large stakes the following day.

Houdini naturally rejected their offer but the men were determined. When, in the middle of the night he was informed that there was a telegram for him, he got up but

as he made his way to the telegram office, the men intercepted him and led him at gunpoint to the gambling establishment.

When they arrived, Houdini quickly picked the lock, but as he swung the door open, he knocked the two men down, jumped inside and locked the door from the inside. He waited for them to leave. But one of the men saw him through a cellar window, and opened fire with a pistol. Houdini unconsciously raised his hand to protect himself, and was hit by a bullet that remained lodged in the back of his hand until his death.

THE BIG BREAK

One night, Houdini was playing St. Paul, Minnesota, when a party of theatrical impresarios was in attendance. Among them was Martin Beck (1868 – 1940), who ran the Orpheum Vaudeville Circuit—owners of the best theaters in America's Midwest and West Coast.

Having watched Houdini, Beck bought a ticket for the following night's performance. This time he brought with him three sets of handcuffs to try out on Houdini. Needless to say, Houdini escaped from each of them with ease. Impressed, Beck telegrammed Houdini, making him an offer he couldn't refuse:

You can open Omaha March twenty-six sixty dollars, will see act probably make you proposition for all next season.

It was a big break and, apart from the money, the prospect of ongoing work was enticement enough for Houdini to accept the offer without hesitation.

A GIANT LEAP FORWARD

When they met, Beck advised Houdini to drop the magic from his act and perform just the escapes and, of course, "Metamorphosis." Unhappy to fully comply with Beck's request, he dropped several elements from the act, but retained his card trickery.

Finally, Houdini stepped out of the lavishly appointed dressing rooms, and onto the stage of the Creighton-Orpheum Theater, Omaha, Nebraska. He realized that he had finally made the giant leap forward in his career for which he had worked so hard all those years.

Houdini's act was a sensation. One critic described him as every bit as good as Alexander Herrmann or Harry Kellar. He was equally successful at the next stop in the tour, in Kansas City, where he performed his handcuff escape for the first time in full view of the audience.

It was a triumph. He started off getting billed as "The Wizard of Shackles, A Man of Marvels" but he changed that to the stage name he ultimately retained for the remainder of his career—"The King of Handcuffs."

GENTLEMEN OF THE PRESS

Moving on to San Francisco, their new-found situation enabled the Houdinis to take a step up in their accommodation. They booked a hotel room for six dollars a week, considerably more than they would normally spend. What's more, their room had a stove and running water.

As usual, the following day, Houdini made his way to the main police station. He escaped from restraints in front of an aghast audience of four hundred police officers. Copious press coverage of his escapades ensured sell-outs every night of his two-week run at the theater. He was just as successful in Los Angeles, after another performance at police headquarters to publicize the shows.

Of course, Houdini's relationship with the gentlemen of the press was key to his success. He generated his own news, and the press loved it. Double-page spreads with photographs appeared in newspapers in which he often ridiculed the spiritualists:

> *Anyone can do the escape act if they know how. This being aided by spirits in a dark cabinet is all bosh. Of course one must do the act out of sight of the audience, just as I do the escape from the handcuffs at the Orpheum, or after people had seen how simple it is, they would not pay to see it again.*

He even began to explain how he did some of his own tricks, but only after he had dropped them from his act. In this way, he stopped other performers from imitating his act. It was a very clever tactic.

PROFESSOR BENZON REVEALS ALL

As the Los Angeles engagement was coming to an end, a story appeared in a San Francisco newspaper in which an English card magician, "Professor Benzon," explained how he thought the handcuff escapes were done. The English conjuror claimed Houdini had a key secreted in his mouth.

Houdini was fuming, especially when the story appeared in a Los Angeles newspaper. To debunk Professor Benzon's outrageous claims, he returned to the San Francisco police station. In front of an audience, he stripped naked, and was examined by a police surgeon to ensure that nothing was hidden in any of his body orifices.

ELABORATE RUSE

Houdini then proceeded to escape from ten pairs of police handcuffs that were also locked onto leg-irons. To make matters even more difficult, his arms were locked in a crossover position. He also escaped from a heavy leather strap used in asylums.

After Houdini had completed all his stunts, he threw down a challenge to his accuser to escape from the handcuffs. The reward, if he was successful, would be the customary $100. Naturally, there was a point behind all this effort, namely that it enabled Houdini to announce he had been engaged for another week at the Orpheum Theater.

In the end, it is entirely possible that "Professor Benzon" had been in on the whole commotion from the start, and it was just an elaborate Houdini ruse to gain publicity for the shows at the Orpheum. Whether it was or not, it certainly worked—the theater was packed every night.

MARTIN BECK

Vaudeville theater owner, manager, and booking agent, Martin Beck (1868 – 1940), was born in Northern Slovakia, in the Austro-Hungarian Empire. At 16, he embarked on a ship bound for the United States with a group of actors at Bremen in Germany. In America, he worked initially as a waiter in a Chicago beer garden before joining the Schiller Vaudeville Company. He traveled to San Francisco where, in 1889, he became a United States citizen.

He found work with Morris Meyerfeld Jr. (1855 – 1935), who had purchased the Orpheum Theater in San Francisco in 1899. Together they began to buy more theaters and six years later, Beck was running the business. In 1910, he established a booking agency, United Booking Offices, with British theater impresario, Alfred Butt (1878 – 1962).

In 1913, Beck built the Palace Theater in New York which became the most important vaudeville venue in the country, and it still operates today. In 1923, after he had been voted out of the presidency of the Orpheum Vaudeville Circuit, Beck built the Martin Beck Theater, in Manhattan, which opened in 1924. It was designed to be the most opulent theater of its time, with dressing rooms for two hundred actors. The theater is still open for business today at 302 West 45th Street in Broadway. It was renamed the Al Hirschfeld Theater in 2003.

Martin Beck died in 1940, at the age of 72.

THE MIGHTY MISSISSIPPI

In September 1899, Houdini was performing in St. Louis, Missouri, when he announced he had devised a sensational, new underwater escape stunt, designed to garner even more publicity for his shows. He would be shackled at the ankles, and handcuffed at the wrists, and then he was going to leap from the 88-feet high Eads Bridge into one of the world's greatest rivers—the mighty Mississippi.

I know I can do it, and I will ... There is absolutely no question in my mind of my ability to free myself of the irons while I am underwater. That is an old trick of mine.

He also declared that he had another new trick. Similarly shackled and handcuffed, he would be placed in a bag, and then in a basket. The lid would be closed and the whole thing would be dropped into a large, deep tank of water on the stage. After about a minute, the basket would be raised and inside would be found the empty sack and the cast-off shackles. Houdini, meanwhile, would be swimming in a leisurely manner in the tank.

These two new underwater stunts soon formed a major part of his regular repertoire. He dived into rivers across the country for many years after that, always shackled and bound, but forever resurfacing unscathed.

THE FIRST STRAITJACKET

Houdini was full of good ideas. It was an imaginative and innovative time for him. Just a few months later, he added the first straitjacket to the restraints he used in police station stunts. It proved to be a complex escape.

The strap of the straitjacket was wrapped tightly around his body three times. His mouth was taped over, and a handkerchief bound around it, to ensure he could not conceal a key or implement.

It took at least a quarter of an hour to strap him up, and yet Houdini was always able to free himself within a few minutes.

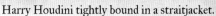
Harry Houdini tightly bound in a straitjacket.

BACK IN THE EAST

Having taken the Orpheum Circuit by storm in the west, it was now time to break through back in the east. In January 1900, Houdini was in Boston, Massachusetts, performing his regular warm-up escapes at police headquarters. But this time he was using an antique pair of handcuffs from the 1800s with a unique lock.

First, before he extricated himself from the antique cuffs, he commenced the routine with what was (for Houdini anyway) a fairly standard safe-vault escape. He stripped to his underwear as usual, was examined by the local police doctor, and his mouth was taped firmly shut.

He was then slapped into regulation handcuffs, and leg-irons were attached to his ankles. After being escorted to a large vault, the leg-iron on one of his legs was secured around the bars inside the vault. The safe was locked shut with Houdini inside—but not for long. It took him precisely eleven minutes and twenty seconds to get out again, swinging the handcuffs triumphantly as he emerged.

A SPELLBINDING SENSATION

Houdini next brought out the hundred-year-old handcuffs, a plug having been inserted into the lock to ensure that he would not be able to open it with a key or pick it. Once more, the safe-door closed on him. Nine minutes later he re-emerged, the handcuffs dangling from his hand. It had not been easy, however, and his hands were bleeding, covered in cuts and sores.

As ever, everyone was in awe of the great escape artist and the press wrote him up in glowing terms. He was a spellbinding sensation. After the first week, he was promoted to top of the bill, but this did not stop him from chasing even more publicity. He escaped from more handcuffs around town, and onstage accepted every challenge that came his way.

THE STAR OF THE SHOW

The act had always been known as "The Houdinis," with Bess being included in their billing. But once they began appearing on the vaudeville circuit, they became an act with just one star—"Houdini, the King of Handcuffs."

Bess was relegated to the magician's assistant, her name dropped entirely from the posters. Houdini claimed that Bess had suggested this fundamental change. She now performed only in Metamorphosis, and spent the rest of her time sewing and adding to her collection of dolls.

THE CONSTANT FEAR

Houdini had well and truly made it. His scrapbook was full of articles from newspapers featuring him making an escape or publicizing his show. They shouted that he was as good as, if not better than, the greatest magicians of the time. His image and name were used to sell everything from clothing to meat. It was paying, too. He was earning around $400 a week (roughly $11,600 in today's dollars).

Fame brought more stringent challenges. Houdini had a constant fear that people were either seeking to expose him as a fraud, or trying to trip him up on stage with increasingly tricky restraints. Two men in Philadelphia, for instance, threw down a challenge as he was about to perform Metamorphosis.

The men used their own string to bind his hands, and waterlogged string to tie the neck of the bag. They then used huge amounts of strong rope to tie the trunk. Interestingly, however, the audience was not happy, believing what the men were doing was totally unfair. Nonetheless, Houdini still performed the escape trick pretty quickly.

A 1906 poster advertising Houdini as The World's Handcuff King and Prison Breaker.

THE REAL HARRY HOUDINI

Harry Houdini's great strength and powerful physique were, of course, well known to anyone who had seen his publicity shots. Only those backstage knew the real Houdini.

The King of Handcuffs had a perpetual fear of exposure, worrying it was only a matter of time before he was caught out by a member of the audience. It was that intense nervous energy which helped the great magician steel himself each evening when he stepped out onto the stage.

The expressive words of an anonymous journalist from *The Omaha Daily News* captured Houdini perfectly during his tour of America in 1900:

The real Harry Houdini, who chats with his friends in the wings before and after his turn, is a serious sort of chap. He has the physique of a young lion. His muscles are like steel. He has a nervous, artistic temperament. His hazel eyes are wonderfully eloquent and sympathetic. Before he makes his appearance at each performance, Houdini roams about the theater like a restless tiger. In his hands he carries a deck of cards with which he does a succession of wonderful tricks. He does this not to entertain the people with whom he is conversing, but to keep his fingers supple and agile ... Before he goes on the stage he is all fire and excitement. When he comes off he is perfectly exhausted. Dark circles show around his eyes, and his face is pale under the rouge. He is glad it is over again. Why? Because Houdini says that someday a man will step upon that stage with a pair of handcuffs, whose lock he cannot unfasten. And when that time comes he will have to lay aside his scepter as King of Handcuffs. No circus performer enters the ring with the trepidation felt by Houdini when he steps toward the footlights. But he smiles and the audience remarks how confident he looks.

CHAPTER 6

THE WORLD'S GREATEST MYSTIFIER

Performers who made a name for themselves in the capitals of Europe were much prized and highly paid in New York. Houdini was earning more money than ever, and could count on being able to do so for some time to come, if he wanted. Instead, he took the advice of Martin Beck to travel to Europe and try his act over there.

Beck was convinced Houdini would be a barnstorming success. There was no one in Europe doing what he was doing. Thus, on June 9, 1900, Harry and Bess disembarked from a steamship in Southampton, England, before heading for London. They took a room in a boarding house for American visiting entertainers, at 10 Keppel Street, in the Bloomsbury area of central London.

SCOTLAND YARD'S FINEST

Some have claimed that Houdini spent weeks scouring the theaters of London trying to obtain an engagement. The truth is, Harry Day (1880 – 1939), a British theater owner, and Labour Party politician, helped Houdini get work. Four days after arriving, he auditioned on June 13, at the West End theater, the Alhambra, the city's premier music hall. C. Dundas Slater (1852 – 1912), manager of the Alhambra, offered him a contract on condition that he could escape from handcuffs at Scotland Yard, the headquarters of the city's Metropolitan Police. Legend has it that Superintendent William Melville (1850 – 1918) of Scotland Yard's Special Branch, locked a pair of London's finest handcuffs around Houdini's wrists, after circling his arms around a pillar.

Melville told Houdini that he and Slater were off to lunch and they would return in a couple of hours. As the pair were about to leave, Houdini said, "I'll go with you." The cuffs fell to the floor, to the wide-eyed amazement of the superintendent and the theater manager. Houdini signed a contract for a two-week engagement at the Alhambra at $300 a week.

MR. HOUDINI'S SLIPPERINESS

Slater arranged for a special press preview of Houdini's act to boost publicity. He asked the reporters to bring along whatever restraints they could find, to try out on the young escape artist. A journalist from *The London Evening Sun* brought an old, rusted set of leg-irons. A manacled Houdini disappeared behind his escape screen.

Three minutes later, he reappeared, brandishing the rusty leg-irons for all to see. Houdini defeated everything they threw at him, before rounding off the act with some card tricks, and a preview of Metamorphosis. The gentlemen of the press went wild, and did him proud in their publications the following day. *The Morning Herald* reported:

> *It was a remarkably clever exhibition by Mr. Harry Houdini, who describes himself as the World's Greatest Mystifier and King of Handcuffs. Perhaps the highest tribute to Mr. Houdini's slipperiness is the fact that he has completely mystified the police of America, who have given him many testimonials.*

HARRY DAY

C. DUNDAS SLATER

Harry Day (1880 – 1939) was born Edward Lewis Levy in the United States. But he changed his name to the less Jewish-sounding Harry Day. He worked in America, selling tickets for Barnum & Bailey's Traveling Circus before moving on to employment as a bill poster. Having emigrated to Britain, he bought theaters in Bedford, Bristol, and Dover. He was briefly Harry Houdini's manager, securing him the all-important first audition at the Alhambra Theater in London.

In 1924, Day was elected Member of Parliament for the constituency of Southwark Central in London. He remained politically active until his death in 1939, at the age of 50.

Charles Dundas Slater (1852 – 1912) was one of the pre-eminent theater managers of his time. He managed London's Empire Theater from 1889 to 1895 and was business manager of the Alhambra Theater until 1907. He can be seen briefly in the Lumière brothers' film *Londres, Entrée du cinématographe* of 1896. In his later years, Slater managed the London Coliseum but poor health and failing eyesight resulted in his dismissal in 1912.

One day in July 1912, Slater ordered a taxi to take him to Charing Cross Hospital in London, but during the journey he took out a revolver and shot himself in the head. It was said that when he shot himself he was temporarily insane as a result of his dismissal from the Coliseum.

From left to right: Joe Hyman, Harry Day, Lord Northcliffe, and Charles Dundas Slater, in 1911.

THE GREAT CIRNOC

At Houdini's evening performance, the audience was eager to see this American Handcuff King. He followed the wonderful female Chinese conjurer, Suee Seen (1863 – ?), who had worked as assistant to Alexander Herrmann, dressed as a little boy. In reality, she was Olive "Dot" Path, an American woman who worked with her husband, Chung Ling Soo, alias William Robinson, who died during a bullet-catching act in 1918.

When Suee Seen had finished, Houdini took to the stage in white tie and tails, with his normally untidy hair smoothed into a center parting. But before he could even so much as introduce himself, an angry man jumped onto the stage shouting that Houdini had stolen the title of "Handcuff King." The title rightly belonged to him—"The Great Cirnoc."

Cirnoc was part of an act who were also billing themselves as "The Handcuff Kings." The Cirnoc family had advertised themselves as "Masters of Locks" since 1872. Cirnoc declared Houdini was a fraud, and even claimed that he had never been to the United States. At that point, US Senator Chauncey M. Depew (1834 – 1928), from New York, leapt to Houdini's defense. The senator stood up and confirmed that he had seen Houdini perform in America several years previously.

THE BEAN GIANT

The audience applauded the senator as he sat down. Houdini, bolstered by this vote of confidence, asked Bess to bring on "The Bean Giant"—a set of handcuffs invented by Captain Bean of Boston. Bean had offered $500 to anyone who could escape from these handcuffs. Houdini had succeeded, but forfeited the prize when he refused to give away the secret of how he did it. Houdini now used the handcuffs as part of his act.

He held out the Bean Giant to The Great Cirnoc and offered him $500 if he could escape. When Cirnoc requested that Houdini escape from it first, he retired to his cabinet and swiftly obliged. He used a customized

long key he had kept hidden, because it was impossible to reach the handcuffs with the normal key.

The cuffs were then put on the wrists of the English escape artist. Houdini handed him the normal key but, he was, of course, unable to reach the handcuffs with it. The Great Cirnoc was defeated. He gallantly shook Houdini's proffered hand, and, somewhat humbled, he left the stage.

HIDDEN HELPER

The newspapers loved all the showmanship, and couldn't get enough of Houdini. The engagement at the Alhambra was a huge success, and C. Dundas Slater extended Houdini's contract right through to the end of August 1900.

When people began to suggest that Houdini had a hidden helper inside his cabinet, he offered to make his escape in full view of the audience. A group of challengers who were police officers, chained and manacled him in such a way that he was forced into a kneeling position. Houdini's only request was that he be allowed to keep his hands behind his back, out of sight. He was quick to free himself of all his fetters.

SELL-OUT SHOWS

C. Dundas Slater was eager to keep Houdini performing at the London Alhambra for as long as possible. But Houdini had already agreed to perform in Germany, opening at the Central Theater, Dresden, in September. So Slater had to be patient. However, Houdini was concerned to learn that his German engagement could be ended in an instant by a hostile audience. The theater manager in Dresden informed him that when German crowds did not like a performer, they would whistle and jeer, and his contract would be terminated.

Houdini need not have worried. The Dresden audience loved the act, and cheered him from his first handcuff escape. The shows were a sell-out for the entire month,

CHUNG LING SOO

Chung Ling Soo was the stage name of the American magician William Robinson (1861 – 1918), who carefully protected his on-stage Chinese persona, never speaking while performing, and always using an interpreter when he spoke to reporters. Only close friends and other magicians knew the truth.

Born in Westchester, New York, to parents of Scottish descent, he was brought up in Manhattan. Robinson took part in his first magic show at the age of 14, and not long after, he launched his own professional vaudeville career. Initially using the name "Robinson, the Man of Mystery," he changed his stage name to "Achmed Ben Ali," and began performing what was known as "black art" illusions.

In 1898, Robinson wrote and published a book, *Spirit Slate Writing and Kindred Phenomena,* that exposed the tricks of mediums. Two years later, Chung Ling Soo was born when an agent was searching for a Chinese magician to perform at the Folies Bergère in Paris. He based his act on the illusions of Chinese stage magician Ching Ling Foo, wearing traditional Chinese clothing, shaving his facial hair and sporting a Manchurian pigtail.

The greatest illusion performed by Soo was "Condemned to Death by the Boxers." His assistants dressed as Boxers—late nineteenth century Chinese nationalist revolutionaries—shot a bullet marked by a member of the audience at the magician. He seemed to snatch the bullet from the air, and then dropped it onto a plate. Sometimes, he would pretend to have been hit, and on those occasions, he spat the bullet onto the plate.

On March 23, 1918, while performing this trick at the Wood Green Empire in London, the gun malfunctioned and Soo was shot in the lung. As he fell to the ground, he was heard to speak for the first time on-stage in perfect English. "Oh my God," he said, "Something's happened. Lower the curtain." He died the next morning, and the public were shocked to learn that Chung Ling Soo was not actually Chinese after all.

breaking all house records. As usual, along the way, he staged a few publicity stunts outside the venue, on one occasion escaping from heavy leg-irons and manacles at the Mathilda Gasse Prison.

VERY MUCH IN DEMAND

Although the Dresden theater wanted to keep Houdini on, he was already booked to play the Wintergarten in Berlin, where the shows were sold-out in advance, even before he arrived in the city. The local police actually stopped the Wintergarten selling any more tickets, as they feared that the crowds could get out of hand.

Again, the act was a huge success, and the Wintergarten wanted to extend Houdini's run of shows. But he was very much in demand elsewhere. His next venue, Ronacher's in Vienna refused to delay their engagement, and after Vienna, C. Dundas Slater who had made a return booking with Houdini back at the Alhambra in London, was also refusing to delay his shows.

The Wintergarten, therefore, offered to pay Ronacher's what they would be paying Houdini—4,000 deutschmarks, about $1,000—if they could continue his engagement.

PALE IMITATIONS

Seeing the huge success being enjoyed by Houdini, other performers began to introduce handcuff escapes into their acts. The Great Cirnoc was still trying to outdo him but, having opened in Dresden at the same time as Houdini, his show had quickly closed. It wasn't just the tricks that attracted the crowds, it was Houdini and his charismatic showmanship.

Meanwhile, the Circus Busch in Berlin were incensed when they failed to get Houdini to perform for them, even after offering to pay the penalty he would incur if he abandoned the Wintergarten in mid-engagement. Hopping mad, they went ahead and introduced a pale imitation of Houdini's act, employing an escape artist called "Hermann."

ALL HELL BROKE LOOSE

Houdini went to watch Hermann perform, and caused quite a stir when he jumped into the circus ring. He offered Hermann 5,000 deutschmarks if he was able to escape from a pair of Houdini's own handcuffs. And another 5,000 deutschmarks if Houdini failed to escape from Hermann's handcuffs. Moreover, he offered a further 5,000 deutschmarks, if Hermann could perform the stunt that Houdini had performed in the Berlin central police station—escaping while wearing no clothes. That was 15,000 deutschmarks altogether that Houdini was offering.

All hell broke loose. Hermann lost his head, shouting angrily to the audience that Houdini was a fake. He was not even an American, he was a Hungarian charlatan. Houdini pulled out his US passport and brandished it at him. The audience loved it, and went mad with applause. In the end, Houdini kept all his money, and Hermann was shown up as an imposter. Of course, all the pandemonium was massive publicity for Houdini's own shows.

OFFICIAL AUTHORIZED HOUDINI

With Houdini at the top of his game, he had to put up with an army of pretenders, cheats, con men, and second-rate imposters. They were all stealing and copying his tricks, and performing them in public as if they were their own!

Imitation might be the greatest form of flattery, but Houdini's patience had run out. He was determined to exert control over his own work, and decided to take on the fakes and fraudsters at their own game. He cleverly commissioned his own legitimate imitation act, performed by his brother Dash. A Houdini tribute act, officially authorized by the great man himself, would surely put an end to the tricksters and frauds. He wired a simple message to his brother in New York:

COME OVER THE APPLES ARE RIPE.

BROTHERS AT WAR

Dash left America immediately, quitting his job as a nightclub bouncer. When he arrived he found that Houdini had everything prepared. Dash was to perform an exact duplicate of his brother's show. All artistes needed a stage name, and they came up with "Hardeen." Soon Hardeen was being described as "the best copy of Houdini in the profession today."

But Houdini was still very often angered by imitators, and did his best to damage and undermine them. Hardeen, although his brother and to a large extent his creation, was no exception. Houdini was furious when Hardeen undertook a particularly successful tour of England in 1911. Bess had to calm him down, and make peace between the warring brothers.

EXPOSING THE EXPOSER

One of Hardeen's tasks was to dissuade Houdini imitators from copying his brother. He wrote a warning letter to a magician named Albert Hill, performing as "Hilbert," telling him to stop "working both mine and my brother's tricks." Hill replied immediately, saying:

> Please accept my assurance that I will make no pretence to originality. I may add that I desire to carefully avoid any conflict with either yourself or your brother.

Sometimes Hardeen was less patient, and rather more force was used to dissuade people from copying Houdini. This was when his experience as a nightclub bouncer came into its own.

Hilbert, however, continued to perform Houdini's tricks. He also created an act in which he "exposed" the secrets, demonstrating how Houdini did them. Things came to a head one day when both men's shows were in the same town.

Houdini rented a shop window next to the theater where Hilbert was performing, and sent his assistant Franz Kukol and another associate dressed as magicians to the shop. Every half-hour, they ruined Hilbert's show by performing his act in the window— exposing the exposer, as it were.

Theodore "Dash" Hardeen, 1905.

CHAPTER 7

BRING YOUR OWN PADLOCKS

Despite Hardeen's persuasive presence and muscular attentions, still the imitators appeared. Some of the pretenders were even using stage names that sounded very similar to Harry Houdini, such as Harry Rudini, Harry Blondini, and Harry Mourdini. These fake soubriquets were deliberately designed to confuse the paying public, which made the one-and-only authentic Harry Houdini even more exasperated.

CHAMPION OF ALL CHAMPIONS

Houdini was well-equipped at all times to deal with charlatans and fraudsters. He always carried what he described as "handcuff-king-defeaters." These were special handcuffs that were nearly impossible to escape from. But

Engelberto Kleppini.

as one friend from the old days in the dime museums said, he never used such tactics unless someone "first tried to 'do' him."

One such trickster who tried it on with Houdini was the self-styled "Champion of all Champions of Handcuff Kings"—a man named Engelberto Kleppini. He first made the mistake of claiming that he had escaped from Houdini's handcuffs. Worse still, he went on to claim that Houdini had failed to escape from his. It was an elementary error that he was soon to regret.

THE FALSE MOUSTACHE

Kleppini was performing in Dortmund in Germany when an old man with a moustache jumped to his feet and shouted that what Kleppini was claiming was untrue. When challenged, the old man—Houdini in disguise—leapt into the center of the circus ring in which the show was taking place, ripped off his false moustache, and shouted "I am Houdini!"

He offered Kleppini 5,000 deutschmarks if he would permit Houdini to handcuff him. But the circus boss refused to back his man with the same amount and Houdini had to return to his seat. The audience were disgusted and many walked out. A few nights later, however, the challenge was on. The circus manager had visited Houdini and arranged it.

THE FRENCH LETTER CUFFS

When asked which handcuffs would be used, Houdini told the manager to choose whichever one he wanted from a dozen pairs. He chose a pair of French "letter cuffs" that could only be opened when the correct combination of letters were selected. He innocently asked Houdini what would open them, and Houdini replied "CLEFS," which is French for "keys."

The night when the challenge was to take place, Houdini spread out the dozen pairs of cuffs, and invited Kleppini to choose whichever he wanted. As Houdini had anticipated, he chose the same set as the manager. Houdini locked them over Kleppini's wrists and told the audience that there was no possibility he would ever escape from them.

FRAUD IS THE KEY

At 9:00 p.m., Kleppini entered the cabinet, and by 11:00 p.m., with the hall nearly empty, he was still there. Solidly locked into the letter cuffs, Kleppini decamped to his dressing room to try to escape, while Houdini waited. At 1:00 a.m., Kleppini finally admitted defeat.

Houdini gathered together the circus owner and a news reporter. Eventually Kleppini had to confess that the manager had told him that the key word to open the cuffs was "CLEFS." But when he tried to use that codeword they would not open. Houdini laughed and explained triumphantly that he had changed the letters. They now spelled out "FRAUD."

No matter how many imitators and fakes Houdini took down, however, they kept on coming. Such was his fame and their desire to make a fraudulent fortune by riding on his magical coattails.

PRIDE AND BRAVADO

Soon Houdini and Bess were back in London, performing at the Alhambra, billed above the expensive ballets that the theater was renowned for. This was highly unusual, and Houdini, full of pride and bravado over the hugely successful season of London shows, wrote in a letter to a friend:

It would be boastful to tell you how successful we are over here.

Next, they traveled back to Germany to perform in Leipzig, from where he wrote:

We closed a 20 weeks' engagement at Alhambra, London, and jumped here to Germany and stay here at least 6 more months, and at an excellent salary, no not an excellent salary but an "exorbitant" or newspaper salary.

CLUMSY IS CLEVER

To be honest, Houdini's act was still a little rough around the edges at this time, and nowhere near as accomplished as it would later become. But, he always knew the precise mechanics of how and why it worked.

Naturally, as the star of the show, the success of each trick largely depended on Houdini himself, but he was also well aware of the valuable contribution of a performer's assistants. One time he revealed the secret of the real role the assistants played in the theatricals of a magic trick:

To avert suspicion from our assistants, we make them seem as awkward and clumsy as possible. We have them drop things, stumble over chairs, and make mistakes of a minor nature. We want you to get the idea that these men play no real part in the performance of our tricks; whereas, of course, they are most important cogs in our work. Once I was sitting next to a woman who kept exclaiming at the clumsiness of one of the cleverest assistants I have ever seen. Instead of the magician doing all the work, the assistant was really doing nine-tenths of the tricks. Yet he acted his part so well that this woman finally said, "My! How clumsy that man is! I wonder why the magician keeps him?"

FEEDBACK FORM

Houdini was also very thorough when it came to preparation. He was highly critical, and he also liked to make various review notes. He put together a form that would record how his show went in the numerous places he played. It had headings such as:

OPPOSITION · WEATHER · COMPLAINTS · RECOMMENDATIONS · REMARKS REGARDING BILLING · WORKING OF SPECIAL NIGHTS.

LIFE ON THE ROAD

It was a tough life on the road. The constant moving from place to place was relentless, and Houdini began to feel the strain of it all. At the age of only 27 in 1901, he was already a veteran—old before his time. He wrote around then:

> *I am not well as the perpetual worry and excitement are beginning to tell on me and I am afraid that if I dont [sic] take a rest soon Ill [sic] be all done up. You know for the last 11 years Ive [sic] had the same strain over & over day in & day out & before this luck streak I had to do 8 to 12 shows a day.*

There were always the theatrical "digs," or boarding houses, of England, to ease the stress and strain of touring. Later, Houdini would look back fondly at his time in these English theatrical institutions:

> *The "digs" for my wife ... and myself never cost more than £6 per week, including tips, often considerably less, and the table and the service was in some ways superior to the best hotels, including, as it did, pheasants, cream, and all the "fixins" ... To my mind no more comfortable form of housing for the itinerant has ever been devised.*

But Germany was slightly less welcoming:

> *It was the custom for acrobats to travel fourth class. This class of cars then had no cross seats, but were furnished with benches along the sides and during night runs the thrifty tumblers would spread their tumbling pads on the floor and sell sleeping privileges at so much per place.*

WHAT'S MY NAME?

There is little doubt that Houdini was highly adept at publicity, and without it, he would probably not have become quite so famous. But, publicity is pointless if it is not backed up by a good act. Long before TV or radio advertising was available, his live-show career was dependent on a mixture of fliers, posters, and publicity stunts.

One time, while on tour in Paris, he lined up a row of seven bald men wearing hats, seated on chairs outside a pavement café. At regular intervals during the day, the men would all remove their headgear and bow to the people passing by, their heads spelled out "H-O-U-D-I-N-I."

A TOUGH NIGHT IN BLACKBURN

When Houdini came to town, posters would appear in advance announcing the show, with the added instruction—*"BRING YOUR OWN PADLOCKS."* Audience participation was an essential part of Houdini's appeal to the people who attended the shows. But it could be a risky aspect of the performance, of course. Famously, one night in October 1902, in Blackburn in the north of England, audience participation was taken to the limit.

Before every show, Houdini offered a reward of £25 to any person who could provide a set of restraints from which he could not break free. The challenge that night in Blackburn was taken up by Mr. Ralph Hodgson, a former soldier. Hodgson wanted to provide a set of irons, but stipulated that he himself should be allowed to put them on Houdini. The magician agreed. As part of the pre-show hype, the money was deposited with the local newspaper. An act that always generated more PR for the show.

On October 24, the two men met at a packed theater. Hodgson arrived weighed down with six pairs of heavy irons, chains and padlocks. Houdini was immediately alert to the fact that these were not the "regulation" irons from which he normally escaped. There had been additions to these, string being wrapped around them, and he could see that they had been tampered with in other ways to make them practically impossible to escape from.

EUROPE'S ECLIPSING SENSATION
HOUDINI

THE WORLD'S HANDCUFF KING

MATINEE EVERY DAY TO SEAT THE CROWDS

AND PRISON BREAKER

HOUDINI INVITES YOU TO BRING YOUR OWN REGULATION HANDCUFFS, & ETC-

1906 poster printed by U.S. Lithographic Co. Russell-Morgan Print, inviting spectators to bring their own handcuffs.

LOCKED SOLID

The audience cheered Houdini to the rafters when he agreed, nonetheless, to give it a go. He would just need a little more time. Hodgson had even brought an assistant, and together they manhandled Houdini while putting the irons around him. Houdini protested that no assistant had been mentioned in their agreement, and the man stepped away.

A pair of irons were fixed over Houdini's upper arms, and his arms were pulled tightly behind his back. A pair of handcuffs was then put on his hands. Further restraints were put on him, his arms being tied tightly to his sides. Then a pair of leg-irons was passed through the chains at the back that bound his arms. These were then fixed to his ankles and more leg-irons were added. Houdini couldn't move—he was locked solid.

Houdini was lifted into his escape cabinet, and the audience held its breath—and waited. Fifteen minutes passed and the cabinet was raised, revealing Houdini on his side. He had not freed himself. He asked if he could be raised up onto his knees, but Hodgson refused. The audience responded to this with boos, so Houdini was lifted to his knees.

BLUE HOUDINI

Another twenty minutes passed before the cabinet was again raised, Houdini complaining that there was no circulation in his arms. He requested that the irons be removed for a moment for him to regain the feeling in his arms, but Hodgson again refused. The audience was baying by now. A doctor stepped forward to check Houdini. He declared that his arms were blue, but Houdini said he just needed a bit more time.

Fifteen minutes more passed. When the cabinet was raised, he was found to have succeeded in removing one hand. The crowd went wild with excitement. The escape went on for a very long time, Houdini emerging every now and then with a progress report of how he was doing.

Eventually, around midnight, his clothes torn, blood streaming down his arms,

Houdini emerged from the cabinet. He threw the last of the irons down onto the stage with a dramatic clatter. For two hours the audience had been staring at the cabinet, urging the American magician to free himself of his shackles. When he eventually did so, they jumped to their feet, cheering and applauding for a full fifteen minutes.

Houdini finally staggered off the stage exhausted. He was determined never to put himself through such an experience again, where he risked losing everything. But the incident also made him realize the full value of keeping an audience in suspense all night.

BRUSHES WITH AUTHORITY

Houdini had a number of run-ins with the German police because, wherever he visited, he was not a man to obey rules and regulations. His first problem arose in Dresden in 1900. Trying to garner column inches as usual, he wanted to be thrown from a boat handcuffed, freeing himself underwater, and emerging triumphant and unfettered. But the police refused to give him permission to perform the stunt.

Houdini gathered the gentlemen of the German press and did it anyway. He was arrested and taken to court. But the magistrate found the only offense he had committed was walking on the grass near the bridge. He was fined a few German pfennigs.

A DEFAMATORY SLUR

In 1902, he got into even hotter water when the police accused him of offenses relating to misrepresentation. The police used this law to prosecute performers who overstated their abilities, and were not actually doing what they promised they would in their acts.

In the *Rheinische Zeitung*, the chief of the Cologne police, Schutzmann Werner Graff called Houdini a fraud. Naturally, Houdini was not about to take that defamatory slur lying down. A demand for an apology was laughed at, forcing Houdini to engage a top Cologne lawyer—he could now afford such

THE IMPENETRABLE LOCK

He charged Graff with slander, but the police chief said he could prove his case by chaining Houdini up, thinking he would not be able to release himself. Houdini was duly chained up, and escaped. He even showed the judge and jury—no one else—how he did it. He won the case, and the police chief received a fine and had to issue a public apology to Houdini.

Graff refused to make the apology, and took the case to a higher court in July 1902. This time, Graff produced a lock that had been made by a master mechanic. When it was locked it could not be opened, not even with the key. It took Houdini just four minutes to break this apparently impenetrable lock.

HIGHEST COURT IN THE LAND

Graff had to pay heavy costs and put an advertisement in all the local newspapers announcing his punishment and apologizing to Houdini. But, he was a stubborn man and again refused to apologize or give up. The next highest court was the Oberlandesgericht, the highest court in the land and its decision would be absolutely final.

Graff argued on this occasion that Houdini had advertised himself as being able to open safes but he had never done this in Germany. The judge obliged by offering Houdini the safe in his own office to be opened. They escorted him to the room and left him. Houdini nervously approached the safe and tried the door. It opened! It had not been locked in the first place.

He waited the requisite amount of time it would take to open a locked safe door before emerging. The case was found in his favor again. Graff was fined 30 deutschmarks and was ordered to pay the costs of the three trials. He also had to apologize, and place an advertisement in the newspapers. Houdini reveled in the huge publicity the case generated, using it in his own advertising material.

QUEEN FOR A DAY

In January 1901, in a London shop window, Houdini had seen a dress that had been made for Queen Victoria who had just died. Thinking that his mother, whom he was missing terribly, would love it, he purchased it. He then wrote to her, inviting her to Europe, ready to surprise her with the dress.

Houdini was performing in Hamburg, Germany, when she arrived, but he had another surprise for her. He took her on a train to Budapest, her home city, where he had booked the best accommodation in the city—the Royal Hotel. He wanted to hold a reception for his mother in the luxurious palm-garden salon in the hotel, but the manager explained that it was not permitted to be used for private parties. Houdini took him to one side.

I revealed to him my plot to crown my little mother and allow her to be Queen Victoria for a few fleeting hours. He immediately consented to be my confederate ...

A magnificent party was held in Cecilia's honor. All her Hungarian relatives were invited. Houdini later wrote:

How my heart warmed, to see the various friends and relatives kneel and pay homage to my mother, every inch a queen, as she sat enthroned in her heavily carved and gilded chair.

The next day, Houdini's mother returned to the United States, while he borrowed the money to pay for his trip back to Germany. He began touring with the Corty-Althoff Circus, performing in Dortmund, Osnabrück, and Cologne. Then, in September, Houdini was in Prague, before returning to Germany, where he played Hanover.

A lithographic illustration of Houdini in the German courtroom, 1902.

The Imperial Police of Cologne slanderously libeled HARRY HOUDINI, stating his advertised tricks were swindles!

HOUDINI answered them by sueing for „An Honorary Public Apology". The Police lost the Case in the three highest Courts, as they were unable to fetter or Chain HOUDINI in an unescapeable manner. He was even successful in opening a special lock that they had constructed which after it had once been locked could not be opened!

First Trial „Königliches Schöffengericht" in Köln. Feb. 26 1902
Second Trial „Königliche Strafkammer" in Köln. July 26 1902
Third Trial „Königliches Oberlandesgericht". Sept. 26 1902

Having lost the case in all three trials the Police were ultimately compelled to publicly advertise „An Honorary Apology" and pay all costs of the trials.

By command of Kaiser WILHELM II. Emperor of Germany.

CHAPTER 8

RINGING THE KREMLIN BELLS

In April 1902, the Houdinis traveled back to the United States on board the German passenger steamer SS *Deutschland*. He had planned to work in America for six weeks that summer, and then return to Europe, where he would make a farewell tour before retiring from show business. In the end, the visit to America lasted only ten days, and was totally manic. He wrote to his friend W.D. LeRoy:

> *I lived 4 months in those 10 days ... slept one night, the rest of the time I was out, and slept in my motor car, while my brothers drove me about.*

WHIRLWIND VISIT

He traveled to Washington where, he told LeRoy, he had a meeting with Martin Beck. The two men took a Pullman to Pittsburgh, before returning to Washington. In actual fact, Houdini had fired Beck in July 1901. It is hard to imagine that, although they remained friends, Houdini and he would have enough to discuss that would merit their railway marathon. But that is what he claimed in his letter to LeRoy.

The remainder of that year was spent performing in Germany and England, living a fairly low-key existence offstage. He and Bess always bought third-class train tickets, and spent as little as they could on accommodation. But he always ensured that he sent money home to his mother, increasing the amount when coal prices rose.

LOVE PLUS MORE

Although we know very little of the intimate details of Houdini and Bess's marriage, we do have a series of loving notes that he wrote to her that make it clear how he felt about her.

He often left her a message when he went out to work early and did not want her to be disturbed:

> *Honey-Baby-Pretty-Lamby, I did not want to awaken you by ordering coffee. My babykins must sleep. So I'll dine at automat. Will return about 2. All my love + more. H.*

He often attached love poems he had written. Sometimes, Bess later wrote, Houdini left her six notes a day. Of course, it could be presumed from this oversolicitous approach that his wife was the type of person that required constant reassurance of his love for her.

One can sense that Houdini is being very careful how he addresses her and what he says. We know from letters to friends that Bess was often fragile, regularly being "sick" or suffering from an attack of "nerves."

Although the couple never had children, probably, it is thought, on account of a medical problem with Bess, Houdini loved them and devoted time on his travels to perform at orphanages.

On one occasion in Edinburgh, Scotland, horrified at the sight of children wearing no shoes in winter, he purchased three hundred pairs of children's shoes. He told the city's children to come to the theater where he was performing, to get a free pair fitted.

MAGICIAN IN MOSCOW

In 1903, Houdini received an invitation to perform his magic show at the Establishment Yard Cabaret, Moscow. As Russia did not welcome Jews, Bess had to claim her husband was Roman Catholic in the travel visa forms they had to complete. Houdini had polished up an opening speech in Russian for the act. He did this wherever he went, and it immediately endeared him to his overseas audiences.

He had also engaged a language teacher to help him learn the words, but when he tried the speech out on the cabaret's manager, he was appalled. What Houdini had been taught was Polish, a language banned in Russia. The speech was hastily re-written.

In order to learn it, Houdini went to a nearby park, where he sat on a bench reciting it. As he got up, he was arrested by a squad of Russian policemen who had been watching him from the bushes, and thought he looked a suspicious character. Houdini was thrown into a cell, and was only freed when the cabaret manager turned up to confirm his identity.

THE SIBERIAN TRANSPORT CELL

This did not stop Houdini from issuing his customary challenge to the Moscow police. Convicts, he noticed, were transported through the streets of the Russian capital, on their way to Siberia, in wagons known as *carettes*, which were little more than traveling prison cells. One of these Siberian Transport Cells would provide him with a novel and dramatic publicity stunt escape.

He approached Moscow Police Chief Lebedoeff for permission to attempt an escape from a locked *carette*. The Police Chief was skeptical, but agreed to it, saying he would even sign an evidential certificate if Houdini escaped. Lebedoeff just had no idea who he was dealing with here.

PADLOCKED IRON BANDS

On May 11, 1903, Houdini removed his clothing and was searched thoroughly, as was the assistant he had engaged, Franz Kukol (1876 – ?), an Austrian mechanic and musician. Kukol would become an invaluable first member of the team of assistants who Houdini assembled around himself.

Outside in the prison yard, the *carette* was also searched. Around Houdini's wrists were padlocked two heavy iron bands, linked by a short metal bar. His ankles were manacled

Harry Houdini was stripped and padlocked in chains before he was secured inside the Siberian Transport Cell.

before he was locked inside the Siberian Transport Cell.

The police chief then announced, much to his own amusement, that the key to unlock the *carette* was kept in Siberia. The chief joked that if Houdini was unable to escape, he had a long, bitterly cold journey ahead of him. The *carette* was next positioned so that the door with its small barred window was tight against a prison wall.

LOCAL HERO

To escape from this small cell was an exceedingly daunting task but, of course, this was the Great Houdini, and he did it—and fast. There are various accounts of how long it took him. One report says forty-five minutes, another twenty-eight minutes. But however long it was, Houdini freed himself quickly.

Standing outside the still-locked door of the *carette*, he grinned in triumph, as he greeted a furious Police Chief Lebedoeff. Houdini never did receive the promised certificate after he escaped. Lebedoeff was a sore loser, and refused to sign it.

MOSCOW SELLS OUT

The escape was a tricky one. The door of the *carette* on the inside was a smooth sheet of steel with no lock. But it was interrupted by a small high six-inch-square window that had four metal bars. The lock on the outside of the door was about two-and-a-half feet below this window. The magician Harry Kellock claimed that Houdini must have worked through the window aperture. According to Kellock, he could have got an arm through the window, reached down and picked the lock.

Another version, however, claimed that he cut into the metal floor of the *carette* with a concealed implement, removed the wooden planks below this and clambered out. He avoided being caught out by the searchers, by having a hollow false finger attached to his hand, inside which were the sharp cutting implements he required. When he had

escaped, he simply pulled back the flooring into place and replaced the planks.

News of the escape at the police station traveled fast. There had been no journalists in the prison to witness it, but word soon spread. The American magician became a popular local hero, especially as he had made fools of the hated secret police. Tickets for the Moscow shows sold out, and the manager of the Establishment Yard Cabaret doubled the length of his booking.

THE COURT OF THE RUSSIAN TSAR

Houdini was in Russia for five months in 1903, playing a number of venues to rave reviews and capacity audiences. His bookings were made by Harry Day who was Houdini's booking agent in Europe for many years. The magician's show even made an impression on the Russian royal family. He explained in an interview many years later:

The superstitious court went mad about me. The Empress with her love of mysticism refused to believe that there was a scientific and mechanical explanation for my magic. [She] begged me to stay and give her the benefit of my gifts, but I refused. I attended a court function where wine was served. It so happens I am a teetotaller. I did not know the elaborate court ceremony. It seems that a refusal to touch the wine served by the emperor is an insult to Russia. I promptly lost my standing at court.

THE KREMLIN BELLS

But Houdini did perform one magnificent trick at the Royal Court while he was still in favor. In front of the Governor General of Moscow, Grand Duke Sergei Alexandrovich (1857 – 1905), son of Tsar Alexander II, and assembled guests, Houdini asked everyone to write on a slip of paper an impossible task for him to undertake.

He then asked the Grand Duke to pick a piece of paper, unravel it, and announce to everyone what it said. It was, indeed, a

GRAND DUKE SERGEI ALEXANDROVICH

The seventh child of Tsar Alexander II (1818 – 81) of Russia, Grand Duke Sergei Alexandrovich (1857 – 1905), became influential during the reigns of his older brother, Tsar Alexander III (1845 – 94), and his successor, Tsar Nicholas II (1868 – 1918). Nicholas was Sergei's nephew and also his brother-in-law, as Sergei married the sister of Nicholas's wife Tsarina Alexandra.

He fought in the Russo-Turkish War of 1877 to 1878 and was decorated by Alexander III for bravery. He also gave him the command of the 1st Battalion Preobrazhensky Life Guard Regiment, and he remained in command of the regiment until 1891, having been promoted to the rank of Major General in 1889. His wife was a granddaughter of Queen Victoria, but the couple had no children.

From 1891 to 1905, the Grand Duke was Governor General of the city of Moscow. During this time, he was heavily criticized for the Khodynka Tragedy of 1896 when, during the festivities for the coronation of Nicholas II, a stampede and crush resulted in 1,389 revelers losing their lives. Criticism was levelled at Sergei because of the poor response of the authorities, and he was nicknamed "the Prince of Khodynka" while the Tsar was dubbed "Nicholas the Bloody."

The Grand Duke expelled Moscow's 20,000 Jews at the start of his time in office, and took repressive measures against students spreading revolutionary ideas. A staunch conservative, he became hated for his reactionary government.

Shortly after his resignation in 1905, a coach carrying him was bombed, and he was literally blown to bits.

difficult task that the Grand Duke picked out. The bells of the Kremlin had not rung for a century, and on the piece of paper was scribbled—"Can you ring the bells of the Kremlin?"

DO OUR BIDDING

Without hesitation, Houdini accepted the challenge. He walked over to a window that offered a view of Kremlin Square, while everyone gathered around, curious to see what he was going to do. He took a handkerchief from his pocket, and sprinkled some magic purple dust on it. He then shook the handkerchief in front of him, at the same time intoning a magic spell:

Powder travel through the night, your assignation before dawn's light, from Seventh Heaven to the deepest Hell, do our bidding and ring the bell!

He leaned forward, pushing open one of the windows, and as he did so, to the amazement of the assembled royals, the Kremlin bells began to peal.

Of course, they did not really peal. In careful preparation for the stunt, Houdini had quietly positioned assistant Franz Kukol on a balcony of their hotel, located on one side of the square. When he waved the handkerchief, his assistant fired a volley of shots at the bells with an air gun. This made it sound as if the bells were truly ringing for the first time in a hundred years.

SECOND-SIGHT DUCHESS

Houdini and Bess were often invited to the Grand Duke's Palace and, in May, they performed their "Second Sight" mind reading act. Obviously, it was not really mind reading at all. Instead, Bess had learned a code that could be communicated by Houdini verbally and by hand and face gestures, wiggling his ears or even by positioning his feet in a certain way.

Houdini with Bess wearing her favorite brooch. Crafted in gold, diamonds, sapphires, rubies, and emeralds, the brooch was a present from Grand Duke Sergei Alexandrovich.

When she did it wearing a blindfold, he used specific words to communicate with her. A word, for instance, corresponding with a number. He even taught the duchess how to do it, and she amazed her guests by performing alongside Houdini.

RETIREMENT FUND

In Europe, Houdini could earn in one week, as much as $1,750, the equivalent of more than $45,000 today. The money was pouring in. Houdini loved Europe, and could not be blamed for thinking it might be a long time before he would appear again in the United States:

> Over here I stay one, two and even six months in one City, and have a GREAT reputation, and in America it means every week jump to another city!! So I will nurse Europe as long as it will accept HOUDINI, and then come home to America, and retire.

DISILLUSIONMENT SETS IN

Houdini would later become seriously disillusioned with the man whose influence had turned him into a magician. In 1909, in fact, he published what he considered an exposé in the book, *The Unmasking of Robert-Houdin.*

His disillusionment may have begun some years earlier, as a result of perceived slights by the French magician's family. Robert-Houdin had died in 1871, before Houdini was born, but in 1902, Houdini discovered that Robert-Houdin's daughter-in-law was living in a Parisian suburb. He wrote to her, saying:

> I, as a representative of American Magicians, do hereby kindly ask your consent to permit me ... to place a wreath on the tomb of Robert-Houdin, also to grant me a few moments, so that I may have the pleasure of thanking you in person for your extreme kindness. Thanking you in advance for your awaited letter, I do hereby sign myself, Harry Houdini.

TRACKING DOWN ROBERT-HOUDIN

There was no reply. It turned out later that she was, in fact, ill at the time, but Houdini was deeply offended. He was nothing if not determined, however. He knew that Robert-Houdin was interred in the town of Blois on the River Loire, and that another daughter Rosalie, a sculptress, lived there with her husband Henri.

He visited them, and was welcomed at their house by Henri, Rosalie being busy. Robert-Houdin had been a clockmaker, and Houdini's later antipathy to the legend of Robert-Houdin is expressed in a description of some clocks he was shown:

> I was soon placed at my ease and shown a great many "Grandfather Clocks" ... Although at the time I thoroughly believed he had made them, I would not now be at all surprised if Robert-Houdin had bought them and had his name engraved on the various articles.

RESPECT FADING FAST

With Henri's blessing, Houdini set off for Robert-Houdin's tomb. He laid a wreath with the message "Honor and Respect to Robert-Houdin from the Magicians of America," and had a photograph taken beside the tomb. The rebuff in Paris and Rosalie's failure to see him still irritated him, however.

His disillusionment with his former hero was compounded the following year in Russia, when he bumped into a Frenchman named Bolin who created stage illusions for a living. Bolin was very knowledgeable about magic, and had met Robert-Houdin.

He told Houdini that the great French magician had exaggerated his achievements in his memoirs. Houdini pounced on this, and began investigating for himself. He began publishing the results of his enquiries in *Conjurers' Monthly Magazine* in 1906.

Harry "Handcuff" Houdini, 1903.

WRETCHED BLACKBURN

On December 14, 1903, Houdini was back in Blackburn, a "wretched town," as he described it, where "the gallery is certainly the worst." That night a young local man named Wilson had brought handcuffs to challenge Houdini. Wilson made a speech from the stage, and then went to walk off, seemingly reluctant to pass over his handcuffs.

Houdini followed him, grabbed the handcuffs off Wilson, and quickly snapped them shut over his own wrists. When Houdini entered his cabinet, however, he discovered that the inside of the lock had been removed. It took him an unusually long time—ten minutes—to free himself.

He emerged to boos of derision, but Houdini snapped the handcuffs onto some rods at the front of the stage. It took Wilson ten minutes to remove them. Houdini was booed, and Wilson was applauded. Perhaps because the audience believed Houdini was trying to make a fool of the young man.

COUNTING COLUMN INCHES

Houdini was very annoyed and irritated by the audience reaction. The local *Standard and Weekly Express* newspaper ran a story suggesting that he was about to walk away from performing altogether:

> *I hear that Houdini, having made his "pile," intends shortly to retire from the stage, for the demand made on him by his performances and the brutality to which he has not infrequently to submit, are making inroads on his health.*

His main publicity platform—the escape from police cells—was also becoming increasingly difficult to organize. Some forces, such as Birmingham in the Midlands, in late December 1903, refused to indulge him.

He did, however, successfully get copious column inches of publicity in Sheffield, Yorkshire, when he escaped from a triple-locked cell, that twenty-five years earlier, had held the infamous English burglar, and murderer, Charles Peace (1832 – 79).

THE ANTIQUE MANACLES

But he was increasingly dismayed by the fall in attendance at his shows. When he returned to London, to perform at the Hippodrome Theater in late February 1904, he tried to drum up public interest by staging an escape from 131 pounds of antique manacles at the offices of the *Weekly Dispatch* newspaper.

The antique manacles had been borrowed from the Chamber of Horrors, built by John Tussaud (1858 – 1943), the great-grandson of Madame Tussaud (1761 – 1850), founder of the famous wax museum. They had even been used as restraints on prisoners at Paris's Bastille prison, and on some of England's most notorious criminals.

But it made no difference to his box office. People were losing interest. In his diary, he wrote:

> *House very poorly visited. Hope business will pick up.*

AVENUES ARE CLOSING

In London, as elsewhere, the police were also becoming more and more tired of Houdini, and were reluctant to help him with publicity. After Bow Street police station refused to assist, he wrote to the Metropolitan Police Commissioner to ask if he would authorize his cell break-outs. The Commissioner's office replied:

> *I am directed by the commissioner to acknowledge receipt of your letter of the 7th, and to say that he regrets being unable to grant you permission to make the attempt of effecting an escape from any police cell in the city.*

With these particular avenues closing, he would now have to come up with something else to drive people to his performances.

A 1903 poster for a Houdini show at the Palace Theater in Halifax, Yorkshire, England.

PART THREE

THE CONSTANT FEAR OF OBLIVION

Never tell the audience how good you are; they will soon find out for themselves.

HARRY HOUDINI

CHAPTER 9

The Right Way To Do Wrong

THE DAILY MIRROR HANDCUFF CHALLENGE

The handcuffs were extraordinary. They were very heavy, a single cuff fastening both wrists. There were two Bramah locks—the Bramah being famed for the difficulty in picking it or tampering with it. The incredible handcuffs were offered to Houdini during a performance at the London Hippodrome in March 1904. He was reluctant to accept the challenge, protesting that they were not "regulation cuffs." The man in possession of the handcuffs announced to the audience:

On behalf of my newspaper, The Daily Illustrated Mirror, I have just challenged Mr. Houdini to permit me to fasten these handcuffs on his wrists. Mr. Houdini declines ... The handcuffs are made of the finest British steel, by a British workman, and being the property of The Daily Illustrated Mirror, has been bought with British gold. Mr. Houdini is evidently afraid of British-made handcuffs, for he will not put on this pair.

TAKING UP THE CHALLENGE

As Houdini proceeded to break free from the normal handcuffs that other challengers had brought, the newspaperman interrupted and asked if he might have one of these pairs. He took the handcuffs to some stairs leading up to the stage, and brought them crashing down on a step. The cuffs sprang open immediately to the delight of the audience.

He turned to the audience and questioned Houdini's right to call himself the "Handcuff King," if he refused to take on his challenge. Houdini could not let this pass. He said he would accept the challenge, but there was insufficient time that evening to undertake an escape from such a device.

The date of March 17 was set, during the matinée performance at the London Hippodrome Theater, when the challenge would take place. Naturally, there was a frenzy of pre-event press coverage—far more than breaking out of a Bow Street police cell could ever have generated.

On the day, 4,000 spectators crammed into the Hippodrome Theater, near Leicester Square, in central London. Houdini came on stage, and asked for a committee of audience members to ensure that everything was above board. He also asked for any of his friends present to come forward.

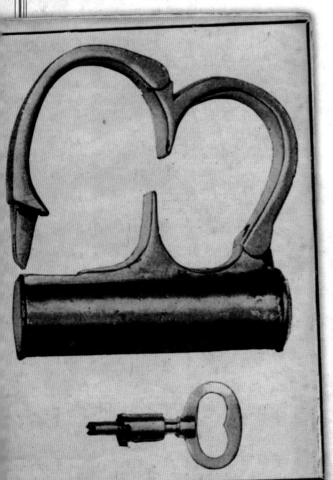

THE SPECIAL PAIR OF HANDCUFFS

The extraordinary Mirror cuffs.

AN EXHAUSTING ORDEAL

By the time the handcuffs were locked—the massive key being turned six times to huge cheers from the audience—around a hundred people were on the stage. Houdini entered his three-feet tall cabinet, where he would secretly perform the escape.

He emerged a few times to examine the lock in the light, and to stretch his limbs, and drink some water. He was provided with a cushion. On another occasion, he emerged to cut off his jacket, using a penknife clenched between his teeth.

After an hour, with some members of the audience yelling at him to give it up, he leapt from the cabinet, the handcuffs dangling from one hand. The crowd went wild with delight as Houdini, exhausted by his ordeal, collapsed in the arms of his friends. He later told the audience, after being carried round the arena on their shoulders:

> *I thought this was my Waterloo, after nineteen years of work. I have not slept for nights. But I will do so tonight!*

However, there was a great deal of muttering, doubters suggesting that anyone could escape from those handcuffs. Houdini, therefore used the *Mirror* to issue a challenge to the world to try to escape from them. Needless to say, no one succeeded.

The truth behind the challenge is probably that the *Mirror* and Houdini concocted the entire stunt between them, to gain publicity for him, and increase the circulation of the newspaper. Houdini had particularly cosy relationships with *The Weekly Dispatch* and the *Mirror*. It is probably no coincidence that they were both owned by Houdini's close friend, Alfred Harmsworth (1865 – 1922).

ESCAPE FROM EVERYTHING

In his live shows, Houdini now introduced a new challenge. In Essen, Germany, in 1902, he had escaped from a packing case, but in advance, he had challenged people to prove that the trunk was not fixed in some way. In May 1904, in London, he picked up a gauntlet thrown down by a company named

The cuffs are locked on Houdini's wrists at the Hippodrome Theater during the Daily Mirror Challenge, 1904.

Howill & Son. They insisted that there was no way he could escape from their specially-made trunk. It was a brilliant idea that he accepted and expanded upon.

From that day on, he always included in his act a challenge to the audience to bring their own trunks, boxes, and sacks for him to escape from. It created amazing tension and anticipation in the audience, and took away the limiting nature of just being the King of Handcuffs. Now, Houdini could escape from everything!

RETURN TO NEW YORK

Finally, it was time to drag himself away from Europe. On May 27, 1904, Harry, Bess, and Hardeen, boarded ship for New York. Coincidentally, Houdini's former manager, Martin Beck, was on board and offered to upgrade them to first class. Houdini declined the offer.

Beck also offered to book him to do some shows back home, but Houdini had been missing his mother, and needed a rest. Therefore, he planned no work before returning to England at the end of August.

During his visit, he bought a New York base for himself and Bess, where his mother, brother Leopold, and sister Gladys, could stay. It would also be large enough to house his burgeoning collection of books on magic, and spiritualism, as well as all the magic memorabilia he had purchased over the years.

TWENTY-SIX ROOMS

He paid $25,000 (around $677,000 today) for a ten-year-old twenty-six-room mansion at 278 West 113th Street in a respectable part of Harlem. One can only imagine how he felt walking through the doors of this huge property, his promise to his father well and truly fulfilled.

He had it decorated, and in his bathroom was a mosaic spelling out "H." The floor of Bess's bathroom had "B" marked out in tiles. In the basement he had a workshop installed where he could work and build props for his shows.

He also at this time purchased a burial plot in the Machpelah Cemetery in Cypress Hills, Queens, and had the remains of his father, and his half-brother Herman, re-interred there. He even rather gruesomely had a look at them before the re-burial, noting in his diary at the time:

> *Saw all that was left of poor father and Herman, nothing but skin and bones. Herman's teeth were in excellent condition.*

Harry Houdini with his mother Cecilia Weiss, and his wife Bess.

EDNA FERBER

American novelist, short-story writer, and playwright, Edna Ferber (1885 – 1968), was born in Kalamazoo, Michigan, to a Hungarian-born Jewish shopkeeper, and his Wisconsin-born wife. At the age of 12, Ferber and her family moved to Appleton, Wisconsin, where she was briefly a student at Lawrence University. She worked for the *Appleton Daily Crescent* and the *Milwaukee Journal* newspapers, but suffered a severe nervous breakdown.

During her recuperation, she wrote a short story, "The Homely Heroine," that was published in *Everybody's Magazine* and, in 1911, she published her first novel, *Dawn O'Hara*. She also wrote the first in a long series of stories that featured a traveling saleswoman named Emma McChesney.

Her work became well-known and, in 1912, she moved to New York. In the coming years, she developed into one of the most influential female writers of her time. She published numerous novels and stories, and became a member of the famous social/literary group, the Algonquin Round Table. Among the other members were Dorothy Parker (1893 – 1967), Groucho Marx (1890 – 1977), and Robert Benchley (1889 – 1945).

Her fiction, drawn from the lives of ordinary Americans and often featuring strong female protagonists, was criticized for being sentimental, but it was hugely popular. She won the 1925

Pulitzer Prize for her novel *So Big*, which sold more than 300,000 copies, and in 1926, her best-known work *Show Boat* was published. It was adapted into an acclaimed musical in 1927. Other works that became films included *Cimarron* (1929) which won the 1931 Academy Award for Best Picture, and *Giant* (1952), famously made into a 1956 film starring James Dean, Elizabeth Taylor, and Rock Hudson. Edna Ferber died in 1968, at age 82.

GOING BACK TO APPLETON

He also made a visit to his old hometown of Appleton, Wisconsin. While there, he was interviewed for the local newspaper by Edna Ferber (1885 – 1968), a young woman who later became a famous author. Her article appeared with a description of Houdini:

> ... a quick and nervous chap, inclined to jump when an unexpected noise is heard and to shut his eyes until they are almost closed, when speaking under excitement. [She felt his forearm, which was] ... amazing, as massive and hard as a granite pillar. His neck, too, is large and corded.

COUP DE THÉÂTRE

Houdini spoke to Edna Ferber about life after performing:

> I think that in a year I may retire. I cannot take my money with me when I die and I wish to enjoy it, with my family, while I live. I should prefer living in Germany to any other country, though I am an American, and am loyal to my country. I like the German people and customs. Why don't I go then? Why it is too far away from my mother, who lives in New York City with a couple of my young brothers.

At the end of the interview, Houdini performed a wonderful *coup de théâtre*. As he had been talking to her, he had been leaning on a vending machine that sold chocolate and chewing gum. "Better give this to the drugstore man," he said, dropping the padlock of the machine into her hand.

NAILING THE BOX OFFICE

At the end of August 1904, as the Houdinis said goodbye to New York and returned to England, retirement seemed a long way off. Houdini's money had now increased, because Harry Day had negotiated his bookings on a percentage of box office receipts. He would almost certainly earn more as he invariably played to capacity audiences.

On September 22, Houdini performed an escape from a box at the zoo in Glasgow, Scotland. Huge crowds turned out to see him and tickets were being re-sold at double, and treble, their original value. A box had been specially constructed by Messrs. J.&G. Findlay.

With Houdini inside, it was nailed and roped shut by eight carpenters, and placed on a raised platform behind a curtain. After fifteen minutes Houdini appeared from behind the curtain, covered in sweat and looking decidedly rumpled. Not a nail on the box had been loosened, and the three ropes that had bound it were still firmly in place. The audience, as ever, cheered wildly.

AN AIR OF INTEGRITY

Eight days later, Houdini was in high dudgeon after a rival advertised an escape from "an unprepared coffin." At a performance on September 30, he brought on stage a coffin and began to explain to the audience how the man had "escaped."

He protested that the coffin was not "unprepared," as the advertisement had trumpeted. It had been interfered with, before being brought onto the stage. The long screws that kept the ends in place had been substituted with shorter screws allowing the man to simply push the ends of the coffin out and slip free. He demonstrated by lying in the coffin and doing it. But then he replaced the short screws with the originals.

The screws were tightened and he climbed in. The lid was clamped on and the committee of audience members, who had been invited to add screws wherever they liked, went to work. Stamps were then pasted over the screws and over the edges of the coffin where the lid met the sides to prevent any tampering.

Houdini appeared in just a couple of minutes, the coffin, stamps and all in pristine condition behind him. His trickery was just that bit cleverer than the other man's, but he was always at pains to present himself as an honest man with an air of integrity.

The Secrets of Houdini
The Right Way to Do Wrong

Houdini became an author in 1906 with the publication of his first book, *The Right Way to Do Wrong: An Exposé of Successful Criminals*, in which he signs himself "Handcuff King and Jail Breaker." In it, he uses findings taken from interviews with criminals and police officers to explain various types of crime, and how crooks and swindlers carry out their nefarious deeds.

Chapter headings included "Income of a Criminal," "Pickpockets at Work," "Begging Letter Swindles," "Burglars' Superstitions," and "Thieves and their Tricks." In a chapter headed "Fake! Fake! Fake!" among several examples of fakery, Houdini talks about spiritualism:

> *Spiritualism has many followers, and at one time I was almost a believer, but this was before I made a thorough investigation, which I have followed up even to the present day. I have never seen a materialization or a manifestation which I cannot fully explain … Spiritualism is really a beautiful belief for those that are honest and believe in it; but as I have visited the greatest spiritualistic meetings in the world, I am sorry to say that no one has ever produced anything for me that would smack of the spiritual.*

Card swindles, burglary, pickpocketing, shoplifting, and safe-cracking, are all discussed with Houdini explaining how criminals go about their business. Throughout, he cautions against criminal activity:

> *To those who read this book, although it will inform them "The Right Way to Do Wrong," all I have to say is one word and that is— "DON'T."*

He knew about many of the techniques explained in the book because he, of course, used them himself. But still, he maintained his aura of honesty. The trickery of others was just that—trickery, implying that there was something dishonest about it.

Houdini, however, as he often announced somewhat pompously, had his "secrets." Indeed, a rumor spread that he had locked his "secrets" in a box, only to be opened many years after his death. This was obviously not true, and his "secrets" are now known by magicians and many others.

In fact they were pretty much known while he was still alive, although, if he felt that too many people knew the secret of a particular trick, he would make public his method of performing it.

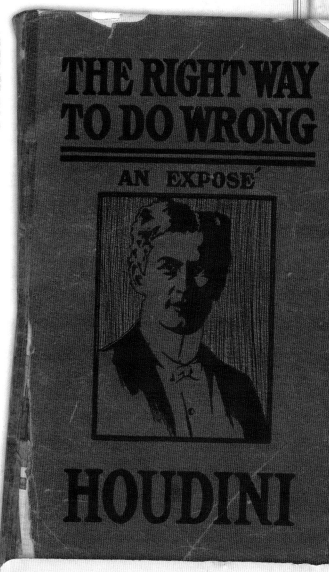

First edition front cover of *The Right Way to Do Wrong*, 1906.

CHAPTER 10

MAKE OR BREAK TIME

In the fall of 1905, Houdini was back in America. He had signed up for a six-week tour that paid him $5,000. As he opened at the Colonial Theater, New York, he felt like he was almost launching his career again. Having not performed in the United States for five years, he was a comparative unknown.

His situation was not helped by the growing band of Houdini imitators that were popping up across the country. He had already made efforts in the past to dissuade people from passing themselves off as him, or at least using his tricks.

In 1903, he had heard that his old partner, Jacob Hyman, was playing under the name "Houdini" in Massachusetts. He dispatched his brother Leopold from New York,

accompanied by a lawyer, to persuade Hyman of the error of his ways.

THE DEFEATER HANDCUFFS

In May 1905 another of Harry's brothers, William, was sent over to Hurtig & Seamon's Music Hall in Manhattan, to talk to another Houdini impersonator, a man named Cunning. William took with him a set of Houdini's special "defeater" handcuffs, designed to flummox imitators. When Cunning called on people to come to the stage with their restraints, William joined them.

There were seven volunteers from the audience with handcuffs which were locked

Houdini (center) and his brothers (left to right) Leopold, Hardeen, William, and Nathan.

on the performer. He was then secured in a steel cage around which a curtain was pulled. Time passed and there was no sign from Cunning. When he did finally stagger out, he had managed to free only one arm.

Cunning tried to walk off the stage, but a melee broke out as William tried to get his handcuffs back. He was tossed off the stage by the stagehands but the audience leapt to William's defense and attacked the stagehands. William was ultimately arrested and spent the night in a prison cell but charges were later dismissed.

CHAOTIC RUCKUS

Houdini, of course, would not let it go. A few nights later, he and Hardeen were in the audience at Hyde and Behman's theater, Brooklyn, to see Cunning's performance. At the request for audience members with handcuffs, Hardeen leapt on stage with five other men. Cunning put on all the handcuffs, but when Hardeen stepped up, Cunning gestured for him to return to his seat.

Hardeen pulled out a $50 note, and said that he bet Cunning could not escape from his handcuffs. Cunning and his assistants began pushing and shouting insults. Houdini went to defend his brother and joined in the argument. Eventually, the curtain was brought down on the whole chaotic ruckus.

NO PUBLICITY IS BAD PUBLICITY

With the theater in uproar, someone punched Hardeen, knocking him out. The audience went mad, and the police were called. Hardeen was dragged from the theater, and charged with disorderly conduct.

The following day in court, Houdini charmed the magistrate, telling him that the entire business was nothing more than an advertising stunt gone wrong. The charges against his brother were dropped. But the old adage "No publicity is bad publicity," turned out to be true. Houdini gained just as much publicity from this escapade as he did from some of his own staged stunts.

PRISON BREAK

Houdini tried to revive the police prison cell escapes in an attempt to drum up the publicity he needed to fill the theaters where he was performing. The importance of these pre-show stunts was shown in a letter from an East Coast booker that he received while in Europe. Lack of publicity was given as a reason for rejecting Houdini's salary demands:

> *... it is absolutely impossible for us to get the cooperation of the police force in tests and experiments in connection with your work and therefore secure the valuable advertising that you are able to do in the west and in Europe.*

Houdini managed, however, to perform some prison breaks in a few US cities. Then he received an invitation from Warden Harris, the governor of the 10th Precinct jail in Washington DC, to test the security of his prison.

Houdini turned up with a bunch of reporters on January 6, 1906. He asked to make his escape from Cell Number Two, a strongly fortified cell that had once held Charles J. Guiteau, the assassin of President James A. Garfield (1831 – 81).

ESCAPE FROM MURDERER'S ROW

Cell Number Two was located in a block of seventeen cells known as Murderer's Row. They were all made of brick, with their doors sunk into the walls, three feet from the outer wall of the corridor that passed them. All the doors in the corridor were heavily barred, and when they were closed, an L-shaped bar stuck out that was angled to the right. It slipped over a steel catch, which in turn tripped a spring that fastened a five-tumbler lock.

However, as in most prisons, one key could unlock all the doors in that particular corridor. Totally naked, to prove that he was not hiding anything, Houdini was locked in Cell Number Two, and was out in two minutes. He was not finished, however. He ran along the corridor to the other cells and opened them all, swapping prisoners around.

The Secrets of Houdini
The Jail Breaks

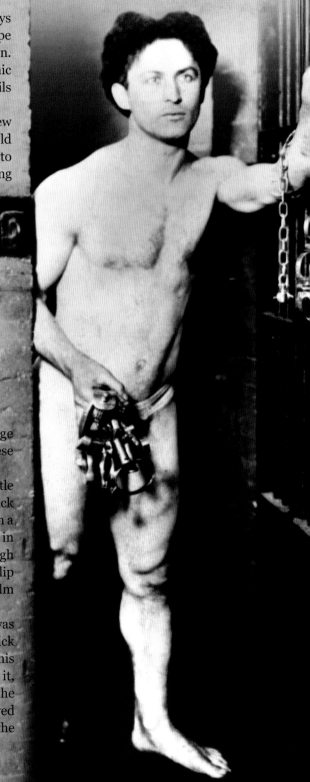

In preparation, Houdini would turn up a few days in advance at a jail he was going to make an escape from. Bess often tagged along to cause a distraction. It has been suggested that he had a photographic memory. That allowed him to memorize the details of a key and make a duplicate.

But it seems more likely he was relying on a few tried and tested methods. There was always the old trick of using a lump of clay or a little box of wax to make an impression of the shape of the key. Visiting a cell in advance also gave him the chance to hide tools or lock-picks in the cell, perhaps in a bar of soap or stuck onto a piece of gum under a shelf or a bench out of sight.

Sometimes, if the stone floor of a prison was too cold or unsanitary, he would use a brilliant piece of subterfuge. A friend had created a shoe with hollow heels in which he could hide his escape tools.

He sometimes brought along his own massive padlocks, convincing the police that it would look better in the papers if he escaped from his own huge padlocks as well as the police-issue ones. But these padlocks were in reality little toolboxes.

Another method of smuggling tools in was a little egg-shaped container that he concealed at the back of his throat. He might even obtain his tools from a friend whose hand he would shake once he was in the cell. He had a habit of shaking hands through the bars. As he did so, he would open a spring clip on a finger ring being worn by the man and palm the key or pick he needed.

One trick he is reputed to have used when he was searched while naked, was to have the key or pick in his hand, and ask his searchers to start with his thick hair. Once they had thoroughly searched it, he would run his palm through it depositing the key there ready to be used later. He even received a key sometimes in a kiss from Bess through the bars of the cell.

Lastly, he broke into the cell containing his clothes, got dressed and strolled nonchalantly into the governor's office, where the crowd of reporters was waiting. They were completely amazed, and even more so when they discovered all the prisoners were in the wrong cells.

NO CONFEDERACY OR COLLUSION

Warden Harris gave Houdini a sparkling letter of commendation. "There was positively no chance," he wrote, "for any confederacy or collusion." The warden dressed it up as a valuable experiment by Houdini, helping to improve the security of the prison. Reports were issued to that effect:

> *The experiment was a valuable one in that the department has been instructed as to the adoption of further security, which will protect any lock from being opened or interfered with … Mr. Houdini impressed his audience as a gentleman and an artist who does not profess to do the impossible.*

The reality was that it was just another publicity stunt designed to sell tickets. As such, it had been entirely successful. How had he done it? Probably by jamming a small wooden wedge into the socket of the lock's spring latch, making the lock appear closed when it was not.

ON TOUR IN AMERICA

At that time Houdini was escaping from anything and everything. No straitjacket, jail cell, safe, or container could hold the great magician. In September 1906, in Washington DC, he broke out of a zinc-lined piano box. In Toledo, Ohio, he was almost beaten by a boiler. While in San Francisco, it took him all of twenty-five minutes to escape from a mail bag.

In January 1907, in Boston, Massachusetts, Houdini agreed to escape from a coffin while manacled. It took him over an hour to get out of the elaborate case—the lid had been nailed down with 6-inch nails!

When he leapt from a bridge in Rochester, a man slightly the worse for wear from drink, plunged in to try to save him. They both managed to make it safely back to the shore. In Passaic, New Jersey, the river he jumped into was so polluted that he was almost defeated. In Pittsburgh, Pennsylvania, a massive crowd of 40,000 spectators watched him jump, in handcuffs, from the 7th Street Bridge.

THE FEAR OF OBLIVION

These stunts all gained publicity for his shows, but things were not going as well as they had in Europe. It was partly because of all the rivals and impersonators. A Canadian handcuff artist turned up in Detroit, performing on the same night as Houdini at another theater. He was described by the Detroit *Times* as "unquestionably better" than the Handcuff King. Houdini was quick to point out that he had never used the *Times* for advertising and that paper had an axe to grind against him.

Needless to say, when he encountered these characters, Houdini destroyed them in characteristic fashion, but they detracted from his originality and hit his audience numbers. He feared the day when his act would be over and a few times he thought he was close to the end of his performing days.

In 1908, when he was way down the bill at a theater in Cleveland, he recalled the fate of some of his predecessors, such as Thomas Nelson Downs, the "King of Koins:"

> *Am not featured. Is this the first step towards oblivion? No attention paid to me … Downs has retired, and is landlording in Marshalltown, Ia. He could not change his act and so died theatrically.*

THOMAS NELSON DOWNS

Thomas Nelson Downs (1867 – 1938) was born in Marshalltown in Iowa, the youngest of a family of six. Completely self-taught, he was expert in card and coin manipulation by the age of 12. At 17, he found a job as a railway telegrapher which gave him a lot of time to practice his skills with card and coins.

In 1895, at age 28, he launched a career in magic. Within two years, Downs was specializing in coin tricks. His act was fairly unique and he soon established himself as a vaudeville artiste. His success took him around the world and he played at royal courts as well as in good venues such as Tony Pastor's New York Theater, and London's Palace Theater.

Downs possessed the remarkable ability to palm up to sixty coins at a time and one of his best-known tricks was "The Miser's Dream," in which he pulled huge numbers of coins out of thin air. It was a trick that had been used many years before by a magician named de Linski, and Jean Eugène Robert-Houdin was performing a version of it entitled "Shower of Money" by 1852.

In 1908, Downs decided to retire to Iowa at the age of 42. He opened a vaudeville house in Marshalltown, and sold magic equipment. He was often visited by other magicians, including Harry Houdini, Chung Ling Soo, and Canadian magician, Dai "The Professor" Vernon (1894 – 1992). T. Nelson Downs died in 1938, age 71. His headstone commemorates him as "King of Koins."

The Secrets of Houdini
The Buried-Alive Coffin Escape

Death fascinated Harry Houdini, after all, he had had his fair share. He had lost his half-brother Herman when he was only 12 years old, and had lost his father too when he was still young. He was known to frequent cemeteries, and must have dreamed up his buried-alive coffin escape during one of his visits.

He had tried to figure out ways to make it work. It would be difficult to shift earth while underground, certainly more difficult than water. So, he devised a method featuring two loose end boards that were held by a catch in the top of the box. When the catch was released the boards would fall into the box, allowing space for him to crawl out and dig his way up through the soil.

In 1917, a challenge was thrown down in California. He would be buried alive, and handcuffed, at a depth of six feet. The actual site of the stunt was vital. The soil needed to be light and sandy, and entirely free of vegetation such as roots. He constantly practiced.

Firstly, he was buried one foot down, then two feet down, and progressively deeper, until he was being entombed six feet down. It was not easy, however, and the people who had challenged him were happy for him to stop at four or five feet. But Houdini dramatically insisted on the full six feet under.

He had to struggle to control the stress he felt. He began the dig once he had released the fake ends of the coffin. Panic began to set in, as he felt the full weight of the soil above him pressing down. When he tried to shout for help he got a mouthful of soil for his efforts.

He dug at the soil, gradually making his way upward and finally pushing through the surface. Although he escaped from plenty more coffins after that, they were always on the surface. He never performed the buried-alive coffin escape again.

BURIED ALIVE

STRAPPED IN STRAIT JACKET

SECURED IN CASKET

BURIED UNDER SAND AND SECURELY LOCKED IN GIANT VAULT

HARRY HOUDINI'S ORIGINAL CREATION

ESCAPING FROM A QUADRUPLE SMOTHERING IMPRISONMENT UNDER TONS OF SAND.

"FREE!"

HOWARD ELCOCK

The Illusion That Never Was! This 1914 illustration of Houdini's "Buried Alive" escape depicts the way he imagined it. In the event, the stunt proved impossible, and the 1917 California challenge was his only attempt.

The Secrets of Houdini
The Milk-Can Escape

By 1908, Houdini was beginning to believe he needed to add a bit more spark to his act—something new and different. It came in the form of a milk-can. Large enough for a man of Houdini's stature to slip into, it was a giant galvanized-iron can that was made in the shape of a very large milk-can. He introduced it into his act on January 27, 1908.

The can held 22 gallons of water and when it was wheeled out onto the stage to be filled, Houdini would go off to put on a bathing costume. He would return to explain to the audience that a man can only live a certain time without air to breathe.

He then clambered into the can, water slopping about, and splashing onto the stage. But before plunging his head down below the surface of the water and being locked in, he first challenged the audience, as an experiment, to hold its breath for as long as possible.

The can was then topped up, and Houdini sank down below the surface out of sight. Of course, having practiced for many years, he was able to hold his breath a lot longer than the audience, and by the time his head reappeared, they had all started breathing again. In fact, Houdini could hold his breath for a remarkable three minutes underwater. It was a lot longer than many of the swimming champions he challenged.

He next had himself handcuffed before ducking under the water again. His assistants filled the can to the brim before screwing the lid on and padlocking it with no fewer than six padlocks. The curtain was drawn to conceal the milk-can and the drama began, the orchestra playing "Sailor Beware."

As time passed, his assistant Franz Kukol added even more drama by appearing with an axe ready to break into the can if necessary. Kukol walked up to the curtain and put his ear to it. Three minutes had passed as he raised his axe.

Just at that moment, Houdini would appear from behind the curtain, water dripping from him, an exhausted smile on his face. He and Kukol stepped up to the can and revealed it to be completely intact, locks in place, and when it was opened it was found to be still brimming with water. Houdini's new stunt was a triumph and brought the full houses back again.

HOW DID HE DO IT?

Of course, Houdini used a special milk-can. The secret of this trick was revealed by a friend a few years after the magician's death. The collar of the can was not really riveted to its body. The rivets were fake, although there were the ends of rivets inside to create the impression that they were real. Furthermore, because the collar was tapered and greased, it was impossible for anyone to pull it off or move it. However, it was easy to push it up from the inside and climb out, thereby leaving the padlocks around the lid intact. There were also two tiny air-holes in the lid of the can. If something untoward were to happen, Houdini would not have been in too much danger.

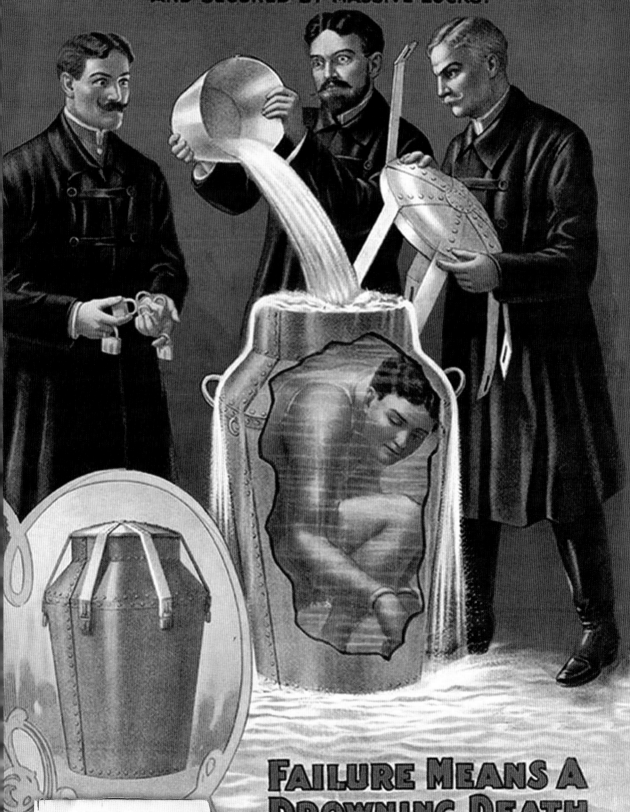

Vintage Milk-Can Escape poster.

CHAPTER 11

THE HIGH-WATER MARK

The year 1912 was a very good time for Harry Houdini. It probably represented the high-water mark of his career in vaudeville. He was offered $1,000 a week for an eight-week stint at Hammerstein's Paradise Roof Garden in New York, a semi-outdoor venue owned by impresario Oscar Hammerstein I (1846 – 1919). It was built on top of the Victoria Theater and the next-door Theater Republic, popularly known at the time as the Belasco Theater.

Houdini had been met with reticence to cover his exploits before by the cynical New York reporters. This time he was determined to win them over. He invented a brand new publicity stunt that he practiced at the Municipal Swimming Pool on 80th Street and the East River.

One of his assistants, Jim Collins (1882 – 1942), had created a hefty packing-case box, weighted with iron, which was designed to be lowered into the river, with a manacled Houdini inside. Collins had used short screws on one of its sides to help Houdini escape, but it would certainly stand up to close inspection.

INTO THE WATER

On the day that Houdini opened at the Paradise Roof Garden, he was to be winched into the East River in the morning, handcuffed and in leg-irons inside the box. As well as the gentlemen of the press, a large crowd turned out to witness the spectacle. Even Houdini's mother made the short trip across town to see her son's big moment.

Harry Houdini after having escaped from a nailed-down packing crate submerged in the East River, New York City.

The police arrived, however, and put a stop to it, declaring it was against the law to jump off New York's piers. Thinking quickly, Houdini spied a nearby tugboat and jumped on board, and his packing case followed him. The obliging tugboat sailed out to the middle of the river, where the pressmen who had accompanied Houdini inspected his handcuffs and leg-irons.

He climbed into the box, and nails were hammered into the lid, closing it solidly against the sides. The box was then winched into the cold East River water while the journalists took out their watches and began to count the seconds. It took him fifty-seven seconds to escape.

IN THE PALM OF HIS HAND

The New York reporters were impressed, cheering him as he spluttered onto the deck of the tug. When they brought the box to the surface it was still intact, and inside were the handcuffs and leg-irons he had been wearing. The headlines that night were all Houdini's.

He finally had New York in the palm of his hand.

During the engagement at the Paradise Roof Garden, Houdini requested his first week's salary be paid to him in gold coins. He took the coins to his house, and poured them into his mother's apron like a character from a fairy tale. His father would have been very proud of him.

THE INTREPID AIRMAN

Houdini had been defying death as part of his act for years. But in 1908 he discovered another daring new way to challenge his own mortality.

In 1903, the American Wright Brothers had undertaken the first powered flight in their craft, the *Wright Flyer I*, near Kitty Hawk in North Carolina. Now, Houdini became fascinated with manned flight, offering the Wright Brothers $5,000 for him to be flown in one of their planes over the West End of London.

Houdini proposed to parachute down, escaping from handcuffs as he plummeted toward the ground. He would land in the middle of Piccadilly Circus. Sadly, this spectacular stunt never happened, but Houdini did not completely put flying out of his mind.

So, when he was in Germany the following year, playing the Hansa Theater in Hamburg, he was delighted to learn that the German aviator Hans Grade (1879–1946) was putting on a demonstration of a new French biplane, the Voisin, at an airfield near the city.

NOTHING WAS IMPOSSIBLE

The Voisin biplane was the very latest in aero-technology. One had recently made a flight near Rheims in France lasting more than an hour and twenty minutes. Houdini hurried out to the airfield and was captivated by the flight. He met Grade, congratulated him, and implored him to tell him where he could purchase such a craft.

It should be remembered that, at this time, no more than a couple of dozen people in the whole world had flown an airplane. Houdini was entering a world of inexperienced pioneers, where no one knew much about anything. If he did manage to buy an airplane, there was no such thing as a school where he could learn to fly. But, of course, this was Harry Houdini. Nothing was impossible.

THE PROUD OWNER

Within a week, he was the proud owner of a French Voisin biplane, bought for the princely sum of $5,000. It had been custom-built for him, and weighed 1,350 pounds, "with Mr. Houdini mounted." The eight-foot, steel-shafted, aluminium propeller was behind the pilot. The aircraft resembled an enlarged powered version of a box kite.

The Voisin was thirty-feet long by about six-feet wide, with four vertical panels that divided the main surface of the aircraft into four large sections. The rudder, used both to stabilize as well as steer the airplane, was at the rear of the craft, positioned in a six-foot square box-shaped tail. It was powered by an impressive E.N.V. 60 or 80 (we do not know which) horsepower engine.

Houdini hired a very good mechanic—a small, stout, Frenchman named Antonio Brassac whom, he hoped, would teach him how to get the craft up into the air, and, more importantly, keep it there. Brassac was a good man to have on the team. He had taught Louis Blériot (1872 – 1936) who, in July 1909, had become the first man to fly across the English Channel in a heavier-than-air craft. Brassac had also built the monoplane Blériot had flown in.

LEARNING TO FLY

Houdini obtained permission from the German Army to train at Husaren Exerzierplatz, Hamburg, on condition that, once he had learned to fly, he would train some of their officers. This was an agreement that would come back to haunt him at the

outbreak of the First World War. The use of military aircraft for the first time in warfare, caused him to complain to Bess:

I taught those fellows to fly, and they may have killed Americans!

Houdini set out early every freezing-cold morning with Brassac to Husaren, where for days the weather was so bad that flying was impossible. But, he sat in the cockpit, Brassac beside him, showing him how to operate the controls.

Finally, the clouds cleared, the ice melted, and the wind dropped. An excited Houdini watched as Brassac swung the propeller. He taxied off down the grass runway to the cheers of the watching German soldiers and began to lift off from the ground until he was airborne.

BROKE ALL TO HELL

Sadly, it did not last long and, after just a few seconds, the plane nose-dived and crashed to the ground. Brassac and the soldiers ran to the damaged plane. The nose had borne the brunt of the impact, which could mean bad news for the pilot. But Houdini walked away from the crash.

The plane had not suffered much damage, even though Houdini scribbled in his diary: "I smashed the machine. Broke propeller all to hell." The engine was undamaged and a new propeller was delivered from Paris within a couple of weeks.

On November 26, 1909, Houdini took to the sky again, and made his first successful flight. At the end of December, however, he had to leave Hamburg. He had been booked to perform in Australia.

But he did not intend to leave behind his new-found passion for aviation. He was to be accompanied by Antonio Brassac and the Voisin biplane. Fully aware that, as yet, no one had flown in Australasia, he was determined to be the first one.

OSCAR HAMMERSTEIN I

Born in Stettin in Prussia, Oscar Hammerstein (1846 – 1919) began playing piano, flute, and violin while still young but, with his father not wanting him to follow a music career, he ran away to Liverpool in England and then to the United States. There, he worked in a cigar factory, working his way up to become a cigar maker and founded the *US Tobacco Journal*. He invented numerous machines relating to cigar manufacture and also worked as a theater manager in German theaters in New York.

Having become rich from cigar manufacture, he built his first theater, the Harlem Opera House in 1889. A year later, he built the Columbus Theater on the same street. The Manhattan Opera House followed in 1893. He built four more theaters in Times Square, and opened Hammerstein's Paradise Roof Garden in 1899.

Hammerstein decided to compete with what he viewed as the unsatisfactory Metropolitan Opera by building two opera houses. He presented contemporary operas and provided them with large budgets, but the productions resulted in financial problems, that led him to the brink of bankruptcy.

Meanwhile, the rival Metropolitan was also heading for financial trouble as it tried to compete with him. This led his son Arthur Hammerstein (1872 – 1955) to do a deal with them. In return for $1.2 million, his company would not stage an opera in the United States for the next ten years.

Hammerstein used the money to build the London Opera House in England to compete with the established Covent Garden's Royal Opera House. But the money ran out within two years, and Hammerstein returned to America.

The final theater he built—his eleventh—was the Lexington Opera House, but it opened as a cinema, as under the ten-year

agreement with the Metropolitan, he was still not allowed to produce opera in America. He sold the Lexington not long afterward. In 1910, he was focussing on drama, and had turned over all his opera buildings, and contracts, to the Metropolitan.

Hammerstein died in 1919, just a year before he was legally able to stage opera productions once more. He was 73 years old.

THE WRIGHT BROTHERS

Aviation pioneers, Orville (1871 – 1948) and Wilbur Wright (1867 – 1912) achieved the first powered, sustained, and controlled airplane flight in 1903. The brothers were born near Millville, Indiana. Their father was a bishop in the Church of the United Brethren in Christ. They developed their lifelong interest in aeronautics after their father brought home for them a model helicopter, based on a design by the French aeronautical pioneer Alphonse Pénaud (1850 – 80).

Wilbur planned to go to Yale University but in the winter of 1885 – 86, he was badly injured playing ice hockey, when another player's stick hit him in the face. The injury plunged him into depression, and he did not graduate from high school, let alone attend university. He retreated into himself, and spent most of his time reading, and caring for his sick mother, who died in 1889 of tuberculosis.

That year, the Wright brothers launched a newspaper, the *West Side News*, Wilbur editing, and Orville being publisher. At the time, bicycles were becoming extremely popular, leading the brothers to open a bicycle shop. They did repairs and sold a machine of their own design.

Wilbur and Orville closely followed the research of the German aviator, Otto Lilienthal (1848 – 96). Following his death in a glider accident, they resolved to start experimenting with flight. They based themselves in Kitty Hawk, North Carolina, an area known for its strong winds. They based their wing design on the angle of a bird's wings, in a concept they called "wing-warping."

Wilbur finally flew their craft on December 17, 1903. He made several flights, the first of 120 feet, lasting 12 seconds, at a speed of 6.8 miles per hour. The second, flown again by Wilbur, traveled 175 feet. The third, piloted this time by Orville, covered 200 feet. A fourth flight, with Wilbur at the controls, covered 852 feet in 59 seconds.

Many in the press, as well as fellow aviation experts, were reluctant to believe them, and some thought the distance inconsequential. However, when the brothers traveled to Europe to demonstrate their flying machine, they became famous. They also became wealthy back in the United States.

Wilbur died of typhoid in 1912, at age 45. Orville succeeded to the presidency of the Wright Company. He made his last flight as a pilot in 1918, and died in 1948, at the age of 77.

Aviation pioneers Wilbur (left) and Orville Wright, 1909.

CHAPTER 12

AVIATION FOR DAREDEVILS

In January 1910, Houdini set off for the other side of the world, but he always suffered badly from seasickness, and the long voyage to Australia was hell for him. It was a place where he had always said he would never perform. He lost twenty-eight pounds in weight. But his discomfort was alleviated somewhat by the wages, and the knowledge that the promoters were paying him for the journey, as well as the performances. He wrote to a friend:

> *So I get paid 12 weeks for resting and 12 for working. That is the only condition I would go all that distance ... It's a bit too far to get back from, shouldst anything happen to my mother.*

LORD NORTHCLIFFE'S VISION

Up until then, large balloons had been used in military operations, but the development of smaller aircraft that could be used for aerial surveillance had rendered them obsolete. Eventually, aircraft developed to such an extent that they had offensive capabilities, the ability to drop explosives on targets. There were those who recognized just how important flight could be for warfare, among them was the English newspaper magnate, Lord Northcliffe (1865 – 1922).

A close friend of Houdini, Northcliffe had been interested in aviation for years, and was convinced that in the next major conflict, airplanes would play a large and possibly decisive role. In 1909, he traveled to France to watch a display by the Wright brothers of their flying machine, but was disappointed that no representatives of the British military were present. He wrote to the British Secretary of State for War, Lord Haldane (1856 – 1928)

bemoaning the British government's lack of interest in this new technology.

With his pleas falling on apparently deaf ears, Northcliffe began to use his newspapers to stimulate interest in aviation, providing financial incentives amounting to around £95,000 for aviators. The most impactful of these was the £1,000 he paid Louis Blériot for his flight across the English Channel.

Following that, the newspapers were full of stories about Britain's lack of preparation for an air attack. By 1910, Northcliffe had come up with a plan to bend public opinion to his way of thinking by encouraging Harry Houdini, the world's greatest daredevil, to become the first to fly in Australia.

FLIGHT INCENTIVES

Houdini was contracted to make ten flights in Australia, each of more than five minutes. For these he would be paid £20,000 (more than £2 million in today's money). He and Brassac had prepared their aircraft, and visited the Voisin factory in Paris to stock up with extra parts.

The following day, they watched a woman pilot fly her airplane into a tree, destroying the craft. At the site of the crash, he bumped into a Belgian who was also traveling to Australia, aiming to be the first to make a powered flight there.

On Thursday, January 6, 1910, they embarked on their long voyage to Australia from Marseille, Bess having enjoyed a shopping spree beforehand. He wrote of her frenzied, pre-departure activity:

> *Bess out early and shopping, buys dresses and hats, happy as a lark. Her trunks full to overflowing. She has no worries.*

WATCHING THE WEATHER

On arrival in Melbourne, Australia, Houdini gave interviews in which he expressed his worries about sharks endangering his underwater stunts, and his retirement. He said that after he had fulfilled the next eighteen months' engagements, he would hang up his handcuffs for good. He immediately set about learning to drive so that he could get out to the airfield at Diggers Rest in the early morning.

The Voisin emerged from its packing crates on February 24, 1910, and they began the ritual of waiting for suitable flying weather. Days passed with Houdini returning to Melbourne to perform to sold-out houses each evening, worrying all the time that someone was going to beat him to the record. Sometimes he would drive out to Diggers Rest immediately after the show, to sleep in the tent where the aircraft was housed, with Brassac.

THE OPPOSITION

Making matters worse for Houdini was the presence of another airplane parked next to his. It was owned by the headmaster of Melbourne's Wesley College, Lawrence Adamson (1860 – 1932), who was determined that the honor of the first flight in Australia should not go to a jumped-up American magician. He had bought a Wright Brothers airplane and hired a British flier, Ralph C. Banks, to pilot his craft.

On March 1, as Houdini waited on the runway, he was astonished to see Banks about to take to the air. Houdini had that morning employed the match test to estimate whether conditions were suitable for flight. If a match was lit and it stayed lit, everything was okay. This morning, however, when Houdini had struck the match, it immediately blew out. The wind was too strong for flying. Banks was pushing his luck.

The British flier took off and flew for about 300 yards but, suddenly caught in a gust of wind, his craft dropped its nose and plummeted toward the ground. The airplane was destroyed, only two wheels and the engine remaining intact. Banks was lucky to escape with just cuts and bruises.

GOING FOR THE RECORD

Finally, on March 18, the sun rose on an almost windless day at Diggers Rest. At just

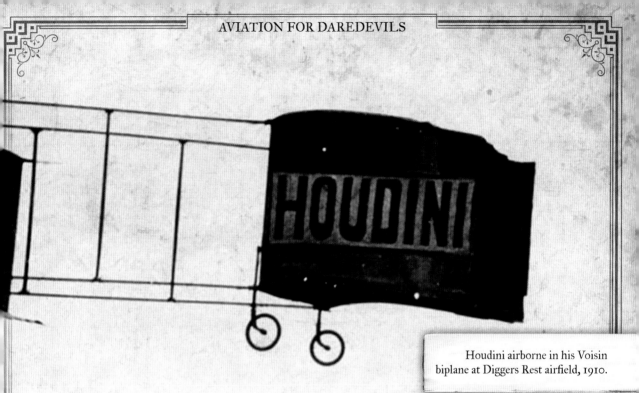

after 8:00 a.m., the Voisin, with *"HOUDINI"* proudly emblazoned on its tail, was wheeled carefully from its tented covering. Brassac checked it over while Houdini clambered into his seat, cap worn backward on his head, aviator-style.

He taxied across the field several times to warm up the engine. Then, always the showman, he returned to where Brassac was standing, asking him to make small adjustments to the rudder. Brassac spun the propeller again, and the engine leapt into life. Houdini eased the airplane forward, taking its speed up to 35 mph. It had traveled around fifty yards when he pushed down on the steering wheel, lifting the Voisin gently into the air.

He took it to a height of around twenty-five feet and started to circle around the field. About a minute after taking off, Houdini eased the airplane down to the ground to make a perfect landing. But he took it up again almost immediately, remaining airborne for a minute longer than his previous flight.

His landing this time was less successful, and the plane landed nose on the ground, tail in the air. Houdini managed to right the craft as Brassac and the other mechanics raced toward him.

AIRBORNE EXHILARATION

His next flight, a few minutes later, took him up to a height of 100 feet, and he made three circuits of the field, lasting around four minutes. He then brought the craft down, executing another perfect landing. He had done it!

Surrounded by photographers, he threw his arms up in a triumphant salute. He got the spectators, including his assistant, Franz Kukol, to sign a piece of paper certifying that he really had flown.

Houdini's place in aviation history was assured. He was the first person to make a controlled, powered flight of an airplane in Australia. He later commented in an interview with the *Sydney Herald*:

As soon as I was aloft all the tension and strain left me. When I was rolling every muscle of me was taut. When she cants over at the turns—you know how she goes when she's rolling—I'm always afraid the wing will break in the air. It was different as soon as I was up. All my muscles relaxed, and I sat back feeling a sense of ease, freedom and exhilaration. That's what it is. Oh she's great. I know what it is to fly in real earnest. She's like a swan. She's a dandy. I can fly now.

BEEN THERE DONE THAT

In characteristic fashion, after achieving the prize for the first flight in Australia, Houdini lost interest in flying. He had been there, and done that. The following year, when he read that a French flier had crashed an airplane of the same design as his, Houdini offered his Voisin for spare parts entirely free of charge.

Being Houdini, he did not make this offer without grabbing some publicity though, and the message was sent to the unfortunate aviator via the *Daily Mirror*. The magician was very irritated when the Frenchman failed to respond.

Houdini did make some spectacular flights later in March 1910, however, at the Rosehill racetrack near Sydney. Having persuaded Brassac to stay on in Australia, he put on a week of flying displays. His engagement at the racetrack proved so popular with the public that he was still doing the airshow in May. But the love affair with flying was over.

AERIAL LEAGUE OF AUSTRALIA

Particularly pleased with the success of Houdini's displays was George Taylor (1872 – 1928), founder of the Aerial League of Australia, who was a champion of the new technologies of aviation and wireless. Taylor had been the first man in Australia to fly a heavier-than-air craft, when he flew a glider in 1909. The Aerial League, founded the same year, was a pressure group that focused on aviation's military applications.

Taylor and the League representatives had been instrumental in persuading Houdini to bring his plane to Australia to promote military aviation. On April 29, the organization honored him at Sydney's town hall. Films of his flights were shown before he rushed in, having just finished a show in a theater in another part of town. They presented him with a trophy, a commemorative scroll, and an elaborate wooden plaque.

TANGLING WITH THE RED BARON

The Aerial League was delighted. Aviation was on the tip of everyone's tongues, and was getting widespread press coverage. Their strategy was successful. The following year Australia's Minister of Defence established an aviation training school. Four flying machines were ordered from the British government and Australia's air force was launched.

The Australian Flying Corps, as it was known by 1916, fought alongside British aircraft in the Middle East during the First World War. Its Third Squadron was tangling with the German Air Force on the day the famous German pilot, Manfred von Richthofen—"The Red Baron"—was shot down and killed.

NEVER BETRAY HOUDINI

Performing in Australia, Houdini was now reluctant to accept handcuff challenges, preferring to present what he termed "mysteries" such as escaping from a straitjacket or getting out of the milk-can. In Sydney, at the end of March, Bess returned to performing "Metamorphosis" with him.

Houdini's act was by now a very complex production, and he needed a team to make it happen. Franz Kukol was the manager. He dealt with the bureaucrats in the countries where Houdini performed, and also arranged the music. Bess was in charge of wardrobe, and Jim Collins was employed to help Houdini produce his ideas on stage.

Jim Collins was a master mechanic and cabinet-maker. He had a talent for making himself almost invisible too, rendering him an invaluable accomplice in Houdini's stunts. There were also two general assistants—Jim Vickery and, when Houdini was performing in Europe, George Brooks. As with anyone who created a piece of magic equipment for Houdini or sold him a trick, they were all forced to sign a non-disclosure clause that read:

I the undersigned do solemnly swear on my sacred honor as a man as long as I live I shall never divulge the secret or secrets of Harry Houdini, or any thing I may make for him and the secret of the can. I further swear never to betray Houdini ... So help me God almighty and may he keep me steadfast.

THE HOUDINI TOURING SHOW

When traveling by rail, as they mostly did, Houdini's touring team occupied two carriages. One contained the personnel, the other all the baggage and props. Houdini's library of around one-hundred books also traveled with them. When they arrived at a theater, the group took up three dressing rooms.

Houdini himself occupied the star dressing room, his team of assistants was in the second, and the third was for all their equipment. The third room was also something of a workshop, where implements could be tweaked, keys could be cut, and new props could be made.

None of the theater's permanent stage crew had signed the non-disclosure oath, so it was imperative that they did not witness anything on stage during the performance. Thus, the stage was always blocked off with screens.

Another important member of the team remained back home in Houdini's property in New York. John W. Sargent was a former magician who took care of Houdini's magic collection, and acted as his secretary. Sargent, who had performed as "Sargent the Merry Magician," had been President of the Society of American Magicians from 1905 to 1906.

The Houdini touring team usually wore ceremonial officers' coats on stage, and were entirely subservient to the great man. Although, now and then, he would lose his temper and fire them. At no point were such dismissals taken seriously, however, and all was usually forgotten by the following day.

LOSING ALL RESTRAINT

In January 1913, the Houdini traveling show was in England, pulling in full-houses with the usual crowd-pleasing combination of tricks, stunts, illusions, and escapes. One particular night in the city of Hull, in the north of England, Houdini escaped from a seabag, a type of restraint used in days gone-by to incarcerate sailors who had gone insane at sea.

The forerunner of the modern straitjacket, the seabag was made from leather and canvas. It was long enough, and strong enough, to imprison a deranged sailor from the neck down to the feet. Heavy leather straps were bound around the bag, restraining the ankles, the knees, the chest, and the neck.

To huge acclaim, Houdini freed himself from the seabag in twenty minutes. When interviewed the following day, it was suggested that he was showing signs of wear and tear caused by his escapes. Houdini, agreeing with the reporter, said that the intense stress he put on his body would one day catch up with him. He did not expect to live long.

THE WATER TORTURE CELL

On the same 1913 tour, Houdini made preparations to launch his new stage-sensation, "The Chinese Water Torture Cell" in England. He alerted everyone in an advertisement in *The Strand Magazine*, saying:

I wish to warn managers and the Profession in General that I have invented another sensation viz. THE WATER TORTURE CELL which is the greatest feat that I have ever attempted in a strenuous career and hereby wish to give notice that I have a SPECIAL LICENSE FROM THE LORD CHAMBERLAIN (granted May 2nd 1912) as a Stage Play and I will certainly stop anyone from infringing my rights.

The Secrets of Houdini
The Chinese Water Torture Cell

"The Chinese Water Torture Cell"—or "the old Upside-Down," as Houdini nicknamed it—was one of his greatest and most dramatic tricks. It was also one of the most dangerous. It consisted of a mahogany and glass box with a cage around it, attended by two of his assistants, clad in black rubber coats.

Houdini made a great show of examining the box, and explaining its workings to the audience. He told them about the cover and its grill, through which his feet would extend. It fastened him in place, upside-down in the tank, preventing him from turning round when he was immersed in the water.

Adding some dangerous drama to the trick, he explained that the front of the tank was made of glass, just in case anything went wrong. An assistant would always be standing by with an axe, ready to rush in and smash the glass.

THE DIVER

He then invited a committee of audience members to come and check it out. While they were inspecting the apparatus, Houdini changed into a blue bathing costume offstage. If one of the committee suggested that there might be a trapdoor under the tank, Houdini immediately ordered it to be moved to another part of the stage.

The assistants began to fill the tank with water, using buckets and a hose. When this was completed, Houdini threw off his robe and lay down on his back while audience members placed his feet in the holes in the stocks that fitted over the top of the tank.

He was then slowly winched up and suspended, upside-down above the tank, dangling from the grill. He was next lowered into the water, two assistants guiding him into the cell with water lapping over the sides onto the stage. Meanwhile, the orchestra struck up a tune called *The Diver*.

THE GREAT ESCAPE

The assistants quickly snapped locks on the lid and curtains were drawn around the apparatus. The audience held its breath. Franz Kukol stood to one side, axe at the ready.

After just forty seconds, the curtains were flung open and a dripping wet Houdini leapt out. He climbed up the side of the tank and sat at the top, dangling his feet in the water, just to prove that the tank was still full.

First performed in Berlin in the fall of 1912, the Chinese Water Torture Cell was one of the greatest magic tricks ever devised. It had everything—drama, danger, and spectacle.

HOUDINI UPSIDE DOWN

Interestingly, Houdini had performed it once before, on April 29, 1911, at the Southampton Hippodrome to an audience of one. The performance had not been advertised, and the price of a ticket was hugely expensive—a guinea.

Houdini presented it as a play in one act and two scenes that he called *Challenged* or *Houdini Upside-Down*. This enabled him cleverly to copyright the trick as a play, rather than having to patent it as a magic stunt.

It had cost around $20,000 for Collins to create the cabinet for the Chinese Water Torture Cell, according to Houdini's brother, Hardeen. It was worth every dollar. Houdini immodestly described it to a friend as "without doubt the greatest spectacular thing ever witnessed on the stage."

The fraudsters and imitators were not to be denied, however. After Houdini left Germany, a woman performer known as "Undina"—close enough to "Houdini" in a German accent—began performing the trick. An injunction was obtained, and a court prohibited her from ever performing it again.

HOW DID HE DO IT?

When Houdini was immersed in the cell, some of its water cascaded out leaving a small pocket of air between the surface of the water and the lid into which his feet were fitted. The holes through which his feet protruded were large enough for him to twist himself in such a way that he could slip his feet out.

He then brought his feet down to his chest and flipped over, righting himself and enabling him to breathe the air trapped in the pocket. The lid through which his feet had stuck was hinged so that it would open. Houdini opened it, climbed out and closed it again. The curtain then opened and he triumphantly presented himself to the cheering audience.

One of Houdini's greatest tricks, The Chinese Water Torture Cell was first developed in 1911, and remained a dramatic feature of his act until his death in 1926.

PART FOUR

HANGING HIGH IN THE SKY

No prison can hold me;
no hand or leg irons or steel locks
can shackle me. No ropes or chains
can keep me from my freedom.

Harry Houdini

CHAPTER 13

An Angel on Earth

Houdini had traveled back to Europe after Hammerstein's Paradise Roof Garden, but committed himself to a two-week stint back there in 1913, even though it meant a long return voyage that would take as long as his booking. The press had been ecstatic about his performances, the *New York Times*, for example gushing:

> It is [Houdini's] act and practically his act alone, which gives the present bill its one gleam of intense interest and originality. Owing to this man's wonderful flubdub and personality, one follows his entrances and exits as breath-batedly as if he were pushing himself through the small and hindermost entrance of a Yale lock. And he would get himself out of there—that's the wonder of the man.

THE PASSING OF CECILIA

On July 7, 1913, Houdini dined with friends, and the following day he sailed for Europe, to perform in Copenhagen, Denmark. Leaving from Hoboken, New Jersey, he had a difficult time saying farewell to his increasingly frail mother. He kept saying goodbye, boarding the vessel, and then running back down the gangplank to do it all again. Cecilia became concerned that the ship was going to sail without him.

Meanwhile, Houdini's brother Hardeen was performing in Asbury Park, New Jersey, from July 14. He invited his mother to accompany him so that she could have a holiday. They lodged at the Imperial Hotel, and Hardeen, engaged by the Lyric Theater, began his performances and stunts—leaping in handcuffs from the pier, donning the straitjacket, and climbing into the milk-can.

But on July 14, Cecilia suffered a stroke that paralyzed her. Theo telephoned Gladys who was still in New York, to give her the bad news, and she hurried to her mother's bedside. But there was little that could be done. On July 16, 1913, Hardeen completed his act at the Lyric and rushed to be with his mother. That night, Cecilia Weiss passed away, at age 72.

DEEP SHOCK

While his mother was dying, Houdini was performing for members of the Danish Royal Family who were attending his show at the Circus Beketow in Copenhagen. As ever, he charmed his audience with his attempts at their language, and his act was received with wild cheers and applause.

At noon the following day, as he talked to members of the Danish press, he was passed a cablegram. He ripped it open and, after reading it, collapsed to the floor.

He failed to perform that evening, and a doctor told him he needed to rest. He was in deep shock which had also antagonized an old kidney problem, originally caused by the stresses he placed on his body in his escapes. He refused to rest. He could not be seen to show any weakness whatsoever. It would damage his aura of invincibility.

For the next three nights, he took to the stage and performed his act in excruciating pain. Finally, he stopped and rested for two weeks, but the kidney issue remained with him for the rest of his life. At night, he often lay with a cushion under the affected side to have any chance of sleep.

MY DARLING MOTHER

Houdini told his brothers to wait until he came home to hold the funeral. He arrived back in New York on July 29, and went straight to the house, where his mother still lay in her coffin. He later wrote:

> *She looked so dainty and restful, only a small spot on Her cheek, and the Face which haunted me with love all my Life is still and quiet, and when She does not answer me I know that God is taking Her to His bosom and giving Her the peace which she denied herself on this earth. And tomorrow Mother will be laid alongside of Her best friend, one for whom she mourned ever since he obeyed the mighty command ... And I know if there is a Meeting Place, Both are Happy in this event, which leaves all us children miserable, unhappy, and mindfull [sic] of sorrow.*

The funeral was held the following day and a distraught Houdini's diary read:

> *This day Cecilia Weiss, geboren Steiner, my darling Mother, was laid to rest alongside of her husband and my father. (As we stood on the deck, July 8, Mother asked me to bring back a pair of warm woollen house slippers and she said, "Nicht vergess', nummer 6." In Bremen I bought the slippers on our return journey and they were placed with her when she was laid to rest.)*

THE RESTLESS SOUL

Houdini spent a terrible month restlessly visiting his mother's grave. Bess later said that he lost something during this time, a youthful joyousness that he never recovered. Around this time, he adopted the birth date of April 6 that his mother had preferred for him, instead of his real birthday, March 24.

> *It hurts me to think I can't talk it over with Darling Mother and as SHE always wrote me on April 6th, that will be my adopted birthdate.*

He had her letters, which he had saved over the years, transcribed into good German and typed out to make them more legible. The clock he had given her was stopped at the time of her death and never re-wound. Cards were printed and sent out to friends, on which were a photograph of Cecilia and the legend:

> *If God ever permitted an Angel to walk the earth in human form, it was my Mother.*

Houdini had new writing paper printed with a thick black border. Worse still, normally a workaholic, he completely lost interest in working. He wrote a despairing letter to Hardeen/Dash:

> *Dash, I knew that I loved Mother, but that my very existence seems to have expired with HER, is simply writing my innermost thoughts ... With all my efforts, I try and still my lounging, as I know positively that Mother would not like the way she PASSING AWAY has affected me, but what can I do?*

Goodbye Mama! Houdini kisses his mother farewell.

NOTHING TO FORGIVE

Houdini was obsessed with his mother's death. Apparently, she had tried to say something at the end. Dash thought it may have been "Forgive ..." But what was there to forgive?

Years later, Bess wrote that Houdini and his mother had created a code that could be transmitted from beyond the grave. In fact, Houdini did this throughout his life with friends, each having a separate code word, the expression of which would provide proof of life beyond the grave.

The code Bess suggested that Cecilia and Harry had devised was "Forgive." Or perhaps she was asking Harry to forgive his brother Nathan. A word from his mother would have made that happen.

FAMILY FEUD

Houdini never really got on with his brother Nathan, who appeared to be a fairly incompetent businessman. He had married a woman named Sadie Glantz, but the marriage had foundered. Sadie now lived with one of Houdini's other brothers, Leopold, at Houdini's house at 278 West 113th Street, where Leopold also had radiology consulting rooms.

Harry and Bess Houdini at the grave of his beloved mother, Cecilia Weiss, *c.* 1915.

Houdini was fond of them both. It was his wish that Nathan, who had found another girlfriend, should divorce Sadie, and let Leopold marry her, which eventually came to pass. But in 1917, a family feud broke out between Houdini and Leopold.

He took a picture of himself, Bess, his mother, Bess's mother, and Leopold, taken together in London and cut off Leopold's head with scissors. He scribbled on the reverse of the photo:

> *This is the picture from which Houdini later cut off his brother's picture, because he thot [sic] that an act of his brother had hastened his mother's death.*

NO WAY BACK

There was no way back for Leopold. Houdini never forgave him, and signaled his displeasure in his will, in 1924:

> *It is my express desire, intention and direction that no part of either the principal or income of my Estate shall ever directly or indirectly go to Sadie Glantz Weiss, the divorced wife of my brother Nathan Joseph Weiss and the present wife of my brother Doctor Leopold Davis Weiss.*

Furthermore, Leopold was to receive nothing until Sadie died. He was also removed from the list of family members who could be buried in the family plot at Machpelah Cemetery. The nature of the offense committed by Sadie and Leopold that so upset him, was never revealed.

MANY A BITTER TEAR

Eventually, the spell was broken and in September 1913, Houdini left for Europe. He opened the tour on September 16, at Nuremberg, Germany, where he recorded that his "Act works beautifully." But he was still having a tough time on account of his mother's death, reading her letters and making himself sad:

> *Many a bitter tear I am shedding. In the entire lot of letters, which I have saved since 1900, each is a love story, a prayer to God to protect her children, a plea that we should be good human beings.*

In Germany, Houdini ran into trouble, being hauled up before the court for failing to obtain police permission for his two manacled leaps into the Dutzendteich Lake in Nuremburg. The judge fined him 50 deutschmarks, and an additional 20 deutschmarks for walking on the grass. Houdini duly noted that, although the police had refused to grant permission, the city authorities still put additional buses into service to bring crowds of spectators to witness the event.

THE TERRIBLE BLOW

Houdini traveled on to France. In November 1913, he performed in Paris, but he was still not himself, and that month had only accepted one challenge. He wrote despairingly to his brother:

> *Dash its [sic] TOUGH, and I can't seem to get over it ... Time heals all Wounds, but a long time will have to pass before it will heal the terrible blow which MOTHER tried to save me from knowing.*

It was a puzzling comment, the significance of which will probably never be known. Perhaps it was connected with Leopold and Sadie. Or perhaps there was some other "terrible blow" in Houdini's family history, that remains to be uncovered.

Uncharacteristically, Houdini cancelled the December Paris shows, and instead traveled to Monte Carlo with Bess. His interest in the gambling tables at the casino did not last long, although he did win 2,000 francs. His mother remained on his mind, and he often woke in the night, crying out, "Mama, are you there?"

CHAPTER 14

CHANGING THE HISTORY OF MAGIC

For a number of years, Houdini had been dreaming up a different type of show, in which he would perform only magic tricks. There would be no escapes or spectacles. To that end, he had been trawling the catalogs and shops of magicians and dealers in Europe. He even purchased "Dr. Lynn's Palingenesia," the illusion that had made such a deep and lasting impression on the young Ehrich Weiss back in Milwaukee.

It was originated by Thomas Tobin (1844–83) in 1872. Tobin was a chemist, architectural apprentice, and scientific lecturer at a London college. In his spare time, he had created a number of magic illusions.

As well as "Dr. Lynn's Palingenesia," Tobin had developed the "Cabinet of Proteus," in which people appeared and disappeared from a large cabinet, and conceived the "Oracle of Delphi," an illusion in which a disembodied talking head can be seen floating in space.

THE CRYSTAL CASH BOX

Houdini's mother's death in 1913 had derailed his plans for the show, but by April the following year it was coming together in his head. He put it on as a trial in several provincial English theaters, and in June began alternating it with his usual show for a week. It began with the Robert-Houdin trick, "The Traveling Coins," but Houdini had changed the name to "The Crystal Cash Box."

It said a lot about Houdini that he was not above using a trick devised by the man whose reputation he had tried to destroy in *The Unmasking of Robert-Houdin*. The illusion seemed to make coins travel invisibly through the air into a box that was suspended over the stage by two ribbons. Houdini showed the box to the audience, proving that it was empty.

He then walked to the other side of the stage, while it swung in the air. Picking up a handful of coins, he threw them toward the box. They disappeared as they apparently crossed the stage before rattling into the still swinging box. When he had thrown all the coins, Houdini walked back to the box, opened the lid and took out the coins that he had held in his hand a few minutes before.

PYRAMIDS AND CUBES

He followed up with two more illusions—"Goodbye Winter," and "Hello Summer." Houdini had bought them from the English magician Charles Morritt (1861 – 1936) who created many illusions during his career. In the "Goodbye Winter" illusion, Houdini made an audience member disappear, and in "Hello Summer," he brought a beautiful "Fairy Queen Gardener" out of a pyramid-shaped box.

He also performed Buatier De Kolta's "Marvelous Cube." In this illusion, a small suitcase was brought onto the stage. Houdini informed the audience that it contained a young lady. He reached into the case and brought out an eight-inch square black dice that he put on a low table. Houdini then took a step away from it and it miraculously began to swell. The cube continued to grow until it was a cubic yard in size. Houdini approached it and lifted it off the table and a young woman materialized.

BUATIER DE KOLTA

Born Joseph Buatier, French magician Buatier De Kolta (1847 – 1903), a contemporary of Jean Eugène Robert-Houdin, performed in England and the United States during the 1870s and 1880s. Many of the brilliant illusions that he devised are still being performed in one form or another by magicians today—tricks such as "Multiplying Billiard Balls" in which billiard balls appear and disappear; the "Marvelous Cube;" and the "Vanishing Bird Cage" in which a bird cage and a small bird disappear between the magician's hands. He is mostly remembered for the illusion of the "De Kolta Chair," also known as the "Vanishing Lady." A woman who is seated in a chair, covered by a large cloth disappears. It is an illusion that has been used by the hugely successful contemporary illusionist, David Copperfield (born 1956).

LOVING HIS OWN WORK

The show climaxed with Houdini's *pièce de resistance*, "Metamorphosis," and Bess was back at work for the first time since they had performed in Sydney. He very much enjoyed the show, describing it in his diary at one point as "Best show I ever presented. Bess works magnificently." He added that the critics agreed.

But his audiences did not concur. Neither did the managers of the theaters where he was booked to perform. They wanted to see the Handcuff King and escape artist. Reluctantly, Houdini put all his magic tricks back into storage, and returned to giving the crowd what they wanted. Nonetheless, he told a friend, "… I'm determined to give a good magical show before I die."

AN EXTRAORDINARY YOUNG MAN

In 1914, the great magician made the acquaintance of the remarkable teenage amateur escapologist, Randolph Douglas (1895 – 1956). Douglas was a big Houdini fan, and performed his own escapes under the stage name "The Great Randini."

As a boy, Douglas had started buying locks and figuring out how they worked. He even had his own straitjacket, and planned a career following in his hero Harry Houdini's footsteps. However, letters from Douglas's possessions show that the relationship between the two men was more than simply that of superstar and super-fan. Douglas had many ideas for new illusions, and is said to have devised tricks for Houdini.

On this occasion, Douglas had a new trick he wanted to show Houdini, who had been performing in Nottingham, England. Houdini hired a car to drive thirty-two miles to the city of Sheffield, where Douglas lived with his mother.

CHANGING THE HISTORY OF MAGIC

They all had dinner together, then Douglas led Houdini upstairs to the attic of the house. There, he requested Houdini to strap him into a straitjacket. Houdini thought the young man was merely going to show him that he, too, could escape from a straitjacket. However Douglas went on to do something even more extraordinary. Something no one had ever done before.

Douglas asked his mother to tie a length of strong rope around his ankles and thread it through a block and tackle. Houdini helped her hoist Douglas up into the air, upside down. Suspended by his ankles from the roof beams of the house, Douglas proceeded to spectacularly escape from the straitjacket, hanging upside down in mid air in front of Houdini's eyes. The great man was so amazed, he decided there and then to incorporate the new idea into his own performance.

Douglas's ingenious invention had changed the course of the history of magic. By combining supreme athleticism, strength, and a genius for escapology, Douglas had created an iconic straitjacket escape for Houdini, that would become a legendary cornerstone of future outdoor spectacular shows, attracting huge crowds wherever it was performed.

MEETING TEDDY ROOSEVELT

In the summer of 1914, Houdini boarded the largest passenger ship in the world, the German-owned SS *Imperator*. It so happened that among the passengers was Theodore Roosevelt (1858 – 1919) who had been President of the United States from 1901 to 1909. As soon as Houdini found out that the former president was on board, he was determined to make his acquaintance. He managed it using one of his tricks.

The event was a benefit for the German Sailors Home and the Magicians Club of London, and it took place in the ship's Grand Salon. The evening's entertainment had begun with some Puccini played by the Ritz Carlton Orchestra, followed by some opera pieces. Next was Houdini who began with some close-up magic tricks with cards and handkerchiefs.

He then launched into the stunt that he hoped would impress the ex-President who was seated next to the well-known American composer and conductor, Victor Herbert (1859 – 1924). Houdini proposed that he would conduct a séance, but it would be a séance with a difference in that it would be conducted with the lights on.

ASK THE SPIRIT WORLD

He distributed pieces of paper, pencils and envelopes at random around the room before asking those who had received them to write a question on the paper that they would like someone from the spirit world to answer. The pieces of paper were then folded and deposited in the envelopes so that there was no possibility of Houdini seeing what had been written. Roosevelt was, of course, one of the people who was given a piece of paper.

As the former president was writing his question, Houdini approached him holding an *Atlas of the World*. Roosevelt had been writing with the paper in his hand. Houdini invited him to use the *Atlas* to lean on. Roosevelt wrote his question, sealed it in the envelope and passed it to Houdini. Houdini put it in a hat and placed the other envelopes in the hat. He picked up two slates and walked back to Roosevelt's table asking the audience if they would mind if he used the ex-president's question. The audience did not seem to have a problem with this.

THE RIVER OF DOUBT

Houdini confirmed that Roosevelt had

written down a question and also that the two slates were blank. Houdini asked him to place his envelope between the two slates and then asked him to inform the audience what his question had been. Roosevelt turned to the others in the room and said, "Where was I last Christmas?"

Houdini separated the slates and held them up for the audience to see. On one could be seen a chalked and colored map of Brazil, the River of Doubt in the Amazon highlighted. On the other slate was written "Near the Andes." It was signed by W.T. Stead, a famous English newspaper editor, and ardent spiritualist, who had drowned when the *Titanic* had sunk in April 1912. The audience was amazed and Roosevelt was ecstatic.

ONLY HOKUS POKUS

The following morning, as the two men were having a stroll out on the ship's deck, Roosevelt turned to Houdini and asked him if it really had been a spirit who answered that previous night. Taken aback that a man who had led the life that Roosevelt had should think that there might have been some truth in the illusion, Houdini could only answer, "No Colonel, it was hokus pokus."

Houdini had begun planning this trick even before he had boarded ship. He had been told Roosevelt was going to be on the vessel and also knew that Roosevelt was in London after a long trip to South America. The story of the adventure was going to be published in *The London Telegraph* and Houdini made sure he visited the *Telegraph's* offices in London to get a preview of what Roosevelt had written. He also obtained maps from his journalist friends.

WILDFIRE SENSATION

On the night of the performance, Houdini filled the hat with envelopes that all asked the same question—Roosevelt's question, "Where was I last Christmas?" Earlier that day, he had taken a couple of books from the

Grand Salon, and razored off the cloth of the back and front covers, inserting a piece of paper and a sheet of carbon paper inside. He left a small string on the edge with which to open the covers and the books were returned to the salon.

The idea was that when Roosevelt leaned on the book to write his question, the imprint on the carbon would go through to the paper revealing exactly what Roosevelt had asked. He was delighted when he saw that Roosevelt had actually written the question with which he had seeded the hat. The event was a sensation that spread like wildfire across the ship and beyond. In fact, by the time Houdini disembarked in New York it was in all the newspapers.

Interestingly, a photograph was taken of Houdini and the former president on the deck of the ship. In the original there are five other men, but Houdini later had them cropped out of the picture so that it looked like just him and the president posing for the photographer.

Harry Houdini with Theodore Roosevelt (center) and others aboard the Hamburg-American liner *Imperator* in 1914.

Secrets of Houdini
Walking Through a Brick Wall

The American rights to this illusion were purchased by Houdini from the English magician, Sidney Josolyne in 1914. A version of it had first been performed in 1898 in Alaska, using blocks of ice, by the magician known as "Alexander" who was born Claude Alexander Conlin (1880 – 1954).

The brick wall was introduced by P.T. Selbit on June 15, 1914, at Maskelyne and Devant's Egyptian Hall in London. Houdini performed it just a few times during his week's engagement at Hammerstein's in New York in July 1914. It is speculated that he dropped it from his act because firstly, it was not a stunt of his devising, and secondly because too many people knew how it was done.

As he performed his act, bricklayers erected a brick wall nine feet high and ten feet wide on the stage. It was built at right angles to the front of the stage, so the audience could see both sides of the wall. Furthermore, it was constructed on a large rug to prohibit the use of a trap door. When the bricklayers had finished their work, Houdini invited audience members onto the stage to inspect it, knock it with a hammer and confirm that it was, indeed, a solid brick wall.

Houdini then stood on one side of the wall and a screen was brought onto the stage and placed in front of him, blocking the audience's view of him. Then, a second screen was wheeled on and positioned on the other side of the wall.

Houdini raised his hands above the screens and shouted "Here I am!" but when the screen was removed, he had disappeared. The screen on the other side of the wall was then removed and there stood Houdini, having apparently walked through the wall from one side to the other.

HOW DID HE DO IT?

There are two versions of how this trick may have been achieved. One suggests that the screen was wheeled in front of Houdini by men dressed in working clothes. After the screen had been put in front of him, Houdini quickly changed into similar working clothes and as the assistants walked around the back end of the wall, to place the second screen in position on the other side, Houdini simply joined them and then hid behind that screen where he changed into his stage clothes. The hands the audience saw were mechanical hands that made them believe Houdini was still there.

The other suggestion as to how he did it, involved the rug that, rather than preventing the use of a trap door was actually enabling him to use one. There was a long trap under the wall that opened downward at the center, and when it was sprung, a sheet under the stage formed a V or hammock shaped space through which Houdini crawled to the other side.

Houdini stands solemnly, after passing through from the other side of the brick wall.

CHAPTER 15

The Straitjacket King

In January 1915, Houdini planned to travel and perform across Europe, moving on to Russia before traveling to Japan on the Trans-Siberian Railroad. He made elaborate plans for a tour of the Far East, performing in Japan and China.

He would be using a specially designed railway carriage that would open up to six times its length with seating for five-hundred people around it. But the First World War (1914 – 18) put an end to his plans, and he had to remain in America for the duration of the war.

PERVASIVE PRESENCE

Back in New York, Houdini found it difficult to live in his own house. His late mother's presence seemed to pervade every room. Bess and he, therefore, moved to Dash's house in Flatbush. It was a decision that might have been difficult for Dash's wife and two children, but Houdini ruled the roost, where his brother was concerned.

This arrangement lasted three and a half years before Houdini and Bess moved out. During that time, he did not achieve a great deal apart from having a tombstone made for the family plot at the Machpelah Cemetery.

WEISSES ONLY

By 1916, a sculptor had been working for a year on the design. Unveiled in October 1916, it was an Exedra, a semi-circular wall of granite against which a stone figure of a weeping woman kneels with *"WEISS"* inscribed on a central block of stone.

Houdini made a list of who would have the right to be laid to rest there and the offending pair, Leopold and Sadie, did not make the list. His other brothers and sisters would be allowed to be buried there, but their spouses and children would not. It was "Weisses only," with one exception—Bess.

THERAPEUTIC MOURNING

This was obviously a form of therapy for Houdini, as he continued to mourn his mother's passing. He wrote a letter to Bess detailing how she should behave in the event that he should die first. If she were to marry again, he advised, she should make sure her new husband "sign away his marriage right in everything, otherwise do not marry him."

For Houdini, it was evidently an important letter, shown by the fact that he frequently re-read it and re-signed it. He also stipulated in another letter, that, on his death, all his mother's letters should be placed in a bag and "used as a pillow for my head in my coffin."

TOUR DE FORCE

When Houdini eventually returned to performing, he introduced even more risks and melodrama into his stunts, gambling everything for the publicity they brought him. He had adapted Randolph Douglas's straitjacket escape to be part of the promotional build-up to his live touring show—but being Houdini, he had scaled it up somewhat.

Instead of being suspended by his ankles from the roof beams of a house, he dangled precariously from a block-and-tackle hoist, mounted high up on the outside of tall buildings. Vast crowds gathered to witness Houdini being straitjacketed by strong men on the ground, turned upside-down, and then lifted up high into the air to perform his remarkable escape.

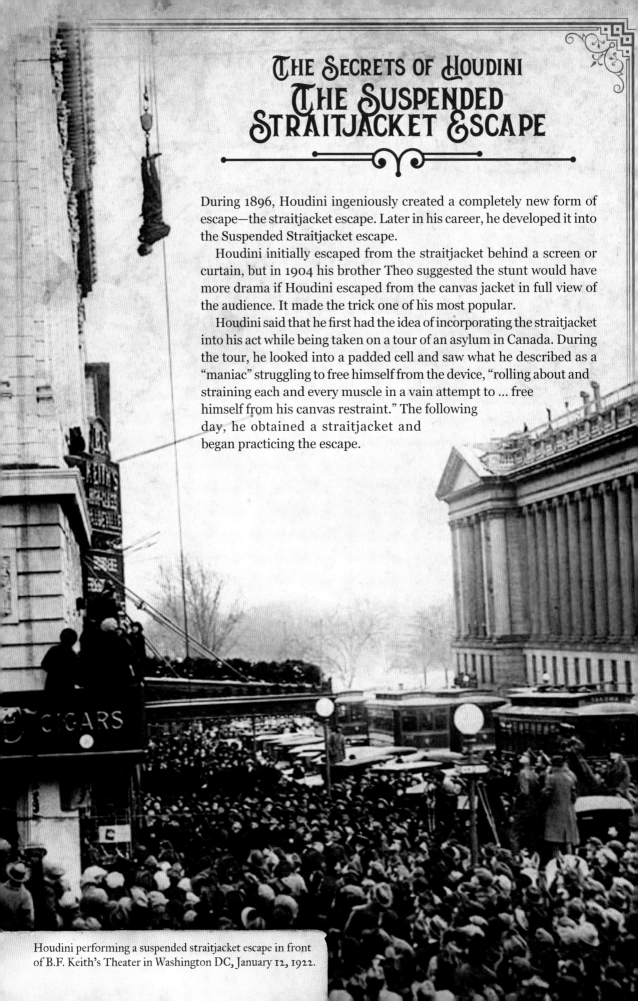

The Secrets of Houdini
The Suspended Straitjacket Escape

During 1896, Houdini ingeniously created a completely new form of escape—the straitjacket escape. Later in his career, he developed it into the Suspended Straitjacket escape.

Houdini initially escaped from the straitjacket behind a screen or curtain, but in 1904 his brother Theo suggested the stunt would have more drama if Houdini escaped from the canvas jacket in full view of the audience. It made the trick one of his most popular.

Houdini said that he first had the idea of incorporating the straitjacket into his act while being taken on a tour of an asylum in Canada. During the tour, he looked into a padded cell and saw what he described as a "maniac" struggling to free himself from the device, "rolling about and straining each and every muscle in a vain attempt to … free himself from his canvas restraint." The following day, he obtained a straitjacket and began practicing the escape.

Houdini performing a suspended straitjacket escape in front of B.F. Keith's Theater in Washington DC, January 12, 1922.

Houdini first performed the suspended straitjacket escape in Kansas City in September 1915, after which it rapidly became his signature *tour de force*.

DANGER AND DRAMA

But it was hugely dangerous. Not only was there an increased chance of him plunging to certain death, but there was also a real prospect of being swung violently by the wind into the side of the building, while helpless with his arms bound in the straitjacket. One newspaper account of just such a perilous performance conveys the danger and drama of the escape:

A number of times his body, held taut by the straitjacket, was swung towards the building by the wind, while a murmur of fear arose from the crowd. A minute, two minutes passed, and the crowd roared. Houdini's body, held rigid by the straitjacket, was beginning to move. Slowly, but surely, the man who has startled the entire world by his feats and by his magic, began to work himself free from the instrument of torture.

The wind continued to swing his body back and forth as it hung suspended in mid-air. Again the wind swung him towards the building, but once more he narrowly escaped being dashed against the brick wall. A roar from the crowd and the straitjacket slowly floated to the ground!!! Houdini waved his hands to the cheering crowd as he was lowered to the street again. Although the temperature was rather low, he was perspiring freely when he was released from the ropes that bound his ankles.

CLOSE TO COLLAPSE

He regularly performed this incredibly dangerous stunt during a long tour he embarked upon in 1915. He dangled from the Los Angeles *Tribune* building, the Kansas City *Post* building, the San Antonio *Express* building, and many others. But it was a massively exhausting stunt to perform, and the stress and danger were starting to take their toll. Speaking around this time, a worn-out Houdini was close to collapse:

I don't know how long this thing can last. I have given myself from one to eight years, and that's a liberal estimate. I am now forty-two years of age. I feel like I am fifty-two years, and some of the time much older—just as I do this afternoon. I have been told that it is hardening of the arteries. Perhaps it is. Whatever it is I am getting old and yet I have no particular regrets. Some time or another we all grow tired. I have been tired for a long time.

SWARMS OF PEOPLE

The suspended straitjacket stunts drew immense crowds from miles around. On April 20, 1916, Houdini performed an escape from the top of the Munsey Building on Washington DC's Pennsylvania Avenue. Between 13th and 15th Streets, people thronged, craning their necks for a better view. Men climbed lampposts to get a vantage point and people hung out of the windows of the surrounding buildings.

The Police Department estimated that some 100,000 spectators turned out to see Houdini that day. Swarms of people stretched for block after block, it was thought to represent the single largest crowd in the city's history for anything that was not a presidential inauguration. Even Houdini must have gasped in amazement, as he buckled up the straitjacket.

TALKING ABOUT QUITTING

But it was exhausting, and Houdini was just almost ready to hang up his handcuffs for good. Before the Washington stunt, he had once again talked about quitting, saying:

I've about reached the limit, it seems to me. For the last thirty years ... I've been getting out of all sorts of things human ingenuity has devised to confine a human being. Up to date there hasn't been anything made that confined my activities to any alarming extent. But some day some chap is going to make one. And I'm going to quit with a clean record before he comes along. I've about made up my mind that this is the last stunt I'll perform. Hereafter I intend to work entirely with my brain. See these gray hairs? They mean something. I'm not as young as I was. I've had to work to keep ahead of the procession. I'll still be entertaining the public for many years to come. But I intend to do it along lines not quite so spectacular. As an escapist extraordinary I feel that I'm about through.

A GREAT HONOR

But while he was in Washington, Houdini got a boost when he was accorded what he considered one of the greatest honors of his life. The recently married President Woodrow Wilson (1856 – 1924) attended one of his stage performances and the following day, when Houdini was seated in the visitors' gallery in the Senate during a tour, Vice President Thomas R. Marshall (1854 – 1925) saw Houdini and waved to him.

Suddenly, the business of the Senate ceased as all the other senators turned and waved to Houdini. When he was invited to the vice president's chambers, the business of the House again stopped as senators piled into the rooms and corridors trying to catch a glimpse of him. Houdini would later describe this amazing experience as "the proudest day of my life."

FIRST WORLD WAR

On April 6—his adopted birthdate—1917, Houdini turned 43, and on that same day President Wilson declared war on Germany and its allies. Houdini immediately decided to get involved. During his 1916 tour, he had tried to persuade local magic groups where he performed to join the Society of American Magicians (SAM).

Having succeeded in getting groups from Buffalo, Kansas City, Pittsburgh and Detroit to join, he now introduced a proposal at a meeting of SAM that "its members collectively and individually do hereby tender their loyalty to the President of the United States of America and express a desire to render such service to the country as may be within their province." The resolution was sent to President Wilson.

On June 2, 1917, Houdini was elected president of SAM and took over editorship of the society's magazine, *M-U-M* (Magic, Unity, Might). It soon featured pieces on the contributions to the war effort made by members of the organization.

WE MUST WIN

Houdini was excited by the thought of making a contribution, cancelling his fall vaudeville season and devoting his energies to entertaining the troops and raising money for the war effort. As he said in a letter to R.H. Burnside, the manager of the Hippodrome Theater:

My heart is in this work, for it is not a question of "Will we win" or "Will we lose." We must win and that is all there is to it.

Houdini featured in a National Vaudeville Association benefit at the Hippodrome that starred some of the greatest stars of the stage, including singer and comedian, Sophie Tucker (1887 – 1966), singer Eva Tanguay (1878 – 1947) and comedian Eddie Foy (1856 – 1928). Houdini, of course, stole the show, marching into the theater accompanied by a company of US Marines. His escape that night from a straitjacket was his fastest ever at one minute and twenty-three seconds.

GOLD COINS AND LIBERTY BONDS

Next came a fund-raising tour for the Red Cross and a tour of troop camps. During his visits to the camps he performed his "Money for Nothing" trick in which he made $5 gold coins materialize out of the air. Each of these was given to a soldier who was about to be sent to fight in Europe. Legend has it that he personally gave away around $7,000 (today worth about $250,000).

When the US Treasury announced the issue of Liberty Bonds to raise funds for the war, Houdini threw his efforts into a series of fund-raisers, and in a year he sold a million dollars' worth of Liberty Bonds. He also funded the building of a hospital ward named in honor of his mother. On November 11, 1917, he organized a "Carnival of Magic" benefit for the families of those who had lost their lives when the *Antilles* transport vessel had been sunk by a German torpedo.

ANTI-GERMAN SENTIMENTS

He had, of course, taught German soldiers to fly and worried about that, imagining those same fliers killing American troops from the air in France. He destroyed all the photographs of that time and also expunged all evidence of his flights in Germany, instead placing his early flights in Australia.

He played up his anti-German sentiments, telling a story of how he had forced the German Kaiser into making a public apology, and he used the same manacles from the German courtroom during his lectures to the troops. He also went out of his way to give his place of birth as Appleton, Wisconsin, instead of Hungary, appending his false birth date and his invented place of birth to his signature.

TEACHING THE TROOPS

Houdini wrote to US Secretary of War Newton D. Baker (1871 – 1937) in February 1918 offering to teach troops how to extricate themselves from restraints if captured. He was at that time performing his "Vanishing Elephant" trick in *Cheer Up*, a patriotic show at the Hippodrome, and his classes in escaping from

restraints took place during the show's intermission.

Officers also made appointments to bring in their troops for escape lessons. *Billboard* magazine described the theater as being "daily besieged by hosts of boys in khaki." His engagement in *Cheer Up* was extended to an amazing nineteen weeks, the longest booking in his entire career to-date. The theater held 5,000 people and the huge stage could entertain an entire circus.

President Woodrow Wilson at his desk in the Oval Office *c.* 1913.

SUSPENDED STRAITJACKET ESCAPE IN PITTSBURGH

The venue for these daredevil straitjacket escapes was usually the top of the building of the leading newspaper of whatever city Houdini found himself in. By doing this, of course, he was guaranteed blanket coverage in the press, including breath-taking photographs. It was free advertising for his touring show. The result was full houses wherever he played. The Pittsburgh *Sun* described Houdini's breath-taking performance at its offices:

> *Urbane, smiling, the elusive Houdini appeared in the office ... at 12 o'clock. The two attendants from Mayview [a local psychiatric hospital] awaited him, and with them the straitjacket, in a satchel. Houdini shook hands with both men, speaking humorously of his position as a substitute for the deranged persons the two attendants ordinarily handle ... "Treat me," he advised, smiling, "as you would the most dangerous of the criminal insane."*

> *It was almost 12.30 o'clock. Houdini glanced out of the window, and again his characteristic, quiet smile came to his face as he saw the Wood Street and Liberty Avenue congested from wall to wall ... Then, a white-clad attendant on each side, he went downstairs to the street to be bound. A suppressed shout came from the crowd as he appeared in the doorway of the* Sun *building.*

> *Above him, like a gallows, a single beam projected from a window at the top of the building, and a rope swung clear, coiling in sinister fashion at his feet. Houdini had removed the outer clothing from the upper part of his body. "Ready," he said. The two attendants pressed close.*

On the afternoon of November 6, 1916, Houdini performed his world-famous suspended straitjacket escape high above the streets of Pittsburgh while thousands watched in awe.

His arms were inserted in the long, closed sleeves of the straitjacket. One of the attendants clasped him about the body, as if fearing he would make some mad effort to escape. The other standing behind him, fastened strap after strap … "Make it tight," came the quiet word from the prisoner.

The man's knees went up for the purchase in the small of Houdini's back. Using apparently every ounce of strength in his broad-shouldered six-foot body, the attendant drew the big strap through the buckle until it would not yield even a sixteenth of an inch more. He caught it there and made it fast.

Then the arms of the prisoner were crossed over his body, and the ends of those closed sleeves were brought around in back. Again the knee was brought into use. Again the strap was pulled to its highest tension … Then Houdini's ankles were fastened to the rope, by a special appliance that prevented injury, but insured safety.

A word was spoken. The two attendants seized the bound man's body. Workmen drew the rope steadily through the pulleys. Houdini's feet went up, and as his body cleared the platform it was released. The handcuff king dangled head downward. Each moment he was drawn higher, swaying slightly, spinning dizzily …

Then he hung still. Only for a second. While watchers gleamed in the crowd below, the handcuff king was seen to struggle, not frantically, but with a steady systematic swelling and contracting of muscles, and almost imperceptible lithe wriggling of the torso. The struggle went on. One minute— two—then three—Would he do it? …

From above came an inarticulate shout. The muffled arms writhed one after another over Houdini's head. His hand, still encased in the sleeves of the straitjacket, fumbled quickly and effectively with the buckles at his back. Another contortion and the straitjacket slipped down over his chest, over his head and was flung from his arms to the street, in a crumpled heap.

CHAPTER 16

THE MASTER MAGICIAN

Houdini's morose musings about his age and what the future might hold were no empty gestures. He was getting older and he could not carry on as he had been forever. Apart from his own physical condition, he was also very aware that people would tire of his tricks, of his dangling from buildings or escaping from milk-cans. He had to find something new.

MOTORCYCLE MADNESS

But first, he dreamed up another stunt after making the acquaintance of a sales assistant in a sporting goods store in Fort Worth, Texas. The boy's brother, Ormer Locklear, was a stunt motorbike rider and Houdini thought it would attract a crowd, and column inches in the press, if he were to get Locklear to drag him bound, behind his motorbike down the city's Main Street.

Locklear had to be persuaded, but eventually Houdini, dressed in quilted overalls for protection, and wearing a hood, had his hands tied behind him and lay down in the street. A rope was tied around his ankles and then tied to the motorcycle. In front of him was the paved street and on either side of it stood a large crowd.

A starting pistol was fired and the motorbike set off, Houdini being trailed behind him like a sack of garbage. Locklear gradually speeded up, but Houdini had quickly freed his hands from the rope that bound them, and untied the rope that was attached to the motorbike.

MASTER OF MISDIRECTION

In his stage act, part of Houdini's performance was controlling the audience—how it felt, what it was hearing, and what it was looking at. He was truly a master of misdirection, an art that was vital to his performance, taking the audience's attention away from where the trickery was happening and onto something else. He wrote of this:

Suppose I want to use a short flight of steps from the stage down to the audience. I never have a carpet on them, because while I am transferring a watch or producing an egg from a hat while I tramp heavily, and so draw your attention to my feet. If I think the audience is watching me too closely, I signal my assistant to drop something, or to make some sudden movement. If I want a chair, table or basket brought on the stage, and don't want you to see it, I simply walk to the opposite side of the stage ... All the magicians know that the average person never raises or lowers his eyes very much. Most people just look on a straight level. Therefore, whenever we use tables fitted up with magic devices, we always raise them slightly above the level of the eye, so that when you think you are looking at the top of the table you are not. Really to see the top you would have to raise your eyes; and as this would be an effort you just don't do it.

MEETING SARAH BERNHARDT

In 1917, Houdini saw the chance for more free publicity. The great actress, Sarah Bernhardt (1844 – 1923)—one of the most famous people in the world at the time—was to receive an honor for her acting. A bronze statuette, specially designed for the occasion, was to be presented at a grand reception at the Metropolitan Opera House in New York.

Bernhardt, however, was shocked to receive the $350 bill for its manufacture. Understandably upset, she returned the statuette immediately to its maker. Houdini

THE CHAMPION OF THE WORLD

In an incident that has gone down in legend, Houdini took on the World Heavyweight Boxing Champion, Jess Willard (1881 – 1968) on the night of November 30, 1915. But this was no fist fight, it was a verbal brawl that sent the crowd crazy.

Houdini was performing at the Los Angeles Orpheum when he was informed that Jess Willard, a.k.a the Pottawatomie Giant, was in the audience. At six feet seven inches tall, and 256 pounds, Willard had won the title in April of that year, when he knocked out Jack Johnson in the 26th round of a heavyweight contest in Havana, Cuba.

Houdini invited Willard to join the members of the audience inspecting the apparatus onstage. Willard, known to be sulky and aggressive, told Houdini he would rather not, but Houdini refused to take no for an answer. Willard continued to reject Houdini's requests and began to lose his temper.

The audience got increasingly worked up by the argument. They took Houdini's side, with the magician provoking them into booing Willard every time he said no. Willard shouted at one point, "Go on wid the show, you faker, you four-flusher. Everyone knows you're a four-flusher." Many speculate that Willard's words were even more offensive, and filled with expletives. Houdini, also enraged by this time, replied:

> … you have no right to slur my reputation … Let me tell you one thing, and don't forget this, that I will be Harry Houdini when you are not the Heavyweight Champion of the World.

Eventually, with the boos and hisses of the crowd ringing in his ears, the giant boxer was forced to exit the theater.

True to Houdini's words, Jess Willard lost the heavyweight title to Jack Dempsey in 1919 in one of the biggest defeats ever, and after being knocked out by Luis Ángel Firpo in 1923, he retired from the fight game. Jess Willard died in 1968, at age 81.

Heavyweight Champion Jesse Willard, 1915.

SARAH BERNHARDT

French stage and early film actress Sarah Bernhardt (1844 – 1923), was described as "the most famous actress the world has ever known." Having made her name on French stages in the 1870s, she was soon in demand around the world, earning the nickname "The Divine Sarah."

Born Rosine Bernhardt in Paris, France, Sarah never knew her father and her mother was a courtesan known as "Youle." She eventually became a student at the Comédie Française where she made her acting debut in 1862. However, she was asked to leave after slapping another actress who had pushed her younger sister. She moved to Belgium where she became the mistress of Henri, Prince de Ligne (1824 – 71) and gave birth to a son.

The prince's family forbade him from marrying her and she returned to France where she became a courtesan, earning considerable amounts of money and acquiring the coffin she famously often slept in. She began acting at the Théâtre de l'Odéon in 1866. During the Franco-Prussian War of 1870 – 71, she converted the theater into a temporary hospital and helped to take care of wounded soldiers. She returned to the Comédie Française in 1872.

By the end of the 1870s, she was in demand all over Europe, and increased her fame in the early years of the 1880s with a 31-city tour of the United States and Canada. During that decade, she performed also in South America, Italy, Egypt, Turkey, Sweden, Norway, and Russia. In the early 1890s she made it to New Zealand, Hawaii, and Samoa. She visited America again and would make nine tours of the United States altogether.

She took over theaters in Paris in the 1890s, including the Théâtre de la Renaissance and the Théâtre des Nations that was re-named the Théatre Sarah Bernhardt, staging successful plays there including Shakespeare's *Hamlet* which ran for four hours but received rave reviews. She was one of the earliest film actresses, starring in the two-minute-long *Le Duel d'Hamlet* in 1900 and went on to star in eight movies and two biographical films.

Bernhardt married Greek actor Aristides Damala (1855 – 1889) but the marriage did not last due to his morphine addiction. She is also said to have enjoyed an affair with the future King Edward VII of Great Britain (1841 – 1910) while he was still Prince of Wales.

After losing her leg she continued to perform, often using a wooden prosthetic limb. She even undertook an American tour in 1915, and played in her own productions until her death in 1923, at the age of 79.

read about the incident in the newspapers and offered to cover the cost of the statuette. It paid off many times over in publicity and he formed an association with Miss Bernhardt.

The actress was approaching the twilight of her career, and had had to have a leg amputated after an injury sustained when she was performing in Rio de Janeiro. Still she toured, but her incapacity distressed her greatly, as she demonstrated when she met Houdini.

Miss Bernhardt believed that he possessed magic powers, and begged him to restore her leg. Houdini was shocked, but she was serious. He told her she was asking the impossible. She replied that that was what he was famous for doing—the impossible.

TEMPLE OF MYSTERIES

Houdini began to dream of emulating his erstwhile hero Robert-Houdin, and open his own theater where magic would be performed. He actually located a place, a small 300-seater theater near Times Square, that he thought suitable. He planned to re-design it in the style of Maskelyne and Cook's Egyptian Hall in London. The "Temple of Mysteries" would employ the latest technology, including "talking machines" that could be operated by the weight of a person on specific parts of the floor.

He claimed that there were a number of producers and impresarios—including Oscar Hammerstein and Charles Dillingham (1868 – 1934), creator of *Cheer Up*—who were willing to provide him with financial support for the venture. Ultimately, however, they were unwilling in such uncertain times to put up the money.

FINANCIAL CRISIS

Houdini was also dismayed by the failure of a business venture in which he had invested. He had put $4,900 into a new process for developing film stock, and had raised a further $100,000 from friends. However, the Film Development Company was failing

and Houdini had to put large sums of cash into it to keep it afloat. Coupled with the money he had lost through cancelling his vaudeville engagements, plus the money he was plowing into the war effort, Houdini was for the first time facing a crisis in his finances.

Having moved from Hardeen's house in Flatbush back to his own home at 278 West 113th Street, he was conscious of the need to continue to earn big money, especially as by this time, many people depended on him, including his family and growing staff.

THE NEW PHENOMENON

Houdini was also very aware of the new phenomenon of moving pictures that was replacing vaudeville in the public's affections. As early as 1908, on the Keith Theater circuit in England, Houdini had been pushed down to second-top of the bill. The top act had been the Kinetograph which showed "Interesting and Humorous Motion Pictures," and a melodrama entitled *And the Villain Still Pursued Her*.

The Kinetograph was a motion picture camera that had been devised by William Kennedy Dickson (1860 – 1935) at Thomas Edison's West Orange facility in New Jersey. The great American inventor had the whole of vaudeville looking anxiously over their shoulders at the advent of the movies.

THE FORTHCOMING ATTRACTION

The cinema was clearly coming soon, and Houdini knew he needed to move with the times. He had appeared in a motion picture in Paris as early as 1901, and started wondering seriously about a career in films.

In June 1913, he asked an ex-manager, E.F. Albee (1857 – 1930) about his prospects. Albee was old school, and advised against it. "Your value in vaudeville," he told him, "would be very much lessened on account of your name being advertised as extensively as it would be in motion picture houses."

Meetings in 1915 with Universal Film explored the possibilities of making an

The Secrets of Houdini
The Vanishing Elephant Trick

Houdini only ever performed this startling illusion in New York City, possibly because of the scarcity of an elephant with which to do it. He had said:

People are much more interested in seeing things disappear than seeing them appear. When you make things appear they say, "Oh he had it on him all the time!" But when you make things disappear they are amazed.

He first made the elephant vanish on January 7, 1918, at the Hippodrome Theater, New York, which at the time possessed the largest stage in the world. A large cabinet was wheeled onto the stage which Houdini led the elephant into, before blinds were dropped around it.

Stagehands then turned the cabinet sideways and two circular panels were dropped which permitted the audience to see right through the cabinet. The elephant had disappeared. The reviews were ecstatic. *Variety* wrote "So Mr. Houdini puts his title of premier escape artist behind him and becomes The Master Magician," while *Billboard* magazine said:

Houdini's prodigious presentation of perfect prestidigitation at the New York Hippodrome, where twice daily he causes an elephant to vanish in thin air in about ten seconds, has amazed New York ... When a magician can become the big feature of the Hippodrome Show of Wonders, and he is billed like a circus, the art is certainly on the boom. What are you going to do next, Harry?

HOW DID HE DO IT?

No one in the audience had a perfect view of the cabinet holding the elephant and at the moment of the disappearance, Houdini performed a dramatic feat of misdirection by firing a gun.

The audience blinked and jumped at the gunshot, and a roller pulled a sheet of dark cloth up rapidly in front of the elephant, making it appear to have vanished. Another version suggests that as the cabinet was turned by the stagehands, its trainer moved the animal to the back and a black curtain fell over both of them.

When Houdini opened the front curtain, he had the cabinet turned again so that no one in the audience had very long to see the interior. What they saw was the circular light from the back, the darkened interior of the cabinet and no elephant.

Houdini performing at the Hippodrome, New York, 1918.

CHARMIAN LONDON

In 1916, Houdini had befriended the author Jack London (1876 – 1916) and his wife Charmian (1871 – 1955). The two men got on well, possibly because they shared similar backgrounds. Both were self-educated, and before making their names and their fortunes, both had known poverty.

London had written bestsellers such as *The Sea Wolf, White Fang,* and *The Call of the Wild,* and was a lover of the outdoors. Unlike Houdini, he was also a socialist who had divorced his first wife after having an affair with Charmian Kittredge, a woman who was five years older than him. They enjoyed an open marriage.

Houdini was shocked by London's early death, at the age of 40. In October 1917, while visiting New York, Charmian went to see Houdini perform. The two met after the show, and Charmain wrote him an intriguing letter afterward, to let him know that she was staying in the city for a while, and hinting she was available for future get-togethers:

> *Someday, at exactly the right time and place, I shall tell you more about the past year and the other remarkable experience I have had that I've really carved out for myself. This is your letter. Please destroy it (but don't forget it.)*

They remained in touch and she relates in her diary that a "declaration" Houdini had made over the telephone "rather shakes me up." She began to write about him as her "Magic Lover." Houdini noted at the time that he had "Been having a hard time with my private affairs" but the only real clues to their affair can be found in Charmian's diary.

She says that Houdini declared himself to be "mad about you," that he had said, "I give *all* of myself to you." He even brought his mother into it and we must accept that he could give no greater praise to someone than when he said: "I would have told her—my mother—about you."

At the end of April 1918, Charmian was getting ready to return to California and Houdini seems to have been getting desperate. She wrote: "Poor, sad, lonely thing. He is *very* alone, and worse than he had feared." But soon she was gone and all he had left was what he described as the "magic of memory."

adaptation of Jules Verne's novel *20,000 Leagues Under the Sea*. The film would exploit Houdini's underwater capabilities, but they failed to agree on a contract. Houdini admitted that he asked for too much money.

In 1917, he agreed to star in a motion picture being made by the Williamson brothers, who had also been involved in the Verne adaptation. They were pioneers of underwater photography, their father having invented a deep-sea tube.

Houdini planned to leave for the Bahamas to make the movie, and was going to receive "the biggest money ever paid for a single picture." The film was to be called *The Marvelous Adventures of Houdini: The Justly Celebrated Elusive American*. He worked on the script with the Williamsons, but both the war in Europe and a dispute between the Wiliamsons derailed the project. In the end nothing came of it.

QUENTIN LOCKE, MASTER DETECTIVE

It took Houdini until 1918 to make the acquaintance of Californian film producer B.A. Rolfe (1879 – 1956). Rolfe convinced Houdini to star in a fifteen-part silent-movie serial. The ending of each weekly installment was planned as a cliff-hanger to keep the audience wanting more.

Rolfe employed the very successful writing team of Arthur Reeve (1880 – 1936), and Charles Logue (1889 – 1938). Houdini worked closely with them to create the script for *The Master Mystery*, in which he played the part of Quentin Locke, an undercover agent for the American Justice Department.

His nemesis was a shadowy operation called International Patents Inc., owned by an evil tycoon with a beautiful daughter, Eva, played by Marguerite Marsh (1888 – 1925). There was also a monstrous steel robot, "The Automaton," played by Floyd Buckley (1877 – 1956).

A THRILLING OUTCOME

Like all Houdini's films, the plot was a showcase for his amazing escapology skills. Houdini has to rescue the heroine from perilous situations with death-defying acts of courage. He is repeatedly trapped in life-threatening scenarios from which he always dramatically escapes.

Filmed in the summer of 1918, Houdini literally threw himself into the performance. He bursts out of straitjackets. He frees himself from handcuffs. He escapes from an electric chair. He even avoids a river of corrosive acid threatening to consume him, while lying bound on the floor. In one spectacular escape, while hanging from his thumbs, he uses his legs to choke a man, and his toes to loosen his restraints and free himself!

By the time filming was complete, he had suffered seven black eyes, and broken his left wrist. But he was thrilled with the end-result.

NO CAMERA TRICKS

Although the escapes were always miraculous, much more imagination would be needed in the plot and character for future Houdini movies to keep the audience on the edge of their seats.

One of the problems was that the death-defying scenes were no longer being performed live in front of an audience whom Houdini could manipulate. The increasingly savvy cinema crowds of the early 1920s were well aware of the possibility of faking the escapes using camera trickery, and they did not believe Houdini when he said that his tricks on film were real.

ANXIOUS GLANCES

There was never much passion either with his young, glamorous, leading ladies, as Houdini was so obsessed with his own propriety. If Bess was not present, he would not even touch the female lead. He wanted no suggestive rumors circulating that he had done anything salacious with the young starlets. He paid his leading ladies five dollars for a kiss on film.

One director is reputed to have been so frustrated by a wasted morning trying to get a kiss with some passion, that he asked Bess to leave the set, adding "Whenever we get him to the point of kissing the girl he spoils the shot by glancing anxiously at you."

BLOCKBUSTER

Nonetheless, the movie was a huge success. On its opening weekend in New York, the lines stretched round the block, and thousands were turned away from the theaters. In Boston, legend has it that the picture house doors were locked, and five-thousand people were left outside unable to get in. Houdini himself made extensive personal appearances to promote the film—fifteen in one day in New England. There were even some reviews that complimented his acting. A *New York Telegraph* critic wrote:

> *As a screen actor, Houdini also wins laurels, playing his scenes with the heroine in a manner which reflects great credit on him.*

B·A·ROLFE PRESENTS HOUDINI IN The MASTER MYSTERY

BY ARTHUR B. REEVE AND CHARLES A. LOGUE DIRECTED BY BURTON KING

Movie poster for Episode 8 of the film serial *The Master Mystery* (1919).

CHAPTER 17

THE MAGIC OF THE MOVIES

Released on March 1, 1919, by Octagon Films, *The Master Mystery* movie serial was a massive money-maker, probably because of Houdini's fame. Now he was faced with a major predicament. He had been working on plans for a brand-new live spectacular stage illusion called "Buried Alive." But progress was slow and the dangerous illusion was hard work for an aging magician in his mid-forties—performing on stage was a young man's game.

SERIOUSLY TEMPTED

Not only that, but his live stage performances were starting to look old-fashioned and dull compared to the excitement of the movies. Houdini was seriously tempted to swap his dangerous stage show for the easy money that the movies offered. His return to film was assured when he was contracted by Famous Players-Lasky to star in two more pictures. This time, he turned to the work of Edgar Allan Poe for inspiration, but was unable to match the substance of the great story-teller.

Houdini summed up the stories by saying that they "contained the desired amount of mysticism, danger and opportunity for physical exertion." It was hardly the best summation of Poe's weirdly gruesome tales of Gothic fantasy. But as usual, the great magician was full of optimism that his super-prodigious talents would once again succeed:

> *I am told out here in California, where I am working away at my scenarios and productions, that my act is bound to go well in the movies; so if you hear that the Famous Players have made a small fortune during the year 1919, you will know at whose door to lay the credit for it.*

THE HOUDINI TREATMENT

Had Edgar Allan Poe still been alive, he would have been relieved to learn that, in the end, his work never received the anticipated Houdini treatment. The first film Houdini made for Famous Players was *The Grim Game*. The script was written by Arthur Reeve again, this time with John W. Gray.

It was the usual Houdini tale—Houdini has to escape from jail; Houdini climbs a building; Houdini hangs from a rope; Houdini gets re-captured and is taken to the top of a skyscraper; Houdini is put in a straitjacket and dangled from the roof. Excitement was more than guaranteed!

MID-AIR THRILLS

But the excitement got out of hand during the filming of the climactic mid-air plane chase, almost ending in disaster. Houdini was supposed to jump from the wing of one airplane onto another in mid-air. But the stunt went wildly wrong, when the propeller of one plane caught the other. The two planes crash-landed nearby—fortunately, no one was hurt.

The cameraman kept fearlessly filming during the entire episode, and the shots were used in the movie, generating huge publicity. "The Greatest thrill in the greatest thrill picture ever made," the Associated Press headlines shouted. Of course, no one admitted that Houdini had been nowhere near the incident. He had injured his arm and a stunt-double was being used.

The reviews were superlative. "Houdini is honestly a star ..." said *The New York American*. "Houdini has stepped to the front as a film star," said *The New York Herald*. "There is more excitement in one reel of *The*

Grim Game than in any five reels of celluloid I have ever watched," added *The New York Mail*.

❖ THE TIME OF HIS LIFE

Harry and Bess made themselves comfortable in California which they liked very much. They rented a bungalow in Hollywood and stopped moving for a while, an unusual occurrence in a married life that had been spent on the road in Europe and America. Houdini's next silent picture for Lasky was *Terror Island,* shot on Catalina in the fall of 1919.

Houdini was having the time of his life. He became friends with Charlie Chaplin (1889 – 1977) and Fatty Arbuckle (1887 – 1933), and spent some time on a Lasky set with the beautiful young starlet Gloria Swanson

THE GRIM GAME

Harvey Hanford, played by Houdini, is framed for murder by a gang of men who also kidnap his fiancée, the beautiful Mary Cameron, played by Danish actress, Ann Forrest (1895 – 1985). Hanford is arrested and imprisoned for the murder, but manages to escape and sets off in pursuit of the men who had framed him for the crime.

During this pursuit, Houdini effects a number of trademark stunts including an upside-down straitjacket escape, an escape from a bear trap and in one sequence, he rolls under a passing car, catching the transmission bar and hanging on so that he can quickly get to his fiancée.

The kidnappers capture him and chain him up on numerous occasions but he always manages to free himself. The film climaxes in the mid-air plane crash that was almost a disaster during filming, and Hanford is reunited with Mary.

Movie poster for *The Grim Game* (1919).

(1899 – 1983). Best of all, though, his films were bringing his name and his talents to even more people than before and, with his films being distributed internationally, he was receiving fan mail from all over the world. This meant even bigger audiences when he performed on stage ... and even bigger salaries.

SOMEBODY OWES ME AN APOLOGY

The London Palladium offered him $3,750 a week—the largest salary its management had ever offered to a single performer. He had not performed in Britain since 1913, but he could not turn down such an offer.

Therefore, in December 1919, he and Bess set sail for England where he embarked upon his most lucrative tour ever. All was not well, however, and there were some disappointing reviews. The Nottingham *Football News* wrote:

> Somebody in the head office of Moss Empires owes me an apology over the Houdini visit this week. After receiving a long and fulsome screed of preliminary matter (three large type-written pages of it) which, extravagantly worded, contained the definite statement: "He will present his water-torture sensation *AMONG OTHER FEATS*," I felt justified in saying that the show he would give would be well worth seeing, and should not be missed by anyone. In fact, I boomed of the disadvantage of the rest of the bill. No one was more astounded than I was to see on Monday night Houdini's solitary feat, which of itself lasts only three minutes, and no one has more sympathy with the candid remarks of large numbers of the patrons after the act than I have ... Why on earth Houdini should imagine that any audience would be entertained by hearing a long and uncalled-for account of what he had been doing during the last six years I am at a loss to understand ... People go to a Vaudeville house to see a performance ... not to hear a diatribe on the personal pronoun worked around "the story of my life, sir."

MONEY FOR NOTHING

It was not his proudest moment. During this tour, he was onstage for half an hour. He performed the water torture stunt and then gave his long monologue. But it was still phenomenally successful, bringing him more money than he had ever earned on tour. He was certain that his on-screen success had much to do with it, he wrote to a friend:

> Blame it all on the fact I have been successful in the movies. *The Master Mystery* has been showing over a year ... so the people think they know me personally. Have to make speeches every night. It's wonderful to think that after all my hard work, I can draw the Public without killing myself.

RENEWING THEIR VOWS

On June 22, on the twenty-fifth anniversary of their wedding, Houdini announced that he and Bess would be renewing their wedding vows, and he asked Harry Kellar to give Bess away. It gradually turned into a celebration dinner in the main ballroom of the Hotel Alexandra, the best hotel in Hollywood, and the place where Hollywood stars gravitated.

Two hundred guests, including such names as Will Rogers (1879 – 1935) and Fatty Arbuckle, welcomed the couple, who were played into the room with *The Wedding March*. Poor Bess almost fainted from the emotion of the moment, and Houdini had to run to the bar to get her a glass of wine to help revive her.

LOVE IS IN THE AIR

Perhaps she was overcome by the scent of the flowers because the long table at which the guests sat was covered in blooms—orchids, roses, and sweet peas. Fountains sprayed rose-water into the air. Houdini gave Bess a diamond ring and accompanied it with a love note:

> Wear this dear heart. It is my gift to my bride with all the love that it is possible to give.

Early the following morning he added:

> *How wonderful you were! The most beautiful and wonderful of all. You will only surpass yourself, my Dearest, when you will be my Golden Bride. If the years pass as quickly as these twenty-five have done, we ought to begin at once to prepare to celebrate our golden wedding together.*

PRODUCING PICTURES

Unfortunately, *Terror Island* performed badly at the box office and Lasky decided not to renew Houdini's contract. Undaunted, he resolved to produce his own pictures.

He established the company Officers' Mystery Pictures Corp—later the Houdini Picture Corporation—with himself as president and Hardeen as vice president. He raised cash by selling Martinka's magic shop in New York which he had purchased in 1919. Having invested $5,000, he sent another $10,000 while he was performing in Britain.

Although he was not short of ideas, he decided that his next movie would tell a story that he himself had written—*The Man From Beyond*. He played it up as much as he could, taking out advertisements in the trade press saying: "Greatest praise ever bestowed on any production. Territory available. Unlimited exploitation opportunities." But it was not as good as it could have been. One critic wrote:

> *It starts out promisingly, with the assumption that a man encased in a cake of ice for a hundred years may be resuscitated and brought back from the Arctic to civilization to find his sweetheart of a century ago reincarnated as a girl of identical appearance. Many things might be done with this fantastic conception. But none of them is done in* The Man From Beyond. *Mr. Houdini's imagination seems to have run out at the inception of his idea.*

REMEMBER MARK TWAIN

But box office receipts were not bad, mainly because of a scene at Niagara Falls in which

JESSE LASKY

Born in San Francisco, Jesse Lasky (1880 – 1958) began as a vaudeville performer but in 1911 produced two Broadway musicals—*Hello, Paris* and *A La Broadway*. In 1913, he teamed up with his brother-in-law Samuel Goldwyn (1879 – 1974), Cecil B. DeMille (1881 – 1959), and Oscar Apfel (1878 – 1938) to form the Jesse L. Lasky Feature Play Company. In a rented barn near Los Angeles, they made the first Hollywood feature film, *The Squaw Man*, starring Dustin Farnum (1874 – 1929) and directed by DeMille.

The company merged in 1916 with Adolph Zukor's (1873 – 1976) Famous Players Film Company, creating the Famous Players-Lasky Corporation which later became Paramount Pictures. In 1933, during the Depression, the company went into receivership, and Lasky began to produce films with actress Mary Pickford (1892 – 1979). After working as a producer for one of the main studios until 1945, he again formed his own production company, making his last film in 1951 and dying at age 77 in 1958.

Houdini almost plunged over the Falls. He signed for a tour of the Keith Theater circuit at $3,000 a week for the first four shows, and $3,500 a week for the last five performances.

It was still the same old mixture that had so displeased previous correspondents—a film of his jumps from various bridges, talk of his adventures, the Needle Trick, and the Water Torture Cell. It went on until January 22, 1922 and was so successful that the Keith Theater circuit took him on for another five weeks.

On the founding of the Houdini Picture Corporation, one of Houdini's friends had sent him wise counsel about making money:

> My dear old friend, don't be rash but weigh well what you do and if you find the enterprise a "dead one" don't let it swamp you. Remember Mark Twain lost nearly a million in a "dead sure proposition" which was a complete failure.

But the advice fell on deaf ears, and Houdini got ready to make another movie.

DISCOUNTING DOLLARS

Around this time, Houdini was dealing with other business problems, and the Film Development Corporation was not doing well, as he admitted in a letter to Harry Kellar in October 1921:

> I know it displeases you to hear this but I have just discounted between $8,000 and $10,000 worth of notes for the Film Development Corporation. Poor Dash is not well ... He works very hard giving all his time to the laboratory. It will be a Godsend for all of us if we get away from it in a legitimate manner. The only good of the whole thing is that it was the cause of my going into pictures. Let us hope that I have not made a serious mistake. My two pictures are finished. Now I must put them on the market and will see how good they are.

RUBBER STAMPING HOUDINI

The bad news was that his inexperience in the art of producing movies led to the two films running over budget. To pay for this, he had to undertake a nine-week-long tour. He also dreamt up outlandish marketing stunts. A press kit was assembled, filled with reviews and advice to cinema owners as to how they could make the most of *The Man From Beyond*.

He suggested the creation of a rubber stamp reading "Houdini," that could be built into the sole of a boot. The man wearing it would go out into the rush-hour crowds in the morning and leave his imprint for all to see wherever he walked.

PULLING OUT ALL THE STOPS

At the premier of *The Man From Beyond* at the Times Square Theater in April 1922, Houdini performed his Vanishing Elephant stunt to draw the crowds, and tried as hard as he could to make the film successful. But it failed to attract the crowds or the plaudits.

The Niagara Falls scene went down well with the critics, but there was something out of balance in the movie itself. The critic from *Variety* wrote:

> The trouble is that the resumption of high literary meaning in the rest of the story is all bosh. So the net effect is pretty unsatisfactory. Serial melodrama and screen uplift won't mix.

November 1923 saw the release of the second movie, *Haldane of the Secret Service*. Gladys Leslie (1899 – 1976) played the girl, and William J. Humphrey (1875 – 1942) and Richard Carlyle (1914 – 2009) also starred. Houdini once again pulled out all the publicity stops. He printed thousands of tags for doorknobs that read:

> This lock is not HOUDINI-proof. He could pick it as easily as you could pick a daisy. See the Master-Man of Mystery HOUDINI in "Haldane of the Secret Service." A picture that will thrill you to the marrows.

TERROR ISLAND

A woman named Beverley West, played by Lila Lee (1901 – 73), seeks the help of Houdini's character, Harry Harper. Her father is being held captive by South Sea natives. The ransom for his release is an exotic pearl in the shape of a skull that she owns. The natives believe the pearl has been stolen from the idol they worship.

The pearl is also wanted by Job Mourdant, played by Wilton Taylor (1869 – 1925). Mourdant, Beverley's guardian, kidnaps her and sails out into the ocean and Harper, inventor of a submarine used for salvaging sunken ships, follows in hot pursuit. Mourdant throws Beverley overboard and she is captured by the natives. When Harper arrives on the island, he too is captured but, of course, escapes. He watches as the natives lock Beverley into an iron safe that is then thrown into the sea.

Houdini/Harper frees Beverley and gets his hands on the pearl after a fight with a man in a diving suit. The natives are so impressed by Harper's skills as a magician that they release Beverley and her father. The three sail off safely together.

JESSE L. LASKY · PRESENTS

HOUDINI
IN
"TERROR ISLAND"

BY ARTHUR B. REEVE and JOHN W. GREY
DIRECTED BY JAMES CRUZE

A Paramount Artcraft Picture

─── PLAYERS-LASKY CORPORATION

A *Motion Picture News* advertisement for *Terror Island* (1920).

FADING FAST

But the movie theaters remained fairly empty, and the reviews were cruel. *Variety* wrote:

> *Perhaps the renown of Houdini is fading, or more probably the Broadway managers were wise to how bad a film this one is ... There is only one [escape], and that is a poorly staged affair showing the star free himself from a giant water mill ... instead of going in for his specialty Houdini waltzes around in a tuxedo and dress suit.*

Such reviews and the empty cinemas brought an end to the Houdini Picture Corporation.

Productions in the pipeline were shelved, and the company was dissolved. It was all financially disastrous with lawsuits and court cases about the profits made from the successful *Master Mystery* series.

At the end of the day, although Houdini's involvement in film did not create a new career for him, it bolstered his old one. He became even more famous globally and his salary for his performances increased greatly.

Sadly, however, even though he had lost a considerable amount of money, performing on stage was no longer something that he wanted to do.

THE MAN FROM BEYOND

In the Arctic, Howard Hillary has been frozen in ice for a hundred years. He is brought back to civilization, to the home of Professor Strange where he attends the wedding of the professor's daughter Felice. Hillary becomes convinced that Felice is his fiancée from before he was encased in the ice. After disrupting the ceremony, he is committed to a psychiatric hospital from which he escapes. The remainder of the film is spent in a struggle to defeat evil scientists, while at the same time trying to convince Felice that she is actually his long-lost love, as they search for her father who has been abducted.

HOUDINI PICTURE CORPORATION

presents

HOUDINI

in

"THE MAN FROM BEYOND"

Houdini in a cliffhanging scene from *The Man From Beyond* (1921).

HOUDINI PICTURES CORPORATION

presents

HOUDINI

WORLD FAMOUS HANDCUFF KING

IN

'HALDANE OF THE SECRET SERVICE'

WITH
GLADYS LESLIE
AND AN ALL STAR CAST

DISTRIBUTED BY
FILM BOOKING OFFICES
OF AMERICA, INC.

HALDANE OF THE SECRET SERVICE

Heath Haldane Jr. is the son of a US Secret Service agent who has been murdered by an international counterfeiting ring. During his investigation of the ring, he rescues a young woman who is attacked near Washington Square Park in Greenwich Village, New York. He is led by his investigations to a large warehouse located close to the Hudson River which turns out to be the distribution center for the counterfeit currency being manufactured by the gang, but is discovered and taken prisoner.

They tie him up and throw him into the river but he manages to escape, swimming to a transatlantic steamer just leaving for London. In England, he has a secret meeting on Westminster Bridge with officers from Scotland Yard and from there makes for France where he finds the gang's hide-out— an old monastery in a quiet village where the gang-members are masquerading as monks.

He is captured once again and bound to the spokes of an old waterwheel. The ending of the film reveals the identity of the leader of the gang, the mysterious Dr. Yu. Houdini defeats the gang and proposes to the heroine.

Movie art for the film *Haldane of the Secret Service* (1923) starring Houdini.

PART FIVE

A MAGICIAN IN THE SPIRIT WORLD

What the eyes see, the ear hears, and the mind believes.

Harry Houdini

CHAPTER 18

Encountering Sir Arthur Conan Doyle

Sir Arthur Conan Doyle was a remarkable individual. His writing was hugely successful, and he traveled the world, a very famous man. He had killed off his equally famous fictional detective Sherlock Holmes, but such was the uproar and public demand for more Holmes stories, that he had to bring him back to life.

His first wife died in 1906, and a year later he married Jean Leckie, a woman with whom he had been in love for the previous ten years. It was following his re-marriage that Conan Doyle began to fully embrace spiritualism as a religion rather than a curiosity.

Spiritualism became very popular during and after the First World War (1914 – 18), when countless deaths left grieving families grasping for anything that would promise contact with their deceased loved ones. Conan Doyle had himself suffered losses in the conflict—his son Kingsley, two brothers-in-law, and a number of nephews. His mind was filled with questions as to their whereabouts in death.

VOICES IN THE DARKNESS

In September 1919, Conan Doyle and Jean attended a séance featuring the amateur medium Evan Powell. In a hotel room, Powell insisted that Conan Doyle tie him to his chair. Beside him was placed a megaphone in luminous paint.

After the lights were all switched off, a deep voice could be heard. It claimed to belong to a spirit named "Black Hawk" who was Powell's spirit control. The voice announced that "Leely" wished to speak to "the Lady of the Wigwam." "Leely," they presumed, was

a recently dead friend of Jean's—Lily Loder Symonds.

Deeply impressed, the Conan Doyles returned the next night and this time Conan Doyle had what he described as "the supreme moment of my spiritual experience. Almost too sacred for full description." The voice that emerged from the darkness claimed to be that of his dead son Kingsley. Conan Doyle felt a hand on his shoulder and a kiss on his forehead. The voice said "I am so happy."

Conan Doyle was convinced his son had contacted him from the afterlife. From that point on, he was obsessed with promoting spiritualism, and impatient with non-believers.

> *... my wife and I determined that we would, so far as possible, devote the rest of our lives to trying to make people understand that this subject is not to be laughed at, but that it is really the most important thing in the world.*

THE NON-BELIEVER

Finished with movie-making and hoping to retire from the stage, Harry Houdini was interested in writing more books. The first of these would be about spiritualism. He had maintained an interest in the subject and had even been asked to take part in a debate.

It was proposed in late 1919 that he should argue the case on the negative side, against well-known psychic believers, such as Sir Arthur Conan Doyle or the British scientist, Sir Oliver Lodge, who had also become a believer after being contacted by his dead son.

Houdini declined the invitation as he was about to spend six months in England

SIR ARTHUR CONAN DOYLE

Born in Scotland, Sir Arthur Conan Doyle (1859 – 1930) was a writer and physician who is best known for creating the fictional detective, Sherlock Holmes. Conan Doyle studied medicine at the University of Edinburgh, and while studying began writing short stories, some of which were published. Having failed as an ophthalmologist, he began to take his writing more seriously, inventing the character Sherlock Holmes, based loosely on a former university teacher, Joseph Bell (1837 – 1911).

Holmes uses extraordinary powers of deduction to solve crimes, helped by his partner Dr. Watson. First published in *The Strand Magazine* in 1887, the Sherlock Holmes stories became phenomenally successful, both in Britain and in the United States. Conan Doyle was fairly ambivalent toward his creation, planning to kill Holmes off as he was taking over his life. Publishers, however, were prepared to pay exorbitant sums for more stories.

Holmes dies in the story "The Final Problem," but there was a public outcry, and Conan Doyle was forced to revive him for the 1901 novel, *The Hound of the Baskervilles*. In all, Conan Doyle wrote 56 short stories and four novels featuring Sherlock Holmes, the last published in 1927. He also wrote historical fiction stories, and was the author of the well-known 1912 novel *The Lost World,* about an expedition to a prehistoric world where dinosaurs survive.

Conan Doyle was a man with many interests, and he became involved in political campaigning, during the Boer War (1899 – 1902), as well as denouncing the horrific atrocities in the Congo, publishing a book entitled *The Crime of the Congo* in 1909. Several times he stood for election to the British Parliament, but was never successful.

As spiritualism became more widely popular, Conan Doyle embraced it, launching a series of psychic investigations. Greatly influenced by the deaths he saw around him in the First World War, he believed that spiritualism was a "New Revelation" sent by God to help the bereaved on earth.

Conan Doyle became a friend of Harry Houdini, but the two fell out massively in public over psychic medium hoaxers. Conan Doyle always maintained that Houdini himself possessed real magic powers, while Houdini scoffed at Conan Doyle's naivety.

Sir Arthur Conan Doyle died of a heart attack at his home in Crowborough, East Sussex, England, in 1930, at age 71.

fulfilling engagements that had been postponed due to the First World War. In England, he began researching his planned book, but his relationship with spiritualism was a complex one:

> I too would have parted gladly with a large share of my earthly possessions for the solace of one word from my loved departed—just one word that I was sure had been genuinely bestowed by them. In this frame of mind, I began a new line of psychic research in all seriousness and from that time to the present I have never entered a séance room except with an open mind devoutly anxious to learn if intercommunication was within the range of possibilities.

MAKING CONTACT

Disappointed to miss out on meeting the famous author and leading advocate of spiritualism at the debate, Houdini decided to make contact with Sir Arthur Conan Doyle himself. In March 1920, he dispatched a copy of *The Unmasking of Robert-Houdin* to Conan Doyle.

Conan Doyle replied with thanks, adding "Some of our people think that you yourself have some psychic power, but I feel it is art and practice." Conan Doyle also asked a few questions about the Davenport Brothers, American stage illusionists who claimed to be aided by spiritual guides. Houdini replied carefully:

> I am afraid that I cannot say that all their work was accomplished by the spirits ... You will note that I am still a skeptic, but a seeker after the Truth. I am willing to believe, if I can find a Medium who, as you suggest, will not resort to "manipulation" when the Power does not arrive.

BEGUILING CHARMER

Conan Doyle was certainly charmed by Houdini. He found him "far and away the most curious and intriguing character I have ever encountered." He witnessed many of the good qualities that Houdini possessed—his immense physical strength and fortitude, his devotion to his wife and family, and his charitable nature. However, he was baffled by Houdini's frugality:

> While he was giving away his earnings at a rate which alarmed his wife, he would put an indignant comment in his diary because he had been charged two shillings for the pressing of his clothes.

He was also less than impressed by Houdini's outrageous vanity, and his obsession with self-publicity:

> There was no consideration of any sort which would restrain him if he saw his way to an advertisement. Even when he laid flowers on the graves of the dead it was in the prearranged presence of local photographers.

PSYCHIC SCOURGE

Houdini became the scourge of mediums everywhere. He began to turn up at séances in disguise, sometimes wearing a false beard and glasses. At the critical point of the evening, he would leap up dramatically, tear off his disguise, and expose the psychic's trickery.

Being Houdini, of course, the following day it appeared in the newspapers. Such antics made for a difficult relationship with Conan Doyle whom Houdini described as:

> ... a brilliant man and a deep thinker, well versed in every respect, and comes of a gifted family ... He is a great reader who absorbs what he reads but he believes what he sees in print only if it is favorable to Spiritualism.

When the two men met for lunch at Conan Doyle's house, Houdini was on his own, Bess being indisposed, as she often was. Conan Doyle told Houdini that he had now spoken to his dead son six times.

SIMPLY A CONJUROR

Conan Doyle went to see Houdini's show, and the magician later wrote to his friend

THE DAVENPORT BROTHERS

American magicians, Ira (1839 – 1911) and William Davenport (1841 – 77) performed in the late nineteenth century, presenting illusions that were claimed to be supernaturally guided. Spiritualism had become popular in the United States in the 1840s after the Fox sisters had become famous for supposedly receiving communications from the dead.

The Davenports reported that they too received such communications and started touring, demonstrating their powers. Their shows were introduced by a former religious minister who assured the audience that the brothers worked exclusively using spiritual power and that there was no trickery in what they did.

Their best known illusion involved a large box containing a number of musical instruments. The brothers were tied up and put in the box which was closed. The instruments would start to play but when the box was opened again, Ira and William were in exactly the same positions as when it was closed and remained tightly bound. They toured in the United States for ten years before traveling to England where spiritualism was also taking off.

Several magicians, including Jean Eugène Robert-Houdin, sought to expose the Davenports as fakes by writing articles explaining how their tricks were done, and by performing those same illusions in their acts. A couple of amateur magicians also followed them around Britain, and tied up the brothers with a knot that could not be undone. The brothers could not perform their trick, exposing them to an angry audience.

Before he died in 1911, Ira was interviewed by Houdini, telling him that they had never stated that they believed in spiritualism and that the announcements at the start of their performances were just a part of the act. This, of course, contrasted with Houdini's approach which was to make it clear that his feats were achieved by skill and without the intervention of the supernatural.

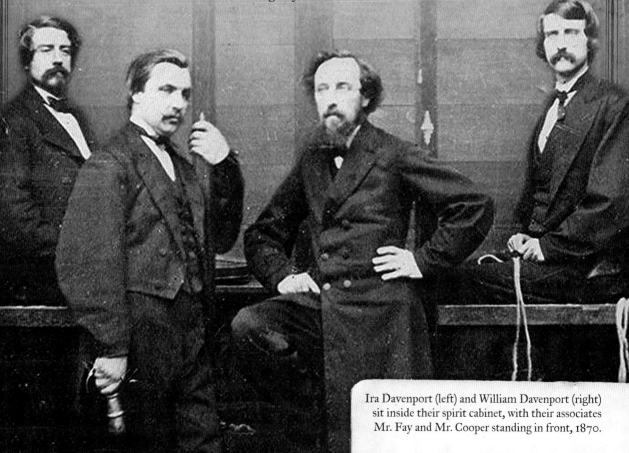

Ira Davenport (left) and William Davenport (right) sit inside their spirit cabinet, with their associates Mr. Fay and Mr. Cooper standing in front, 1870.

Harry Kellar about him:

> [Conan Doyle] saw my performance Friday night. He was so much impressed, that there is little wonder in him believing in Spiritualism so implicitly.

Within a couple of months Conan Doyle really did believe that Houdini possessed occult powers. Naturally, Houdini continued to maintain he was simply a conjuror, and did not possess supernatural powers. But he was unable to prove it without making public his secrets. Conan Doyle wrote to him:

> My dear chap, why go around the world seeking a demonstration of the occult when you are giving one all the time?

THE COTTINGLEY FAIRIES

Houdini began to investigate spirit photography, a process in which the image of a spirit was captured in a photograph. Houdini asked Conan Doyle to let him see some spirit photographs taken by a psychic researcher named Crawford but Conan Doyle did not have them. However, he did have something else:

SPIRIT PHOTOGRAPHY

William H. Mumler (1832 – 84) discovered spirit photography by accident in the 1860s when a photograph he took of himself appeared to include a second person. It was actually a double exposure, as he later learned, but he began working as a medium when he realized there was a market for such pictures.

He would doctor pictures he took, adding deceased loved ones from other photographs. He was exposed as a fraud when it emerged that some of the people he suggested to be spirits were still living.

Nonetheless, other photographers started to sell spirit photographs and spirit photography remained popular into the early twentieth century with practitioners such as Fred A. Hudson, Britain's first spirit photographer. Hudson's photos were exposed as fraudulent in 1872, but people continued to believe in his work. The cleric and spiritualist William Stainton Moses (1839 – 92) claimed that spirit photography used a substance called ectoplasm in which spirits take physical shape.

Arthur Conan Doyle was a strong proponent of spirit photography and when a later photographer William Hope (1863 – 1933) was comprehensively exposed as a fraud by psychic researcher Harry Price (1881 – 1948), Conan Doyle refused to accept the evidence of trickery and tried to clear his name.

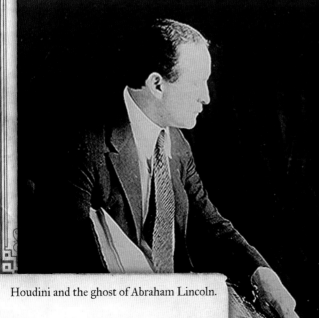

Houdini and the ghost of Abraham Lincoln.

I have something far more precious—two photos, one of a goblin, the other of four fairies in a Yorkshire wood. A fake! You will say. No sir, I think not. However, all inquiry will be made. These I am not allowed to send. The fairies are about eight inches high. In one there is a single goblin dancing. In the other four beautiful, luminous creatures. Yes, it is a revelation.

The "Cottingley Fairies," as they became known, were fakes, as was evident to anyone. One of the girls who took the photographs, finally admitted it years later. A little bit of research at the time would have shown Conan Doyle that the fairy shapes had been cut out of a 1915 children's book. One of his own stories was published in that very same book! Having received this extraordinary letter, Houdini declined to comment.

❖

MIRACLE MONGERS

In England, Houdini attended around a hundred séances and found nothing he had not already seen and exposed. By summer 1921, however, he was asking newspapers to keep his name out of stories about fake mediumship as he could not afford to make enemies of spiritualists while writing his book on the subject.

However, he had another book to sell first—*Miracle Mongers and Their Methods.* The subtitle of the book read: *A Complete Exposé of the Modus Operandi of Fire Eaters,* Heat Resisters, Poison Eaters, Venomous Reptile Defiers, Sword Swallowers, Human Ostriches, Strong Men Etc. In this work, he revealed the secrets of entertainers he encountered back in the days when he was working sideshows and circuses. As he wrote in the preface to the book:

My professional life has been a constant record of disillusion, and many things that seem wonderful to most men are the everyday commonplaces of my business. But I have never been without some seeming marvel to pique my curiosity and challenge my investigation. In this book I have set down some of the stories of strange folk and unusual performers that I have gathered in many years of research.

Reviewers loved the book and critics suggested that fake mediums should be his next target. *Variety* said, "If Houdini doesn't do it, someone else will, sooner or later, but it should be Houdini. He would have the moral support of every clean periodical in the country."

The New York Times loved the book so much that they put his name forward for membership of the Seybert Commission that was looking into the phenomenon of mediums. It concluded eventually that spiritualist mediums were, indeed, engaging in fraud. Others such as his secretary at SAM, Oscar Teale (1847 – 1934), also encouraged him to go after mediums. Teale had exposed many mediums himself years earlier.

Frances Griffiths and the "Cottingley Fairies" in a photograph made in 1917 by her cousin Elsie Wright with paper cutouts and hatpins.

HARRY PRICE

Harry Price (1881 – 1948), British psychic researcher, ghost-buster and author, gained a degree of fame through his investigations into psychic phenomena, and his debunking of fake mediums and spiritualists. Born in London, Price had early experiences with the spiritual world, writing a play at the age of 15 about a poltergeist he encountered at a haunted house in Shropshire, England.

He became a conjurer, joining the Magic Circle in 1922, but his real passion was the investigation of paranormal phenomena. He joined the Society for Psychical Research in 1920, and, with his knowledge of conjuring and magic tricks, was able to expose the trickery of fraudulent mediums, although there were some instances in which he believed the medium to be genuine.

His reputation was established in 1922, with the exposure of the fraudulent spirit photographer William Hope. In 1923, he exposed the Polish medium Jan Guzyk (1875 – 1928) who used his legs to achieve apparently paranormal feats. Price also exposed the "direct voice" mediumship of the American George Valiantine (1874 – 1947). Valiantine claimed to have made contact with the spirit of the Italian composer Luigi Arditi. But Price found that the words the medium claimed to be those of the composer, actually came from an Italian phrase book.

Other famous cases that Price worked on included the mediums Maria Silbert (1866 – 1936), Eileen J. Garrett (1893 – 1970), Austrian medium Rudi Schneider (1908 – 57), and Helen Duncan (1897 – 1956). In 1944, Duncan was one of the last people imprisoned under the British Witchcraft Act 1735, for "falsely claiming to procure spirits."

Price established the National Laboratory of Psychical Research in 1926, its objective "to investigate in a dispassionate manner and by purely scientific means every phase of psychic or alleged psychic phenomena." It became a rival to the Society for Psychical Research and was replaced in 1934 by the University of London Council for Psychical Investigation. English philosopher and broadcaster C.E.M. Joad (1891 – 1953) was chairman, and Price was Honorary Secretary and editor.

Price was best known for his 1929 ghost-busting investigation of Borley Rectory, known as "the most haunted house in England." He reported paranormal activity at the house, claims that were later discredited by the Society for Psychical Research. He died in 1948, at the age of 67.

PARANORMAL ECTOPLASM

Houdini started an investigation of a psychic known as Eva Carrière (1886 – c. 1922). She had launched her career as a medium in Algiers, and had been used by the eminent biologist, Charles Richet (1850 – 1935), to prove that spirits were warm, had hair and breathed out carbon dioxide. Richet devoted many years to the study of psychic phenomena and it was he who had coined the term "ectoplasm."

Eva C. as she was also known, produced ectoplasm from her mouth, and in 1920, Houdini attended several of her séances. However, he was unconvinced by her on the various occasions he watched her. He believed that she got the ectoplasm into her mouth by sleight-of-hand, just as he himself did when performing his East Indian Needles Trick. He wasn't so easily fooled.

Houdini's psychic-busting friend, Harry Price, studied photographs of the ectoplasm that Carrière produced. He suggested that her spiritual materializations did not look real, and indeed, in 1920, it was discovered to be nothing more than chewed up paper.

❖

YOUR FEARSOME FEATS

In the summer of 1920, the Houdinis sailed back to the United States. Knowing that Conan Doyle was planning a lecture tour of America, Houdini wrote offering accommodation while Conan Doyle was in New York. Conan Doyle managed to get out of it by saying that while in the city, he had to be "semi-public for my job's sake." He also took the opportunity to warn Houdini about the dangers of his profession:

All good wishes to you, my dear Houdini. Do drop these dangerous stunts ... For God's sake be careful in these fearsome feats of yours. Surely you could retire now.

❖

A VISIT FROM THE CONAN DOYLES

Sir Arthur arrived in the spring of 1922, and his first lecture, at Carnegie Hall in Manhattan, was sold out. The Conan Doyles then set off on their nationwide tour, but returned to New York City in May. They visited the Houdinis at 278 West 113th Street on May 10. Houdini recorded the event in his diary:

Today at 11 o'clock, Sir Arthur and Lady Doyle came up to 278 for a visit. Sir Arthur was very anxious to see my collection of books and became very much interested. I went all over the house and got together all my rare tracts, and he seemed very much surprised at my collection of literature on Spiritualism.

Houdini invited Sir Arthur to the annual dinner of the Society of American Magicians. It might have been a disaster, a vehement spiritualist among a gathering of magicians. However, Sir Arthur regaled them all with film footage of the dinosaurs from the film that was being made of his novel *The Lost World*.

Eva Carrière performing an ectoplasmic spiritual materialization in 1912.

CHAPTER 19

SÉANCE IN ATLANTIC CITY

The Houdinis joined the Conan Doyles for a weekend in Atlantic City in June during the English family's holiday there. On June 17, 1922, while they were all relaxing on the beach, Sir Arthur suggested that his wife conduct a séance for Houdini, saying that "she has a feeling that she might have a message coming through."

Sir Arthur was desperate to provide the evidence Houdini needed to convert him to a belief in spiritualism. Bess warned Houdini, using the system of signals they had developed, that she knew what was about to transpire. She had spoken to Lady Conan Doyle the previous night at great length about Houdini's relationship with his mother, as he later wrote:

In that manner Mrs. Houdini told me that on the night previously she had gone into detail with Lady Doyle about the great love

I bear for my Mother. She related to her a number of instances, such as, my returning home from long trips, sometimes as far away as Australia, and spending months with my Mother and wearing only the clothes that she had given me because I thought it would please her and give her some happiness.

GRIMMER AND PALER

Nonetheless, Houdini accompanied the Conan Doyles to their suite where Sir Arthur pulled down the blinds. They sat down at a table where they were already provided with pads and pencils.

They placed their hands on the table and Sir Arthur said a short prayer. Houdini later claimed that he was trying to be as objective as possible about the experience and entered into it wholeheartedly.

Sir Arthur Conan Doyle (far left), Lady Conan Doyle (right) and family, with Houdini (center), in Atlantic City at the time of the séance in 1922.

Lady Conan Doyle began writing furiously. Sir Arthur wrote later how he was "tearing sheet after sheet from the block as it was filled up, and tossing each across to Houdini while he sat silent, looking grimmer and paler every moment." The reason was that it was apparently Houdini's mother who was communicating. She began:

> *Oh, my darling, thank God, at last I'm through—I've tried, oh so often—now I am happy. Why, of course, I want to talk to my boy—my own beloved boy—Friends, thank you with all my heart for this.*

On and on went the automatic writing with Cecilia insisting how happy she was in the afterlife. In order to provide Houdini with proof, Sir Arthur suggested that he ask a pertinent question.

Lady Conan Doyle said she did not think that the spirit would answer a direct question. Therefore, Houdini asked "Can my mother read my mind?" The spirit answered that she always read her son's mind. She went on to thank Sir Arthur and to say that her son's eyes would soon be opened. She then bade them farewell.

AMONG THE PROPHETS

After Jean Conan Doyle had stopped writing, Houdini suggested that he should try some automatic writing. Taking the pencil, he unconsciously wrote the name "Powell." Both Houdini and Conan Doyle had close friends of this name. Houdini's Powell was very much alive but was having problems and Conan Doyle's Powell had died the previous week.

Houdini claimed that he had written Powell because his friend was on his mind and he and Bess had argued about his situation. But Sir Arthur insisted that it had to be *his* late friend who had made Houdini write the name:

> *The Spirits have directed you in writing the name of my dear fighting partner in Spiritualism, Dr. Ellis Powell, who has*

> *just died in England. I am the person he is most likely to signal to, and here is his name coming through your hands. Truly Saul is among the Prophets.*

REASONS TO BELIEVE

But when Houdini arrived home, he discovered a letter from his friend Powell. He forwarded it to Sir Arthur, adding the comment "I judge it was just one of those coincidences." Conan Doyle would not let it lie, however.

> *No, the Powell explanation won't do. Not only is he the man who would wish to get to me, but in the evening Mrs. M., the lady medium, got "there is a man here. He wants to say he is sorry he had to speak so abruptly this afternoon."*

Houdini admitted later that he had wanted to believe, especially as the day of the séance was actually his mother's birthday. But he was still skeptical. He wrote:

> *Messages written by Lady Doyle claiming the spirit of my dear mother had control of her hand—my sainted mother could not write English and spoke broken English.*

Furthermore, the messages had begun with Lady Conan Doyle drawing the sign of the cross. Cecilia had, of course, been Jewish and it was, therefore, unlikely that she would have used Christian symbolism in that way.

SPIRIT COMPACTS UNFULFILLED

The Conan Doyles returned home and no more was said about the séance. Their correspondence continued but suddenly in November, Houdini destroyed the relationship when he published a piece attacking spiritualism in the New York *Sun*. The New York General Assembly of Spiritualists had offered a reward of $5,000 to anyone who could produce by "trickery, fraud or deception" eight specific manifestations of spirit power.

Houdini wrote the article in the *Sun* in response to this challenge. It included details about the Atlantic City séance. Entitled "Spirit Compacts Unfulfilled" it contained one section that annoyed Sir Arthur intensely:

> My mind is open. I am perfectly willing to believe, but in the twenty-five years of my investigation and the hundreds of séances which I have attended, I have never seen or heard anything that could convince me that there is a possibility of communication with the loved ones who have gone beyond.

END OF A BEAUTIFUL FRIENDSHIP

Asked for a comment by the newspaper, Sir Arthur declined instead he angrily wrote to Houdini:

> I felt rather sore about it. You have all the right in the world to hold your own opinion, but when you say that you have had no evidence of survival, you say what I cannot reconcile with what I saw with my own eyes. I know, by many examples, the purity of my wife's mediumship, and I saw what you got and what the effect was upon you at the time. ... I have done my best to give you the truth.

Houdini responded:

> You write that you are very sore. I trust that is not with me, because you, having been truthful and manly all your life, naturally must admire the same traits in other human beings ... I know you treat this as a religion but personally I cannot do so, for up to the present time I have never seen or heard anything that could convert me.

Although they both stayed in touch, their friendship was irredeemably damaged. It has been suggested that Sir Arthur's problem was that when he returned to England, he had told people that Houdini had been converted to spiritualism.

This was confirmed by a letter that Houdini received a few weeks after he had replied to Conan Doyle. It was from E. J. Dingwall (1890 – 1986), a researcher for the Society for Psychical Research in England, who wrote:

> Dear Houdini, Is there any truth in the story of Doyle that you got an evidential message from your mother through Lady Doyle? Also that you have become an automatic writer?

THE TRUTH ACCORDING TO HOUDINI

In the years following that séance, Houdini often launched attacks on Sir Arthur in his lectures, berating him for his naivety. In December 1922, he even swore a deposition to the effect that he did not believe in mediums. Conan Doyle, meanwhile, held fast to his views regarding spiritualism, just as Houdini remained a non-believer:

> *THE TRUTH REGARDING SPIRITUAL SÉANCE GIVEN TO HOUDINI BY LADY DOYLE*
>
> *Fully realizing the danger of statements made by investigators of psychic phenomena, and knowing full well my reputation earned, after more than thirty years' experience in the realm of mystery, I can truthfully say that I have never seen a mystery, and have never visited a séance, which I could not fully explain; and I want to go on record regarding the séance given to me by Lady Doyle in the presence of Sir Arthur Conan Doyle, at Atlantic City, June 17, 1922.*

He then gave an account of the séance and confessed that at no point did he feel that his mother's spirit was present in the room. He mentioned that she was unable to speak English and, therefore, questioned how she could have written it so perfectly through Lady Conan Doyle.

He claimed to have written the name Powell not through automatic writing but because he wanted to. The statement concluded with these words:

> I put this on record so that, in case of my death, no one will claim that the spirit of Sir Arthur Conan Doyle's friend Ellis Powell guided my hand.

CONTRADICTING SIR ARTHUR

Sir Arthur Conan Doyle returned to America for another lecture tour, this time visiting the West Coast. Now, he and Houdini really went into battle against one another. The Society of American Magicians, now totally under Houdini's control, offered to replicate any of the phenomena at spiritualist séances. Houdini was ready to offer a contrary opinion to anything that Sir Arthur came out with.

The British writer suggested that the mysterious death of Lord Carnarvon, the leader of the excavations of the tomb of Tutankhamun in Egypt, might have been the work of an evil spirit. Conan Doyle said:

> I think it is possible that some occult influence caused his death. There are many legends about the powers of the old Egyptians, and I know I wouldn't care to go fooling about their tombs and mummies. There are many malevolent spirits.

Houdini was quick to champion the Egyptian authorities' conclusion that Carnarvon actually died of blood poisoning from an insect bite. He also made the very valid point that no other member of the group had died.

STEPPING-UP THE CAMPAIGN

Houdini was now becoming even more serious in his campaign against fraudulent mediums and their tricks. He was paying two investigators—Julia Sawyer who was Bess's niece and Rose Mackenberg. He went so far as to purchase a spiritualist church in Worcester, Massachusetts, where he installed Rose Mackenberg as Reverend F(rances) Raud (for FRAUD). The newspapers loved it.

Sometimes his investigations were serious and complex, however. When he was investigating slate-writing during a séance, words would appear on a slate to which the medium had no prior access. On this

AUTOMATIC WRITING

Automatic writing is a spiritual practice that allows a person to produce writing without consciously being engaged in the act. It is claimed that the words written have come from a subconscious, spiritual or supernatural source.

It was first mentioned in the preface to the third edition of *De l'Intelligence* by French critic and historian Hyppolyte Taine (1828 – 93), published in 1878. Many have claimed to have experienced the phenomenon. The Portuguese poet, Fernando Pessoa (1888 – 1935) said he sometimes felt "owned by something else," his right arm being lifted into the air by something unknown. Georgie Hyde-Lees (1892 – 1968), wife of the Irish poet William Butler Yeats claimed that she could write automatically.

In séances, it is claimed that spirits take control of a writer's hand and guide it in the writing of messages and entire books have even been written this way. Sir Arthur Conan Doyle was a passionate devotee, and believed it was done by the writer's subconscious or by spirits who were communicating through the writer.

The British magician William S. Marriott simulates "automatic writing," inspired by a ghostly guide, 1910.

occasion, Houdini used a mirror that he had fastened to his waistcoat with an elastic band. With this mirror palmed in his hand, he was able to see that the slate was substituted with another on which there was writing, through a sliding panel in the wall behind him.

SCIENTIFIC AMERICAN CHALLENGE

In December 1922, the *Scientific American* magazine offered a reward of $2,500 to anyone who could provide a genuine spirit photograph, with the same amount to the first person to produce a genuine spiritualist phenomenon during a séance.

An eminent committee was assembled to judge the veracity of what was produced. Its members were: Harvard psychologist Dr. William McDougall (1871 – 1938); psychic researcher Hereward Carrington (1880 – 1958); Dr. Daniel Frost Comstock (1883 – 1970), physicist, engineer, and developer of the Technicolor process; Dr. Walter Franklin Prince (1863 – 1934), a minister and psychologist; and Harry Houdini. Sir Arthur was perturbed that Houdini was taking part, and wrote to him:

> *My dear Houdini, I see that you are on the* Scientific American *committee, but how can it be called an Impartial Committee when you have committed yourself to such statements as that some Spiritualists pass away before they realize how they have been deluded, etc.? You have every right to hold such an opinion, but you can't sit on an Impartial Committee afterwards. It becomes biased at once. What I wanted was five good clear-headed men.*

No one provided the committee with much evidence and the magazine was persuaded to increase the reward to $5,000.

MARGERY THE MEDIUM

At this point Dr. Le Roi Crandon came forward suggesting the committee investigate his wife Mrs. Mina Crandon (1888 – 1941), an acquaintance of Sir Arthur Conan Doyle.

Dr. Crandon had become interested in spiritualism through reading a book, *The Psychic Structures of the Goligher Circle* written by Dr. W. J. Crawford (1881 – 1920). It told of a Belfast family, the Golighers who could move objects, he claimed, using material they produced supernaturally that he called "teleplasm."

Dr. Crandon passed the book to his wife and they went to see a medium who told them that Mrs. Crandon possessed psychic powers. They experimented with séances at home and Mina Crandon was apparently able to move a table. They then traveled to Europe to meet the most eminent people in psychic research, including Professor Richet and, of course, Sir Arthur Conan Doyle. Mina Crandon impressed them with her apparent powers.

Dr. Crandon invited the committee of the *Scientific American* to Boston to see Mina Crandon—who called herself "Margery" when operating as a medium—demonstrate her powers. She could make a bugle sound when she had no bugle, was able to stop a clock by concentrating her mind on it and was able to produce things such as a live pigeon and banknotes.

DEALING WITH WALTER

Mina Crandon also had a spirit alter-ego named "Walter," who had been killed by a train several years previously. Walter had a deep, hoarse voice and swore profusely. He could also be difficult, and on one occasion when committee member, Dr. Comstock, brought a mechanical device to a séance for Walter to operate, he proved particularly testy:

> *"How long did it take you to make that thing, Comstock?"*
>
> *"About three days, Walter."*
>
> *"Well, if you expect me to work it in three minutes you're mistaken. I have to experiment and work out things in my sphere just as you do in yours, and I may have to try it forty times before I can do it."*

If you think I'm here just to wander around the room making demonstrations, you're damn mistaken. I have to work hard and gather force for you people here, and light dissipates it just as water interferes with your activities."

Comstock once covered both Dr. and Mrs. Crandon's mouths and noses with his hands "so hard that I must have hurt them," but Walter's voice continued unabated.

Houdini had been sidelined on this investigation, as the committee had decided only to bother him when it felt that there was a serious case in front of them. When he received a letter from Malcolm Bird (1886 – 1964), editor of the magazine, telling him that the $5,000 had been as good as won by Mina Crandon, he was furious that he had not been brought into this investigation earlier.

UNWORLDLY PHENOMENA

Hastening to New York, Houdini confronted Bird and O.D. Munn (1824 – 1907), the *Scientific American's* publisher. He and Munn left for Boston to meet the Crandons. Dr. Crandon, for his part, told Conan Doyle that he and Margery were out to "crucify" Houdini and demonstrate Margery to be "the most extraordinary mediumship in modern history."

The first of Margery's séances attended by Houdini took place on July 23, 1923, and was a tense affair. He was seated to the medium's left, holding her left hand and keeping his right foot in contact with her left foot, so he could be certain they were not being used to create illusions.

The rest of the committee was also present, Malcolm Bird seated on her right. When the room was plunged into darkness, a number of unworldly phenomena were observed. Margery managed to make a bell ring in a box on the floor, Walter threw a megaphone that landed at Houdini's feet and a heavy cabinet in the room was tilted at an angle.

TOTAL TRICKERY

The following day at another séance the box containing the bell fell off the table onto the floor and the table itself was again made to tilt. But Houdini's verdict on Margery was scathing, expressed in a letter to O.D. Munn who was about to publish a positive story in the magazine about their investigation:

Dear Mr. Munn

Please, if I may, allow me to see the exposed article before it is published, as all the other articles were not written as to properly place the real thing before the public. Mr. Bird in your presence, said he believed the medium was fifty per cent genuine, when this evening there was no chance of anything she pretended to have been accomplished by "Walter," but was so done by herself. In fact she is one hundred per cent trickster or fraud judging by the first séance I attended, after forty or more were given … I have been unfairly treated in this case being only called in when according to Mr. Bird's personal statement and in print made, to the effect that the medium, Mrs. Crandon, was fifty per cent genuine … facts such that could not have been written by a competent investigator, and I would like a personally written statement from all those who were present on the Committee to check their findings.

It is worthy of note that Malcolm Bird had spent time with Sir Arthur Conan Doyle in Britain investigating mediums. He was just the type of man that Conan Doyle was happy to see being involved in such an investigation and Bird had been appointed secretary of the committee. He was on record as saying:

[I am] convinced that these phenomena do occur without fraud. I distinctly saw phosphorescent lights, heard trumpet voices and witnessed the movement of material objects under circumstances which satisfied me personally that there was no fraud.

How Did Margery Do It?

Houdini confessed to Harry Price that it had not been easy to detect how the Crandons fooled everyone and, in fact, he went to extraordinary lengths to work it out. Firstly, he tied a silk rubber bandage around his right leg, just below the knee. He wore it all day and by the evening his leg was swollen and painful beneath the bandage. This made it more sensitive and so, whenever Mrs. Crandon/Margery moved her ankle or even flexed the muscles in her leg, he would feel it.

MARJORY'S LEFT FOOT

He noted that she wore silk stockings, and that evening, seated at the table, her skirt was pulled up past her knees. The box containing the bell was positioned on the floor between Houdini's feet, and his right foot was between the box and Mrs. Crandon's left foot. During the séance he claimed to have felt her left ankle against his, as she tried to position it, so that she could raise it over his foot to come into contact with the top of the box.

She said to him that he should press against her ankle so that he could confirm that it was still there but as he pressed she was slowly raising her foot. When she was in a position to touch the top of the box with her foot, the bell rang. But he felt the tendons of her leg flex and tighten as she touched the bell-ringing apparatus. At the end of the ringing, he felt her foot slide back into position.

THE MEGAPHONE

"Walter" requested that an illuminated plaque be put on the lid of the bell-box, and Bird went to find it. Margery's right hand and foot were now free of control and it was "pitch dark," as Houdini later told Bess. While Bird was looking for the plaque, "Walter" suddenly asked for "control."

At this point, Margery put her right hand in Houdini's, leading him to believe that he now held both her hands. Bird was told to stand in the doorway and, at that moment, a cabinet in

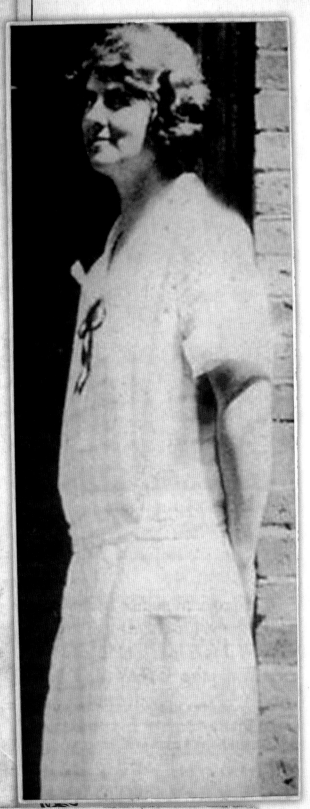

Mina Crandon assumed the persona of "Margery" when communicating with spirits.

the room was knocked over backward. Margery placed her right foot next to Houdini's and told him that he had both her hands and her feet in his control. "Walter" now cried out that the megaphone was "in the air" and requested Houdini to tell him where to throw it. When Houdini replied "Toward me," it landed immediately at his feet.

THE SLICKEST TRICK

Houdini deduced that as soon as Bird left the room, Mrs. Crandon tilted the corner of the cabinet enough with her right hand so that she could get her foot under it. She also picked up the megaphone in the dark with her free right hand and placed it on her head, somewhat like a dunce's cap. She then pushed the cabinet over with her right foot.

To make the megaphone fall at Houdini's feet while he held both her hands, she simply tilted her head and it fell to the floor at his feet. Houdini described it as "the *slickest* ruse I have ever detected."

The spirit medium Margery in a fraud-proof box, with Houdini holding her left hand.

CHAPTER 20

DYING FOR A LIVING

However, Harry Houdini was not yet finished with Mina "Margery" Crandon. He got Jim Collins, his assistant, to build a box large enough to hold her. On August 25, 1924, Margery sat on a chair inside the box, the lid closed and locked, and her head and arms sticking out through holes. Houdini requested that she repeat what had occurred at the séance. Interestingly, Malcolm Bird was prohibited from attending this session as he was suspected by Houdini of passing information to Dr. and Mrs. Crandon that would help them.

The Crandons were unhappy because they believed the box inhibited Mrs. Crandon, claiming that she performed her actions using a pseudopod, a supernormal limb that emerged from between her legs. The first session was unsuccessful as the box broke open. At any rate, somehow Margery succeeded in ringing the bell. They strengthened the locks and began again the following day. After nothing happened, a ruler was found in the box with which the bell could have been rung.

DENYING THE FAKERY

The Crandons accused Houdini of putting it there to discredit them while Houdini accused them of fakery. In fact, a book published in 1959 claims that Jim Collins admitted to throwing the ruler into the box: "I chucked it in the box meself. The Boss told me to do it. 'E wanted to fix her good." However, there are many who dismiss this assertion as total fiction, especially as Houdini and Collins both denied it at the time.

Margery threatened Houdini with a beating by some of her friends if he denounced her from the stage of Keith's Theater in Boston where he was performing. She spoke of not wanting her twelve-year-old son to grow up

believing his mother was a fraud. Houdini's response was—"Then don't be a fraud."

EXPOSING THE TRICKS

The Crandons did not receive the money and Houdini published a pamphlet a few months later entitled: "Houdini Exposes the Tricks Used by the Boston Medium 'Margery' to win the $2,500 prize Offered by the *Scientific American*." The pamphlet charted in great detail with sketches and diagrams how Margery tricked everyone. Houdini wrote:

> *I charge Mrs. Crandon with practicing her feats daily like a professional conjurer. Also that because of her training as a secretary, her long experience as a professional musician, and her athletic build she is not simple and guileless but a shrewd, cunning woman, resourceful in the extreme, and taking advantage of every opportunity to produce a "manifestation."*

A MAGICIAN AMONG THE SPIRITS

In 1924, Houdini published his book *A Magician Among the Spirits*, a social history of spiritualism, taking in the mediums and entertainers involved in it. In the book he discusses, among others, the Fox Sisters, Scottish spiritualist Daniel Dunglas Home (1833 – 86), Italian medium Eusapia Palladino (1854 – 1918) and the medium Henry Slade who was best known for his slate-writing.

Houdini exposed all the tricks and secrets used by mediums and spirit photographers. He chillingly detailed the many deaths that had been caused by spiritualism, often when people foretold a death and then facilitated it. Needless to say, spiritualists were outraged and claims of bias were thrown at him

EUSAPIA PALLADINO

Eusapia Palladino (1854 – 1918), Italian spiritualist and medium, was born into a peasant family in Minervino Murge in the Italian province of Bari. As a young girl, mysterious events seemed to happen around her and when she attended a séance at the house of some friends, a table tilted and levitated when she sat down. She began to hold séances although she is reported to have been afraid of her own powers.

In 1886, she met another spiritualist, Ercole Chiaia (c. 1850 – 1905), who contacted a psychiatrist friend, Cesare Lombroso (1835 – 1909), to interest him in discovering whether Palladino really did possess supernatural powers. Chiaia described her ability to make objects and even herself levitate and to make marks on cards that she was nowhere near. He said that she was able to increase her stature by more than four inches and grow extra limbs. Lombroso investigated her and could find no explanation for her feats.

Séances were held in Milan in 1892 for a group of eminent scientists including Professor Charles Richet. It was deduced that Palladino did, in fact, cheat, taking advantage of every instance of lapsed concentration on the part of those who were controlling her. One of her tricks was to convince the two people holding her arms that each was touching a separate limb when one of them had, in fact, transferred his hand to her other arm, freeing an arm.

This kind of misdirection was helped by the way that she thrashed about when in a trance. There were, however, manifestations that were inexplicable. The sessions were held in a dim red light, and attendees saw and felt what were apparently a number of spectral hands groping outward from behind the cabinet curtain while the medium remained plainly visible in front of them. When her claims were analyzed, however, magicians and skeptics alike concluded that it was all a charade, and none of her phenomena were genuine.

HEREWARD CARRINGTON

Hereward Carrington (1880 – 1958), investigator of psychic phenomena, was born in St. Helier, on the island of Jersey in the British Channel Islands, and emigrated to the United States in 1888. He initially worked as a magazine editor before becoming an assistant to James Hyslop (1854 – 1920), secretary of the American Society for Psychical Research (ASPR), from 1907 to 1908. By that time, he had begun to establish a reputation as an investigator for ASPR. He had to leave ASPR, however, when they could no longer afford to pay him.

He was sent by the English Society for Psychic Research to investigate Eusapia Palladino the Italian medium, whose abilities convinced him of the existence of psychic phenomena. He organized a tour for her in the United States and, in 1909, also wrote a book about her. In 1910, he investigated the case of Esther Cox, known as the Great Amherst Mystery, which featured poltergeist activity.

Carrington was also interested in conjuring and this made him skeptical about some psychic phenomena and he exposed a great many mediums. In fact, in his 1907 book, *The Physical Phenomena of Spiritualism*, he had suggested that 98 percent of physical and mental phenomena were fraudulent. But he did, nonetheless, believe that some of the phenomena in séances were real.

He was involved in a scandal in 1909, when it emerged that he had painted Eusapia Palladino's arm with phosphorescent paint. He claimed it was so that he could keep track of the arm during the séance and that it was not to create the effect of hands emitting light. Carrington stated in 1930:

> I have no particular theory to defend, and no belief to uphold. I am not a convinced spiritualist; at the same time, I am willing to grant that the evidence for survival is remarkably strong.

Although they were not great friends, due to Carrington's support for Margery, Harry Houdini wrote that Carrington's book, *The Physical Phenomena of Spiritualism*, was the best ever written on the subject.

although he was keen to point out that he had always approached the subject with an open mind.

Unfortunately, a number of factual errors were highlighted in the book, for which Houdini had no hesitation in blaming his editors at the publisher Harper and Brothers. He had written a much longer book but they had cut around 100,000 words of the text. He wrote to the novelist Upton Sinclair:

> *The publishing of my book had been so long drawn out that I had a slight premonition that perhaps I would not live to see the book in print if I waited much longer, so I allowed them to rush it, against my judgment, and made some of the very important mistakes, they did not think worthy of correction.*

LAST WILL AND TESTAMENT

Having dispensed with the Crandons, Houdini re-doubled his efforts at debunking fraudulent mediums. He disguised himself and attended séances, leaping up and exposing the trickery of the medium. His two investigators also worked at finding fakers. He demonstrated how spirit photographers plied their craft.

Around this time, Houdini wrote a will. Bess was to receive his dramatic library and all his personal effects while Hardeen was to be left his brother's magical equipment which, the will instructed, was to be burned on Hardeen's death. His vast library of books on spiritualism and the occult was to be donated to the American Society for Psychical Research and his collection of books on magic was to go to the Library of Congress.

His assistants would each receive $500, and SAM would benefit to the tune of $1,000. The remainder of the estate was to be put into a trust for his brothers and sister but nothing was to go to Leopold or Sadie.

HOUDINI IS DOOMED!

If the Conan Doyles could be believed, Houdini's will would be implemented before

long. By this time, Sir Arthur, through the auspices of his wife had obtained his own spiritual guide, a character named "Pheneas." But there was a suspicion in some quarters that perhaps Lady Conan Doyle introduced this spirit as a means of controlling her husband's more naïve moments. His reputation had been badly damaged by the Cottingley Fairies episode, and she did not want it further harmed by similar incidents. But "Pheneas" was also railing at Houdini in his utterances:

> *Houdini is doomed, doomed! A terrible future awaits him. He has done untold harm. It will not be long first. His fate is at hand. He, and all who uphold him, will be, as it were, chained together and cast into the sea. Your friends the Crandons will even in this world reap the reward of their brave work ... In the fearful crisis which is soon to come, America in her sore need will find that she has here a sure and well tested bridge to the spirit world ... They will play a great part in the crisis and it is then that they will wilfully come into their own.*

JUST ANOTHER FAKIR

In 1926, Hereward Carrington was pushing a new act featuring Rahman Bey, described as an Egyptian dervish and fakir. He had the air of the mysterious Middle East about him, although he was actually Italian, and, with the opening up of Tutankhamun's tomb in Egypt by Howard Carter, Egypt was all the rage. Elements of the Middle East were leaking into fashion and design.

Rahman Bey opened at Broadway's Selwyn Theater in May 1926. His act was the usual mix of yogic trickery. He put a steel pin through his cheek, stuck a knife in his neck and put skewers through the skin of his chest. He even performed the old favorite of lying on a bed of nails. All the time, Carrington commentated on what Bey was doing from the side of the stage.

The act ended with a dramatic burial of the performer in a coffin beneath a mound

Sex and Séances

Sex and séances go together, and there is a history of sexual relations between mediums and the very men who investigated them. Sir William Crookes (1832 – 1919), the well-known British chemist, was the patron, for instance, of a beautiful young medium, Florence Cook (1856 – 1904) who claimed to make a spirit named "Katie King" materialize.

King was said to be the daughter of a famous eighteenth century pirate, John King. Funnily enough, Katie actually looked like a young Victorian lady with a handkerchief pinned over her head. Crookes insisted vehemently that the materializations were real, but it later transpired that he and Florence Cook were lovers who used the darkness of the room in which the séance was being held to meet.

In fact, séances often covered for prostitution in both Europe and in the United States. Joseph Rinn, Houdini's childhood friend who also debunked fraudulent mediums, reported that there were upward of a hundred mediums in New York City who were actually prostitutes. Eusapia Palladino often enjoyed relations with her sitters, among them the eminent Cesare Lombroso and Professor Richet.

Eva Carrière claimed to be able to produce large quantities of ectoplasm. She sometimes dispensed with her clothing and ran around the room naked and engaged in sexual activities with her audience.

The highly-regarded German physician Albert Freiherr von Schrenck-Notzing (1862 – 1929) was happy to watch as Eva's sponsor—and mistress—Mademoiselle Bisson inserted her finger into Eva's vagina before a séance to ensure that nothing was concealed there. Eva took so much pleasure from this experience that often at the conclusion of the session she would request another inspection.

Mina Crandon herself was an attractive woman,

described by her biographer as "a slim and pretty woman whose roundness of limb and pertness of attitude men found too attractive for her own good." She dressed well and the fashions of the 1920s were good to her. Malcolm Bird was very taken with her, which might explain why he sided with the Crandons in the tests and was finally excluded by Houdini.

Although Bird actually moved in with the Crandons, the committee member for whom Mrs. Crandon reserved her affections was Hereward Carrington. He is reported to have asked her to run away with him to Egypt.

Florence Cook lies in a trance with a spirit form behind her during a séance at the home of Sir William Crookes.

of sand. He remained there for ten minutes while Carrington delivered a lecture on being buried alive. The coffin was then dug out of the sand and Rahman Bey was cheered by the audience.

It was, ultimately nothing particularly special; nothing new was presented, but Houdini was deeply irritated by it, particularly as he had already exposed such stunts and illusions as Bey performed, when he published his book *Miracle Mongers and Their Methods*.

WHIFF OF THE SUPERNATURAL

Firstly, he was annoyed by Carrington's involvement. Since the Crandon investigation there had been no love lost between the two men. In fact, Houdini had asked that Carrington's role in the Crandon case be investigated. But, he was also deeply irritated by the whiff of the supernatural with which Rahman Bey surrounded himself.

The burial in the coffin was, Houdini felt, simple theft from his act, especially when Bey had himself shut in the coffin and thrown in the Hudson River. This trick malfunctioned, but he did manage to stay underwater in the coffin for an hour in a New York swimming pool.

Carrington issued a challenge to Houdini to do the same and, of course, Houdini immediately accepted. He ordered a box made of galvanized iron that was six and a half feet long, twenty-two inches high and the same wide. He had an alarm fitted in it, in case anything should go awry and even installed a telephone inside.

Rahman Bey claimed that he was able to remain in the box underwater for so long due to the trance into which he put himself. During this trance state his breathing and circulation ceased. Houdini, of course, knew this to be nonsense, and believed that it was really all about controlled breathing. Although he had never quite done anything of this nature before, he had performed tricks in which breathing was the key.

NO SUFFERING

He set about testing himself. In the first attempt, he was not submerged but was able to remain locked in the airtight, strengthened box for an hour and ten minutes. A second test was run on August 4. This time the coffin was lowered into water and Houdini described the effects:

> *This time I was comfortable, somewhat cold. There was plenty of moisture on the inside—I should judge about an inch and a half water on the top of the coffin ... Was much more comfortable than the first test as far as my body was concerned. Started to draw long breaths after about fifty minutes. There was always an irritability there and thought it was simply temperament on my part.*

He signalled for the coffin to be brought up and opened at seventy minutes. It took a further three minutes to unscrew all the fastenings. Then Houdini reported, "There was no suffering."

WHEN BREATH BECOMES AIR

He was nothing if not thorough. The following day another test was executed, this time in the swimming pool at the Shelton Hotel. Beforehand, an unusually gloomy Houdini delivered a somber short speech:

> *If I die, it will be the will of God and my own foolishness. I am going to prove the copybook maxims are wrong when they say a man can live but three minutes without air, [a direct dig at Rahman Bey] and I am not going to pretend to be in a cataleptic state either.*

What Houdini somewhat disingenuously forgot to mention, of course, was that the box contained 34,398 cubic inches of air.

Members of the press thronged around the swimming pool, cameras and notepads at the ready and among them was Hereward Carrington. The coffin was ponderously lowered into the rippling water of the pool, several men standing on it. Inside the box,

Houdini was far from as comfortable as he had been during the second test.

It was warm inside, due to the stuffiness of the pool area. After about fifty minutes he wobbled and was not sure he could remain inside much longer. At an hour, he later reported, he began to pant. Raised from the water, however, and out in the air again, he was exhilarated to learn that he had endured one hour and twelve minutes.

DEATH-DEFYING COFFIN

Houdini announced to all that he was going to make the stunt even more death-defying by having a coffin made that would be fitted with a glass lid. He added this coffin stunt to his act and took it on tour with him.

He also jumped on the Egyptian bandwagon, and there were design elements of his new posters that borrowed from the fashionable Egyptian trend. A sphinx loomed above a sarcophagus containing Houdini. The bold lettering screamed out the message:

"BURIED ALIVE!"

And then, just to rub in the defeat to Bey and Carrington, it added:

Egyptian Fakirs Outdone—

The Greatest Necromancer of the Age—

Perhaps of all times!

HOUDINI AND H.P. LOVECRAFT

In the summer of 1926, Houdini spent the weekends at the Long Island summer home of his lawyer, Bernard Ernst. He was intent on literary pursuits, one of which was a putative autobiography. Another was a novel, *Lucille*. He also began work with the horror writer H.P. Lovecraft (1890 – 1937) on magazine stories. The owner of the magazine *Weird Tales*, J.C. Henneberger, was facing a fall in circulation and believed that adding Harry Houdini's name to the list of the magazine's authors would help lift it out of the doldrums.

The magazine introduced an "Ask Houdini" page and Henneberger approached Lovecraft to ghost write a story that Houdini claimed to have experienced in Egypt but, of course, he had never been there. To secure Lovecraft, Henneberger offered him $100 which was the most money the writer had ever been paid in advance. Short of cash, he accepted.

He listened to what Houdini had to say about the tale, and did some background research before deciding that it was all completely made up. At that point he asked Henneberger if he could use artistic licence on the story. Henneberger said yes, he could do whatever he wanted with it, and Lovecraft got down to work, researching at the Metropolitan Museum of Art and visiting the Egyptian antiquities in the museum's collection.

He finished writing the story, "Imprisoned with the Pharaohs" at the end of February 1924, but he lost the original manuscript a few days later in Union Station in Providence, Rhode Island. He had been on his way to New York to get married the following day. He did, fortunately, have another copy but it had to be retyped, a task he engaged upon the morning of his wedding. By the time he had to set off for the church, he had only managed to do half of it.

The first day of his honeymoon was spent with his new wife reading out from the copy of the story while Lovecraft furiously typed it. "When that manuscript was finished," his wife later wrote, "we were too tired and exhausted for honey-mooning or anything else."

Poster for the death-defying coffin escape evoking
the mystical past of ancient Egypt, 1926.

CHAPTER 21

On the Road Again

The "Greatest Necromancer of the Age" turned 52 in 1926. Houdini was still in robust health and fit as a fiddle. As Sir Arthur Conan Doyle noted:

> *I suppose at that time Houdini was, from an insurance point of view, so far as bodily health goes, the best life of his age in America. He was in constant training and he used neither alcohol or tobacco.*

His insurance company wholeheartedly agreed, ending one letter to him: "Would there were many more like you."

Houdini was about to set off on another huge tour of the United States, although for years he had been insisting that his current tour would be his last. In fact, he seemed this time to be positively luxuriating in the idea of going out on the road again, playing to full houses. He wrote:

> *We all have our hobbies and it is natural that each year I have an inclination to return to my first love—vaudeville—because it was Mr. Albee, of the B.F. Keith Circuit, who gave me an opportunity to make my name known throughout the civilized world as an entertainer. While others go to Palm Springs in the winter for a vacation, I go into vaudeville. I get paid for it, a very good salary, but I don't have to do it.*

CANCER OF SUPERSTITION

For Bess it was different. She was middle-aged now—50 years old—and her drinking was becoming more than just a social habit. Her make-up was thick and her face pale. Living out of a suitcase and taking to the stage and performing Metamorphosis for the umpteenth time was unlikely to fill her with joy. It did not take long for her to fall ill.

While they were in Providence, Rhode Island, fulfilling an engagement, they dined with H.P. Lovecraft and Clifford Eddy Jr. (known as C.M. Eddy Jr., 1896 – 1967) who were working on a book for Houdini called *The Cancer of Superstition*. Eddy was also one of Houdini's team of secret séance investigators.

After dinner, Bess became ill with food poisoning. The doctor ordered her to rest and Houdini organized a nurse, Sophie Rosenblatt, who had worked for the Houdinis before. A female performer from the cast took Bess's roles in the act.

Bess was so bad that Harry sat with her throughout the night of Friday, October 7, finally snatching some sleep in the late afternoon after the Saturday matinee show. He had some business to attend to in New York and after the Saturday night performance, waved the still unwell Bess off with the rest of the cast to Albany where the show was to open on the following Monday.

IMPENDING LAWSUITS

He traveled to New York on the last train out of Providence, to meet, his lawyer Bernard Ernst the following day. Among the pressing matters he had been due to discuss with Ernst were the legal cases that were accumulating from spiritualists that Houdini had denigrated. There were about a million dollars' worth of lawsuits hanging over him. He was so concerned about these that before they set out on tour, he sold his show, complete with costumes, illusions and apparatus to Bess for a dollar.

In fact, when he had been performing in Boston, he had noticed a court stenographer writing down every word he uttered during the last section of the performance in which he exposed spiritualists. Another two people were spotted taking notes and Houdini magnanimously handed them the transcripts of what he was saying and continued with his exposés.

HOUDINI'S PREMONITION

After concluding his meeting with Ernst, Houdini phoned Albany to learn that Bess' condition remained poor but the nurse was going to remain by her bedside through the night. He decided to postpone his train journey to Albany and sometime after midnight put a call through to his friend, the famous mentalist, Joe Dunninger (1892 – 1975). He asked Dunninger if he would help him move some stuff out of his house, requesting that he bring up his car.

Despite the hour and the rain that was pelting down on New York City, Dunninger duly jumped into his car and drove over to 113th Street to find Houdini waiting in the doorway, dressed in old clothes and a beaten-up straw hat. By his side was a man from the Holmes security company, there to ensure that the property's alarm system was not triggered.

It was bundles of tied-up papers and magazines that Houdini wanted moved and after the security guard had helped him load the vehicle and had been tipped fifty cents, Dunninger and Houdini drove off.

They stopped to grab a quick bite to eat but as they returned to the vehicle, Houdini instructed Dunninger to drive through Central Park. At the west park exit at 72nd Street, however, Houdini suddenly clasped

CLIFFORD EDDY JR.

American writer, C.M. Eddy Jr. was best known for the horror, mystery and supernatural short stories he wrote, often for *Weird Tales* magazine. Born in Providence, Rhode Island, he was fascinated by mythology and the occult from an early age. His first published work was a detective story "Sign of the Dragon" that appeared in *Mystery Magazine* in 1919. As well as writing tales of mystery, vampires, ghosts and unexplained happenings, he also wrote songs.

Eddy and his wife Muriel (1896 – 1978)—also a writer—first became friendly with the great horror writer, H.P. Lovecraft in 1918. Lovecraft who also lived in Providence, often visited the couple at their home. He and Eddy edited each other's stories and both carried out work, including ghost-writing and exposes of fake mediums for Harry Houdini. Eddy and Lovecraft went for long walks together while Eddy's wife typed many of Lovecraft's manuscripts.

Eddy worked as a theatrical booking agent for twenty-five years and in later life was a proof-reader for Oxford Press. He also worked as a clerk at the business management office of the Rhode Island State Department of Health. He died in 1967 at the age of 71.

his friend's arm. "Go back, Joe," he said, seeming startled. When Dunninger asked him why, Houdini told him, "Just go back."

Dunninger did as he was asked and they drove through the pouring rain back to the house. On arrival, Houdini got out of the vehicle, removed his hat and stood looking at his house. Returning to the car, he said nothing and they drove off. Dunninger turned to his friend and realized that he was crying and his shoulders were heaving. He said:

> *I've seen the house for the last time, Joe. I'll never see my house again.*

A BROKEN ANKLE

At the opening performance in Albany, Houdini started the second half of the show with the Needles Trick, which was followed by the Water Torture Cell. As usual, he donned his bathing costume and lay down to be shackled into the apparatus that would be fitted into the metal frame of the roof of the water tank. As he was beginning to be hoisted into position above the tank, there was a sudden violent jerk. Houdini heard a crack and grimaced with a sudden shot of pain in his ankle. He made it known to his assistants that they should lower the apparatus. When he was released, a call went out for a doctor.

A Dr. Hannock was in the audience that night, and after examining Houdini in the wings, he concluded that his ankle was probably broken. He ordered the escape artist to go to hospital, but Houdini refused to disappoint those who had paid to see him. He commendably performed the rest of his act, therefore, on one leg.

After the show, the audience gathered at the stage door to cheer him as he left for the hospital. There, doctors confirmed that his ankle had been broken by the hoist's severe jolt and recommended that he rest it for a week. Being Harry Houdini, of course, that was unlikely to happen. He stayed awake all night devising a leg brace that would enable him to perform his act.

AT MCGILL UNIVERSITY

The hall at Montreal's McGill University was crammed to the rafters by 5 p.m. on Tuesday, October 19, 1926, when Houdini limped up the stairs onto the platform, his face pale and drawn with pain. With him were Professor William Tait of the university, Julia Sawyer, and Rose Mackenberg. Professor Tait briefly introduced Houdini who limped over into the center of the platform.

He launched into a lecture on the subject of magic. His tricks and illusions, he told them, were dependent on steely nerves, skill, and perfect coordination. He emphasized, however, as he always did, that they were achieved by natural means and there was nothing supernatural about them. In fact, he said, if people really looked, they would be able to work out how such tricks were done. His work was achieved by not being afraid and by rejecting pain. He proved his point by sterilizing a needle and sticking it through his cheek. There was no sign of any blood.

STILL EXPOSING FRAUDSTERS

He began to warm to his subject, especially when he moved on to the main thrust of the evening, the spiritualist fraudsters who duped people to the tune of many millions of dollars a year. He said that mediums were either themselves deluded, or were psychotic or basically criminals. He laid into the phoney medium, Margery, as well as Lady Conan Doyle. The *Montreal Gazette* ran the headline "*Houdini Assails 'Slickest' Medium—Reiterates Charges Against 'Marjorie' of Boston as Fake—Tilts at Lady Doyle.*" He told his audience that he would go on exposing fraudulent mediums, no matter what.

At the end of the talk, as Houdini conversed with students and faculty members, a young man named Samuel J. Smilovitch approached him with a sketch he had made of him. Houdini was pleased with the sketch and invited "Smiley," as he was nicknamed, to come backstage at the Princess Theater where he was performing, to do a proper drawing of him.

Smiley duly arrived on the morning of Friday, October 22, with a friend Jack Price. At the theater, they met Houdini, accompanied by Bess, the nurse Sophie Rosenblatt, and Bess's niece, Julia Sawyer, who had been working as Houdini's secretary. They went back to Houdini's dressing room where Smiley settled down to draw the magician.

BEATEN TO THE PUNCH

A short while later, there was a knock at the dressing room door and Julia Sawyer brought in a first-year McGill student, J. Gordon Whitehead. It is from Jack Price, Smiley's friend, that we learn what transpired:

Houdini was facing us and lying down on a couch at the time reading some mail, his right side nearest us. The first-year student engaged Houdini more or less continually in a conversation while my friend Mr. Smilovitch continued to sketch Houdini. This student was the first to raise the question of Houdini's strength. My friend and I were not so much interested in his strength as we were in his mental acuteness, his skill, his beliefs and personal experiences. Houdini stated that he had extraordinary muscles in his forearms, in his shoulders and in his back, and he asked all of us present to feel them, which we did.

The first-year McGill student asked Houdini whether it was true that punches in the stomach did not hurt him. Houdini remarked rather unenthusiastically that his stomach could resist much, though he did not speak of it in superlative terms. Thereupon he gave Houdini some hammer-like blows below the belt, first securing Houdini's permission to strike him. Houdini was reclining at the time with his right side nearest Whitehead, and the said student was more or less bending over him. These blows fell on that part of the stomach to the right of the navel, and were struck on the side nearest to us, which was in fact Houdini's right side; I do not remember exactly how many blows were struck. I

am certain, however, of at least four very hard and severe body blows, because at the end of the second or third blow I verbally protested against this sudden onslaught on the part of the first-year student, using the words, "Hey there! You must be crazy, what are you doing?" or words to that effect, but Whitehead continued striking Houdini with all his strength.

Houdini stopped him suddenly in the midst of a punch, with a gesture that he had had enough. At the time Whitehead was striking Houdini, the latter looked as though he was in extreme pain and winced as each blow was struck.

THE SHOW MUST GO ON

Following this incident, Houdini claimed that he had had no chance to prepare himself for Whitehead's punches, and had not anticipated that the student would hit him with such force. He should really have been standing which would have enabled him to withstand the blows more easily, but, of course, his foot injury prevented him from doing that.

Nonetheless, he seemed alright for a while. Only later in the day did he begin to feel some pain in his stomach comparable to that of his injured ankle. But, he performed his show that night. Afterward the pain was worse and he was in agony all through the night. Bess massaged his stomach a little at around two in the morning and he drifted off to sleep.

The following morning, when Bess woke up, she found her husband gone but having left a note referring to a "champagne party" she, Houdini, Julia, and the nurse, had enjoyed in his room:

Champagne coquette

I'll be at the theater about 12.00—

HH

Fall Guy

"Fall guy" referred to the fact that the three women had made him pay the bill. It would be the last of the countless notes that Houdini lovingly wrote to Bess.

The Montreal engagement ended on Saturday, October 23, and the show was due to move on to Detroit, opening at the Garrick Theater the following Monday. They were due to be there for two weeks, but on the train to Detroit, Houdini was still in considerable pain.

Extremely worried, Bess arranged to have a telegram message sent asking for a doctor to examine the magician when he arrived at the hotel. But the train was running late, and it was not possible for their party to check into their hotel before the evening performance.

ACUTE APPENDICITIS

The doctor was telephoned and rushed to the theater where he examined Houdini in his dressing room. He immediately concluded that the star was suffering from acute appendicitis. He told Houdini that an ambulance should be called to get him to hospital at once. Unfortunately, however, Bess was out of earshot when he said this and Houdini chose not to tell her. Houdini told the manager of the theater that he was going to do the show if it was the last one he ever did.

With his ankle injury, the stomach pains and a temperature of 104 degrees, it is a miracle that he managed to perform, and several times that evening he almost collapsed. Understandably, it was a poor performance and he rushed it, just trying to get to the end.

There were two intervals and each time they tried to cool him down with packs of ice in his dressing room. Just before the third act, however, he told Jim Collins that he could do no more and that he should bring down the curtain. Back in his dressing room, he still refused to go to hospital.

They went to their hotel where Bess insisted angrily on calling the hotel doctor. He, in turn, called a surgeon who announced that the magician must be rushed to the nearest hospital at once. Houdini's response was to telephone his own doctor, Dr. William

Stone, in New York. After Stone discussed the case with the doctors present, Houdini was at last persuaded that he should go to hospital.

GOING DOWNHILL FAST

That afternoon, at Grace Hospital in Detroit, Houdini's gangrenous appendix was removed. The surgeon theorized afterward that the appendix had probably ruptured during the journey south and that as he had performed that evening he had begun to suffer from peritonitis.

At last the seriousness of the situation was beginning to hit home, and on Tuesday, October 26, a specialist in post-operative technique from Montreal was engaged. Dr. George Lefevre administered a serum to counter the poisons in Houdini's body and was pleased to see his temperature fall to 99.4 degrees. Jim Collins telegrammed New York with the latest news:

HAS IMPROVED WONDERFULLY DOCTORS PLEASED WITH RESULTS BUT STILL VERY GRAVE BETTER SIGNS DAILY SATURDAY DECIDES THE TURN WILL KEEP YOU INFORMED HOPE BAGGAGE AND ANIMALS STORED OKAY HUNDREDS OF WIRES DAILY FLOWERS AND LETTERS COLLINS

But Houdini's condition quickly deteriorated and his family—apart from the still unforgiven Leopold—was summoned to Detroit. When Dash arrived he was told by Dr. Charles Kennedy that it was unlikely that his brother would live more than another twenty-four hours but the doctor had underestimated Houdini's strength.

Monday, Tuesday, Wednesday, and Thursday passed with him still hanging on. The doctor told Dash that Houdini's bowels had become paralyzed and they would have to operate again. Following that procedure, they were initially optimistic. A bulletin was issued by his doctors:

Mr. Houdini has reacted to the second operation much better than we expected he

would. His condition is very grave, but hope for his entire recovery has not been entirely abandoned. His temperature is 103, pulse 130, and respiration 40.

SOLD RIGHT OUT

Houdini was conscious throughout this time and aware of what was going on. He never at any time thought he was in any danger, talking of a six or seven week lay-off to recuperate before resuming his tour. He even dictated a letter to a friend on Saturday, October 30:

Box offices here are S.R.O. [sold right out] which certainly makes me smug and quite happy. Except that I feel none too well at the moment, but suppose that I will get over this waviness in no time.

But his condition was very serious and on Saturday afternoon Dr. Kennedy told Dash that he had only a matter of a few hours to live. The following morning, at 11 a.m., as his brothers stood around the magician's bed, Houdini reached over and grasped Dash's hand and said:

Dash, I'm getting tired and I can't fight any more.

A sobbing Bess and his sister Gladys were brought into the room. Harry Houdini died in his wife's arms at 1:26 p.m. on the afternoon of Sunday, October 31, 1926, at the age of 52.

Harry Houdini shortly before his death in 1926.

PART SIX

DEAD MEN TELL NO TALES

I always have on my mind
the thought that next year
I must do something greater,
something more wonderful.

Harry Houdini

CHAPTER 22

BREATH IS GONE FOR GOOD

Houdini's death certificate stated his cause of death to be diffuse peritonitis (streptococcic) precipitated by a "ruptured appendicitis." It was believed that this had been caused by the blow to the stomach by the McGill University student, J. Gordon Whitehead.

His props were all put into crates and sent back to New York by Jim Collins. But he had been informed by the shipping company, the Detroit Transfer Co., that one crate had accidentally been left behind. When it was opened, it was discovered that the crate held the bronze casket that Houdini used in his act during his exposé of Rahman Bey.

Coincidentally, Houdini had stipulated in his will that, in the event of his death, he wished to be buried in that casket. His lawyer telephoned to pass on this news and the magician's body was accordingly placed in the casket in which he had lain many times previously during his performances. The casket containing Houdini's body was taken by train to New York.

WELCOME TO THE OTHER SIDE

Meanwhile, the fake medium, Margery, issued a statement about his death, saying:

> We are sorry to hear of the passing of Houdini. He was a virile personality of great determination and undoubted physical courage. We have entertained him and our personal relations with him in this house have always been pleasant. At other times and places we have had our differences.

She was pursued by reporters who tried to elicit confirmation from her that she had placed a curse upon the magician, a curse that had said that he would be dead within a year.

There were stories, however, that her guide "Walter" had communicated to Margery many times in the previous months that he would soon be welcoming Houdini to the other side. It was even suggested by Margery's husband that "Walter" had somehow influenced the young McGill student to punch Houdini.

The press also turned to Sir Arthur Conan Doyle for comment about the demise of his erstwhile friend. He issued a tactful, conciliatory statement, given that he and Houdini had been at loggerheads for so long:

> His death is a great shock and a deep mystery to me. He was a teetotaller, did not smoke, and was one of the cleanest living men I have ever known. I greatly admired him, and cannot understand how the end came for one so youthful. We were great friends.

HOUDINI'S FUNERAL

On November 2, 1926, Houdini's casket arrived at Grand Central Station, New York. It was welcomed by hundreds of people who had somberly gathered there. People wept and men removed their hats as the casket was carried through the station.

The funeral took place two days later at the Elks Club in New York with 2,500 present inside, while thousands gathered outside. The Houdini family were out in force, even Leopold. Bess almost collapsed when they screwed down the coffin lid for the last time.

Rabbi Bernard Drachman described him as possessing "a wondrous power which he never understood and which he never revealed to anyone in life." Another rabbi described him as: "... exceptional, a unique personality, and besides that, he was one of the noblest and sweetest of men."

Following the service, a column of twenty-five cars drove through Manhattan and over the Queensboro Bridge to the Machpelah Cemetery in Queens, home to the Weiss/Houdini family burial plot.

The pallbearers were Houdini's assistants. Jim Collins, Jim Vickery, Frank Williamson, John Arden, Beppo Vitorelli, and Elliott Sandford lowered the coffin into the grave beside his mother. The letters she had written to him were, as he had requested, in a black bag under his head.

THE MYSTERY OF HOUDINI'S DEATH

It was assumed that J. Gordon Whitehead's blows to the stomach were the cause of Houdini's death. The doctors attending Houdini signed off his death as having been caused by "traumatic appendicitis." Such a condition does not exist, however, and it has been suggested that it is medically impossible for such a thing to happen.

One investigator has claimed that after researching medical literature, and discussing the case with doctors, he could find not a single instance of someone suffering from acute appendicitis as a direct result of physical injury. Certainly, other damage can be done, such as the rupturing of the large intestine, but never had anyone come across such a case as a ruptured appendix from a blow. Dr. Charles Kennedy, who attended the dying Houdini, said:

> It is the only case of traumatic appendicitis I have ever seen in my lifetime, but the logic of the thing seemed to indicate that Mr. Houdini died of appendicitis, the direct result of the injury.

ALREADY SUFFERING

It seems more likely that Houdini was already suffering before the blows from Whitehead. The insurance company dealing with his death investigated and found that Abby Wright, manager of the theater in Montreal where Houdini was performing, claimed that the magician was already unwell when he arrived at the theater.

REACTION TO HOUDINI'S DEATH

The death of such a popular figure led to extensive coverage in the press.

> Starting out as a magician, he developed so much that by the end of his career he had fairly earned the title of scientist.

The New York World

> ... a man of wide reading, a collector both of books and of art.

The New York Times

> His death removes a great artist and a useful scientist, and he was both without impairment of the qualities of heart and soul that endeared him to his fellows of the stage and his unnumbered admirers in front of the footlights.

The New York Sun

> Houdini was the greatest showman of our time by far ... he had that something that no one can define that is generally just passed off under the heading of showmanship. But it was in reality, Sense, Shrewdness, Judgment, unmatched ability, Intuition, Personality, and an uncanny knowledge of people.

Will Rogers, actor, humorist and social commentator

> Harry Houdini was a picturesque figure. He was much maligned and generally misunderstood ... His deeds of charity were manifold ... He fought for a principle; this principle was the kernel of magic, its respectability ... He stood as the greatest figure of usefulness to, and representative of, the conjurer in his generation. He was an institution, and we, the exponents of modern magic, owe his memory a debt that we can never repay. His name alone lent dignity to magic.

Charles Carter, "Carter The Great," The Billboard

FULTON OURSLER

Charles Fulton Oursler (1893 – 1952) was an American journalist, playwright and writer, born in Baltimore, Maryland, the son of a city transit worker. While still a teenager, he wrote for the *Baltimore American* before moving to New York City where he became editor of the trade magazine *The Music Trades*.

His short stories began to appear in magazines such as *Detective Story Magazine*, *Mystery Magazine*, *The Black Cat*, and *The Thrill Book*. His stories, written under the pen name Anthony Abbot, often involved magicians and magic. He supported Houdini in the 1920s in his campaign against phony spiritualists, using the pseudonym Samri Frikell, and in 1930 authored the book *Spirit Mediums Exposed*.

During the twenty years from 1921 to 1941, Oursler was Supervising Editor of a number of publications owned by Bernarr Macfadden (1868 – 1955), a man who promulgated the culture of health and fitness through his magazines, but also owned a wide range of other publications and newspapers. Oursler next became a senior editor for *Reader's Digest*.

Oursler wrote a number of novels as himself, and under the name Anthony Abbot, and his play, *The Spider*, was filmed twice, in 1931 and 1945. He died in 1952, at the age of 59.

The nurse Sophie Rosenblatt, who had gone with him to McGill University, had said that she had to get him out of there as quickly as possible. Furthermore, Jack Price had said that each time Whitehead had landed a blow, Houdini had winced as if he had already been in pain.

Professor Tait at the university remarked that he thought the way Houdini sat down at the end of his lecture showed him to be in some discomfort. Of course, it could simply have been the pain in his injured ankle but it may have been another pain.

A letter written by a woman named Gertrude Hills, was published in *The New York Sun* some time later, telling that Houdini had agreed to perform his straitjacket escape in a show for charity during the summer of 1926. As he did so, she said, he injured himself and apparently suffered from a pain in his side for some days after.

Not long afterward, Houdini had an attack of food poisoning that seemed to linger in his body. By the time he set out on his tour, the pain and the food poisoning were still affecting him.

SPIRITUALISTS SAW IT COMING

While in hospital, Houdini had said, "If I die, don't be surprised if phony spiritualists declare a national holiday." And, indeed, the spiritualist world was reacting to his demise. Many reported that they had been receiving predictions of the death of their nemesis for months.

Robert Gysel (1880 – 1938), one of Houdini's investigators into fraudulent mediums, announced that at 10:58 on the night of October 24, 1926, a framed photograph of Houdini that he had hung on his wall inexplicably crashed to the floor, the glass smashing. Margery's "Walter" had already indicated that Houdini's time on earth was limited, and the Crandons had predicted that Houdini would die on Christmas Day 1925.

Sir Arthur Conan Doyle, too, had been forewarned, apparently, by his spirit guide "Pheneas" who had passed on the message: "Houdini is doomed, doomed!" Another medium, a Mrs. Wood, wrote to the novelist Fulton Oursler, who had become a confederate of Houdini's in exposing fraudulent mediums:

> *Three years ago the spirit of Dr. Hyslop said, "The waters are black for Houdini," and he foretold that disaster would befall him while performing before an audience in a theater. Dr. Hyslop now says that the injury is more serious than has been reported, and that Houdini's days as a magician are over.*

Houdini's casket being carried to the hearse, November 4, 1926.

CHAPTER 23

After the Circus Left Town

For Houdini's family and members of his close circle, his death was devastating. For a number of them the entire purpose of their lives had gone, as well as their means of earning a livelihood. Bess was hit very hard. She had been with Harry Houdini since the age of 18, experiencing the ups and downs of his life, the poverty, the riches, the anonymity, and the global fame.

Life had been exciting and she had been a vital part of it. Houdini never denied this fact. But life with an ego the size of her husband's had never been a cakewalk, as is attested to by Bess's increasing reliance on alcohol. She could also be difficult to live with and Houdini lived in dread of her tantrums. But his world had been hers. So what was she to do now?

DEATH AND TAXES

Given the vast amount of money Houdini had earned, one would imagine that there would be no problem. But as he had earned it, so had he spent it. His venture into the movie business had eaten up much of his fortune. His collection of books and magic paraphernalia had been very expensive and, indeed, boxes of books kept arriving for months after his death.

Houdini had wanted to set up a trust, according to the terms of his last will and testament, but there were insufficient funds to do this. Bess, therefore, had to provide money for it as well as pay administration costs and the inheritance taxes that were due.

His library which would have brought in considerable sums if sold, was donated to the Library of Congress.

But there was money from insurance policies that Houdini had taken out, one of them a double-indemnity policy to be paid out in the event of Houdini dying through an accident.

One insurance company carried out a thorough investigation of the circumstances of his death. Houdini's lawyers obtained sworn affidavits from the people and performers who were on tour with him stating that his health had been fine prior to the dressing room incident with Whitehead. The insurance company was satisfied, and made the payment.

After that, all the other insurers also paid out. These payments amounted to around half a million dollars. Taxes had to be paid, but there was plenty left for Mrs. Houdini to live well on.

FROM BEYOND THE GRAVE

She sold the house on 113th Street and moved to a smaller house on Payson Avenue, Inwood, Manhattan. She began to drink heavily, and became miserable, although she helped in the production of Houdini's biography, published in 1928. She also tried to contact her husband in the world beyond the grave.

Every Sunday she would settle down, seated opposite a photograph of him and waited for a signal. At the same time, she offered a reward of $10,000 to any medium who could provide her with a code that Houdini had given her before his death, and known only to him and her. She withdrew the incentive at the end of 1928, by which time only one medium had stepped up.

The Reverend Arthur Ford (1896 – 1971) of Manhattan's First Spiritualist Church, claimed to have been receiving messages from both Houdini's mother, and from the magician himself for the past year. He said in a letter to Bess that Houdini's mother had passed to him the word "Forgive," as the code that she had agreed with her son. Bess replied that this was indeed the code, saying "... this is the first message which I have received that has an appearance of truth."

ROSABELLE BELIEVE

Ford went on tour in Europe and on his return presented Bess with a ten-word code from Houdini. It was:

Rosabelle—answer—tell—pray—answer—look—tell—answer—answer—tell.

During a séance in which Ford's spirit guide "Fletcher" related the code, Bess confirmed it to be correct. Using the secret code that Houdini and Bess had used in their act, the nine words, apart from Rosabelle, spelled out "believe." The message, therefore, was "Rosabelle, believe."

The sensational news that Houdini appeared to have made contact with his wife made headlines in the world's newspapers the following day. Bess was interviewed and insisted that Harry had indeed communicated the code to her. She was going to retrieve it from the safety deposit box in which it was kept the next day.

HOUDINI HOAX

The following day, however, Rea Jaure, a journalist who had been involved, wrote a story with the headline "HOUDINI HOAX EXPOSED." She claimed that Ford and Bess had dreamed up the whole thing together, with a view to going on a money-spinning tour. She went on to prove it.

If Bess had not given Ford the code—and Bess vehemently denied doing this—there were other ways that Ford might have obtained it. The code used in performances

by Houdini and Bess had been made public in the biography of the magician published the previous year.

As for the message, when Houdini had whispered it to Bess on his deathbed, she had not been alone. The nurse Sophie Rosenblatt had been present and she may have overheard it and passed it on.

WAITING FOR HARRY

Bess retreated back to Inwood. She hung around the peripheries of the world of mediums, seeking contact with Harry and later explained that she was not well.

There was a period when I was ill—really mentally ill as well as physically. I wanted so intensely to hear from Harry that spiritualists were able to prey on my mind and make me believe they really had heard from him.

Finally, having received some terrible business advice from a medium, Bess became disillusioned.

Just at this moment along came a man named Charles David Myers, a.k.a Edward Saint (1890 – 1942), who had earned an income both as a living statue and a magician. Her friends introduced the couple and he began to run her affairs.

Soon, a relationship developed, and they moved into a bungalow in Hollywood. Her life still revolved around Houdini, and Bess and Edward Saint worked hard to keep his memory alive.

THE FINAL HOUDINI SÉANCE

What became known as the "Final Houdini Séance" took place on October 31, 1936, ten years after that fateful day in Grace Hospital. Incredibly there was still huge interest in Houdini, and the event was broadcast live by radio around the world. The commentator described the scene:

Over 300 invited guests formed the outer circle, while 13 scientists, occultologists,

ARTHUR FORD

Arthur Ford (1896 – 1971) was born in Florida and was later ordained as a Disciples of Christ minister, serving at a church in Kentucky. During the First World War, he realized he had psychic powers, claiming to hear the names of soldiers who would appear on the casualty list a few days later.

Following the end of the war, he became a traveling spiritualist trance medium with a spirit guide named "Fletcher." He finally settled in New York City where he established a spiritualist church. In 1927, Sir Arthur Conan Doyle attended a lecture given by Ford in Britain and was deeply impressed, saying: "One of the most amazing things I have seen in 41 years of psychic experience ..." However, when Ford was tested by the American Society for Psychical Research, he failed.

Ford's involvement in the Houdini séances caused a huge scandal, and after his death evidence was found to prove that these events were faked. A collection of obituaries, newspaper clippings, and other material, was found disguised as poetry books, that had been used by Ford in researching his clients' backgrounds. This was the material he presented as if it had come to him through "Fletcher."

Evidence was also found of a séance with Bishop James Pike having been faked in 1967. In this séance, Ford had claimed to have contacted Pike's dead son. A biography of Arthur Ford concluded that he cheated, "deliberately as well as unconsciously." He died in 1971, at the age of 75.

newspapermen, world famous magicians, spiritual leaders, boyhood friends of Houdini, joined Madame Houdini in the Inner Circle. Bathed in the weird glow of ruby light, trained observers and spirit mediums joined under controlled conditions to evoke the shade of the late mystifier ... Every facility has been provided tonight, that might aid in opening a pathway to the spirit world. Here in the Inner Circle, reposes a "Medium's Trumpet," a pair of slates with chalk, a writing tablet and pencil, a small bell, and in the center reposes a huge pair of silver handcuffs on a silk cushion. Facing the Inner Circle stands the famous "Houdini Shrine"[a candle burning beside a photograph of her husband], with its doors ajar.

ZERO HOUR HAS PASSED

Edward Saint—described as "Dr." Saint, possibly due to his immaculately groomed appearance, complete with goatee and waxed moustache—was in control of proceedings. They played Elgar's *Pomp and Circumstance*, the music that Houdini used when he made his entrances in his latter years and Saint began to talk:

> Houdini! Are you here? Are you here, Houdini? Please manifest yourself in any way possible ... We have waited, Houdini, oh, so long! Never have you been able to present the evidence you promised. And now—this, the night of nights. The world is listening, Harry ... Levitate the table! Move it! Lift the table! Move it or rap it! Spell out a code, Harry! Please! Ring the bell! Let its tinkle be heard around the world!

There was silence. Finally, Saint turned to Bess and said: "Mrs. Houdini, the zero hour has passed. The ten years are up. Have you reached a decision?" Bess replied solemnly:

> Yes, Houdini did not come through. My last hope is gone. I do not believe that Houdini can come back to me, or to anyone ... The Houdini Shrine has burned for ten years. I now, reverently, turn out the light. It is finished. Good night, Harry!

Bess Houdini with Edward Saint (to her left holding handcuffs), during the final séance, in an effort to contact the spirit of Houdini, 1936.

CHAPTER 24

HOUDINI GOES OFF THE PAGE

BOOKS WRITTEN BY HOUDINI

THE RIGHT WAY TO DO WRONG (1906)

Houdini reveals the tricks of the many different types of criminals.

THE UNMASKING OF ROBERT-HOUDIN (1908)

Houdini's cruel exposure of his former idol as "a mere pretender, a man who waxed great on the brainwork of others, a mechanician who had boldly filched the inventions of the master craftsmen among his predecessors."

HANDCUFF SECRETS (1910)

The secrets of handcuff escapes revealed by the Handcuff King.

MIRACLE MONGERS AND THEIR METHODS (1920)

"A complete exposé of the modus operandi of fire eaters, heat resisters, poison eaters, venomous reptile defiers, sword swallowers, human ostriches, strong men etc."

MAGICAL ROPE TIES AND ESCAPES (1921)

The secrets of magical ways of tying ropes and making escapes from them by the great escaper.

HOUDINI'S PAPER MAGIC (1922)

"The whole art of performing with paper, including paper tearing, paper folding, and paper puzzles."

A MAGICIAN AMONG THE SPIRITS (1924)

A social history of spiritualism, including discussion of the mediums, and entertainers involved in it.

HOUDINI EXPOSES THE TRICKS USED BY THE BOSTON MEDIUM "MARGERY" (1925)

Houdini does not hold back in his exposure of the tricks pulled by "Margery" to win the *Scientific American* prize money.

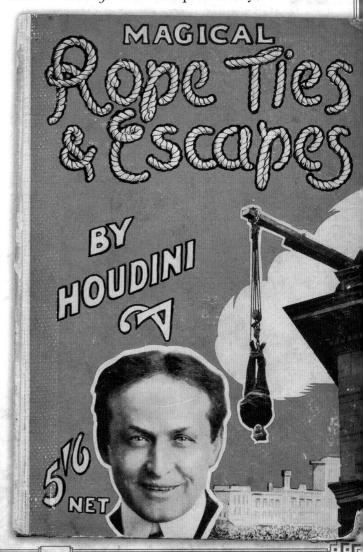

Magical Rope Ties and Escapes book cover, 1921.

BIOGRAPHIES OF HOUDINI

There are countless biographies and books about Harry Houdini. Here is a small selection of the best.

THE LIFE AND MANY DEATHS OF HARRY HOUDINI

Some critics say that this is one of the best books about Houdini. Published in 1993, it is a highly readable and painstakingly researched biography by Ruth Brandon. It is, however, disliked by many Houdini buffs because of the author's theory that Harry was impotent, and that was the reason that he and Bess had no children. Brandon has herself admitted that the theory was no more than "just a guess." In fact, it is known that the couple were childless due to Bess's inability to have children.

HOUDINI!!!: THE CAREER OF EHRICH WEISS

In 1997, Pulitzer Prize-winning author, Kenneth Silverman drew on never before used notebooks, diaries, and unpublished notes and letters to create a compelling and comprehensive biography of the great escape artist. Not only are Houdini's stunts and escapes covered in detail, Silverman also looks deeply into his private life and his friendships with some of the great names of his time.

ESCAPE!: THE STORY OF THE GREAT HOUDINI

Former professional magician Sid Fleishman gave us a fresh and witty biography of the great escape artist in 2006, providing fascinating insider information and investigating Houdini's secrets. Rare photos enrich an accessible, compelling read.

THE SECRET LIFE OF HOUDINI: THE MAKING OF AMERICA'S FIRST SUPERHERO

This major biography of Houdini by William Kalush and Larry Sloman in 2007, was promoted with the information that Houdini might have been a spy. Houdini is said to have sent reports from Germany to Scotland Yard, but that in itself is not proof that he was a spy. This comprehensive biography introduces lots of fascinating new insights into the great man.

HOUDINI AND CONAN DOYLE

Christopher Sandford's account in 2012 of the fractious relationship between Houdini and Conan Doyle shows the magician to be rather scholarly and rational, as well as a man of action. Sandford gained access to some key Houdini diaries and some unpublished writings of Houdini's lawyer, Bernard Ernst, that provide another viewpoint other than that of the two protagonists.

HOUDINI IN FICTION

RAGTIME

Houdini pops up in numerous works of fiction. Perhaps the most famous of these cameo appearances is in the bestselling 1975 novel *Ragtime* by E.L. Doctorow. A number of well-known figures of the time appear in this story, including Henry Ford, Sigmund Freud, and J.P. Morgan. A work of historical fiction, set mainly in New York City between 1902 and 1912, the novel mixes fictional and historical figures. Houdini appears after crashing his car into a telephone pole outside the house of an affluent American family. He reflects on success and mortality, and we see how he was never really accepted by the rich and famous. He grieves for his mother and develops an obsession with communicating with her through spiritualism.

CARTER BEATS THE DEVIL

The 2002 historical thriller *Carter Beats the Devil* by Glen David Gold is another novel in which fictional characters interact with historical figures. The novel revolves around the mysterious death of US President Warren G. Harding and the Carter of the title is the real American magician, Charles Joseph Carter, a.k.a. "Carter The Great." Houdini plays a small but important role in the story as the mentor and inspiration for the hero, and it is he who bestows the sobriquet "Carter The Great" on him.

HARRY HOUDINI MYSTERIES

There are numerous books in which Harry Houdini is a detective, using his great powers to solve mysteries and murders. Daniel Stashower's series, *Harry Houdini Mysteries,* places the young Harry in the midst of nefarious goings-on. Examples include *The Dime Museum Murders, The Houdini Specter,* and *The Floating Lady Murder.*

THE MAN FROM BEYOND

Gabriel Brownstein, author of *The Curious Case of Benjamin Button, Apt. 3W*, threads together historical events and fictionalized characters in his 2012 novel *The Man From Beyond* which takes as its backdrop the 1922 public feud between Sir Arthur Conan Doyle and Harry Houdini. The phony medium "Margery" makes an appearance. When Houdini is feared dead after a stunt to promote his new film, *The Man From Beyond*, goes horribly wrong, Conan Doyle and the book's young reporter heroine Molly Goodman turn detective.

HOUDINI AND THE SÉANCE MURDERS

In *Houdini and the Séance Murders*, author Christopher Farran also turns Sir Arthur Conan Doyle into a detective, but this time his partner is none other than Harry Houdini, the fractious relationship between the two men forgotten as they try to solve a murder committed at a séance. They also get together to investigate the disappearance of a respected judge in a spooky, crumbling mansion in Farran's *Sir Arthur Conan Doyle & Harry Houdini in The Adventure of the Spook House.*

WHO DONE HOUDINI?

Sir Arthur Conan Doyle becomes a suspect when Houdini is murdered in *Who Done Houdini?* by Raymond John. Bizarrely, both Sherlock Holmes and Arthur Conan Doyle are fictional characters in this mystery novel.

THE CONFABULIST

Steven Galloway's *The Confabulist* tells the story of down-and-out Martin Strauss whose life converges with that of Harry Houdini in spectacular and devastating style. Strauss, in this fictional version of real events, is the man who delivers the punch that kills Harry Houdini. But is Houdini really dead?

THE SÉANCE

Iain Lawrence's *The Séance* features Scooter King who performs the illusions that make his mother's séances believable. An admirer of Harry Houdini, he discovers a dead body in the magician's Burmese Torture Tank and sets out to uncover the killer amid the dark world of magic, mediums, and séances.

ESCAPE ARTIST: AN EDNA FERBER MYSTERY

Edna Ferber famously interviewed Harry Houdini in 1904 in Appleton after bumping into him in a drugstore. In Edward Ifkovic's *Escape Artist: An Edna Ferber Mystery*, the nineteen-year-old reporter joins forces with the magician to solve the baffling murder of a beautiful young girl who has mysteriously disappeared from a locked room at the local high school.

EHRICH WEISS CHRONICLES

The *Ehrich Weiss Chronicles* by Marty Chan present the young Houdini in a steampunk New York after he has followed his brother Dash through a strange portal. He becomes Demon Hunter, tracking down dangerous otherworldly visitors to the city. *Demon Gate* and *Infinity Coil* are the first two titles in the series.

CHILDREN'S BOOKS

THE YOUNG HOUDINI

Houdini provides thrills and spills for many authors of children's books. A recent series is *The Young Houdini* written by Simon Nicholson. In *The Magician's Fire, The*

Demon Curse, and *The Silent Assassin*, the young Harry enjoys adventures and mystery with his friends, Arthur and Billie.

HOUDINI AND NATE MYSTERIES

Another series, the *Houdini and Nate Mysteries*, sees a young man named Nate Fuller work with his mentor, Harry Houdini, to fight assassins, deal with spooky late-night gatherings, and solve murders in *Frame-up On the Bowery, Shots at Sea*, and *Danger in the Dark*.

AUDACITY JONES STEALS THE SHOW

Kirby Larson's character, Audacity Jones, attends Miss Maisie's School for Wayward Girls and in *Audacity Jones Steals the Show* our heroine sets off for adventure in the big city with her best friend Bimmy. In New York they meet Houdini who is just about to stage his biggest trick yet—making an elephant disappear. But someone is trying to sabotage the trick and Audacity and Bimmy try to find out who it is in this gripping story.

PIPER HOUDINI: APPRENTICE OF CONEY ISLAND

Harry's fictional niece is the protagonist in *Piper Houdini: Apprentice of Coney Island*. Taken to live with her famous uncle, Piper has to deal with a malevolent force that is threatening New York and on the way encounters real-life historical figures such as Sir Arthur Conan Doyle and Aleister Crowley.

HURRY UP, HOUDINI!

In Mary Pope Osborne's chapter book *Hurry Up, Houdini!* Abracadabra Jack and Annie are on a mission for Merlin the Magician. They use their Magic Tree House to travel back in time to learn the secret of greatness from the greatest escape artist that ever lived—Harry Houdini. Thrills and spills ensue.

HOUDINI IN COMICS

Houdini has made appearances in a number of comics. He stars in Image Comics' *Daring Escapes*, a four-issue limited edition series in which he can travel between time and dimensions. In 2014 and 2015, he appeared in a five-issue series of stories produced by Dynamite Entertainment, entitled *Sherlock Holmes vs Harry Houdini*. In these comics, as the creators say: "Famed detective Sherlock Holmes and brash showman Harry Houdini must combine forces to defeat a mysterious mystic dedicated to destroying Houdini's career and killing anyone who gets in his way."

Houdini has also pops up in numerous other comics including *2000 AD, Herald: Lovecraft and Tesla, Rough Riders* and *Spawn*.

Sherlock Holmes vs Harry Houdini Issue #1 (2014).

CHAPTER 25

Houdini on Stage and Screen

HOUDINI ON STAGE

A planned Houdini musical starring Hugh Jackman failed to materialize, but in recent years there have been several successful stage plays that are inspired by Houdini.

HOUDINI (2013)

BAFTA-winning actor, writer, producer, and director, Stuart Brennan, wrote a play entitled *Houdini* about Harry Houdini—played by Jamie Nichols—and his brother Theo—played by Brennan himself. The play follows Harry and Theo's struggles to find fame and fortune as "The Brothers Houdini," opening with the Coney Island meeting and marriage of Harry and Bess, played by Evanna Lynch. The play follows the relationship of the two brothers, one on the road to global fame, the other constantly in his shadow and features several illusions including The Water Torture Cell, The Bullet Catch (performed by Theo) and Metamorphosis.

A REGULAR LITTLE HOUDINI (2013)

Written by Daniel Llewelyn-Williams, and set in Edwardian times in Newport, South Wales, the award-winning one-man play, *A Regular Little Houdini*, is inspired by the great magician. A dockworker's son who idolizes Harry Houdini, decides to commit himself to a life of magic. He experiences some of the most terrifying events of British industrial history as he practices his escapes on industrial wastelands. His life coincides with the great escape artist, changing not just him but also the community in which he lives.

DEATH AND HARRY HOUDINI (2001)

In *Death and Harry Houdini*, written by Nathan Allen, a ringmaster describes the major events of the escape artist's life, using stunning magic, poignant storytelling and original music. It is all there, the death of Harry's father, the first shows, the meeting with Bess, the struggles on the vaudeville circuit, through to his ultimate success. But all the time Harry can feel Death—wearing a cloak and a gas mask—breathing down his neck and he won't be happy until he has conquered it once and for all.

HOUDINI ON THE BIG SCREEN

We have seen that Harry Houdini made his own movies, first appearing as himself in the 1909 film, *Merveilleux Exploits du Célèbre Houdini à Paris*. His own, later films were, *The Master Mystery* (1918), playing Quentin Locke; *The Grim Game* (1919), playing Harvey Hanford; *Terror Island* (1920), playing Harry Harper; *The Man From Beyond* (1922), playing Howard Hillary; and *Haldane of the Secret Service*, (1922) playing Heath Haldane.

There were a number of later films in which Harry's life was told or in which he makes a fictional appearance. One even includes a real life appearance by Bess Houdini.

RELIGIOUS RACKETEERS (1938)

A wealthy young woman feels guilty because she has not been with her mother when she passed away. She is so desperate that she tries to contact her in the afterlife, becoming involved with a phony medium who is after her money. A reporter, enamored of the young woman, sets out to expose the medium for the fraud that she is. The film famously features a cameo appearance by Bess Houdini at 7 minutes and 30 seconds and then after 67 minutes and 18 seconds.

HOUDINI (1953)

After many years of failed attempts to put Houdini's life on-screen, it finally happened in 1953 with possibly the most successful movie about Houdini. Tony Curtis and Janet Leigh star in this highly fictionalized account of Harry Houdini's life. Directed by George Marshall, it was based on the 1928 book *Houdini: His Life Story* by Harold Kellock. The film re-creates many of Houdini's most famous escapes, including the straitjacket escape—both onstage and suspended from a building—an escape from a safe, a jail escape, and an escape from a metal box underwater in which he becomes trapped in the ice of the frozen river. The film was well-received by critics but the magic community was dismayed by its many fictions, anachronisms and inaccuracies. One Houdini biographer said: "Generally speaking, if any phase of Houdini's life is shown on the screen you can be sure it didn't happen that way."

RAGTIME (1981)

Houdini was going to be played by John Belushi in this Milos Forman-directed adaptation of E.L. Doctorow's bestseller. In the end the role was taken by Jeffrey DuMunn and the part was significantly reduced from the great novel.

FAIRY TALE: A TRUE STORY (1997)

Harvey Keitel plays Houdini in something of a secondary role in this family film about the young girls who created the Cottingley fairies, the hoax that was believed by many including Sir Arthur Conan Doyle—played here by Peter O'Toole—who wrote an entire

book about them—*The Coming of the Fairies*. The film shows Houdini to be involved in the investigation of the fairies' manifestation which is untrue as he had no involvement whatsoever.

DEATH-DEFYING ACTS (2008)

Catherine Zeta-Jones stars as Mary McGarvie and Guy Pearce as Houdini in this story of the magician's obsessive search, during a tour of Scotland in 1926, for a medium who truly can communicate with the dead. McGarvie is a Scottish music hall clairvoyant who, with her daughter (Saoirse Ronan), inveigles her way into Houdini's circle and the two fall in love. Pearce's version of Houdini is highly unlikable; he shouts at hotel staff and his manager (Timothy Spall) in equal measure.

The production, however, is exquisite, and Houdini's stunts and illusions look terrific, evoking the atmosphere of the period. The

Poster for *Death-Defying Acts* starring Catherine Zeta-Jones and Guy Pearce.

magician's tragic death occurs with a fatal punch but it is delivered in public, in the street and he drops down dead immediately. The *Los Angeles Times* said of it: "*Death Defying Acts* is far more diverting and well-crafted than its promotion-free release campaign might suggest. What the film loses in momentum as the romance takes over, it gains in sex appeal as its two attractive actors make their own kind of magic."

HOUDINI ON TELEVISION

THE GREAT HOUDINIS (ALSO KNOWN AS THE GREAT HOUDINI) (1976)

Starring *Starsky & Hutch's* Paul Michael Glaser as Houdini, *The Great Houdinis* was a TV movie. It takes many liberties with the truth but features many real incidents from the magician's life, including Houdini purchasing Queen Victoria's dress for his mother, the Atlantic City séance with Sir Arthur Conan Doyle and his wife and the encounters with Margery the medium. The fatal dressing room punch is also dramatized. In the film, Bess, played by Sally Struthers, is shown to have a liking for alcohol.

VOYAGERS (1982)

Michael Durrell played the role of Harry Houdini in an episode—*Agents of Saturn*—of the short-lived time travel television series *Voyagers*. It was broadcast on the 56th anniversary of the magician's death.

YOUNG HARRY HOUDINI (1987)

Disney produced this entertaining TV movie, telling the story of the "lost years" of Ehrich Weiss, the years after he ran away from home in Appleton. In this colorful story, the young Ehrich finds a mentor in a traveling show—Dr. Tybalt Grimaldi, played by José Ferrer. Love interest is provided by the lovely Calpernia, played by Kerri Green, and Ehrich is inducted into mystic practices by the Native American medicine man, played by J. Reuben Silverbird. We see the older

Houdini perform the Water Torture Cell, and the younger man performing one of his first packing case escapes.

THE REAL GHOSTBUSTERS (1987)

Houdini's spirit harasses a magician, the "Great Calamari" in an old Broadway magic theater in "The Cabinet of Calamari," an episode of the animated series, *The Real Ghostbusters*. When the Ghostbusters are brought in to help, it transpires that Calamari has stolen Houdini's secret notebook.

JEM AND THE HOLOGRAMS (1988)

In Season 3, episode 8 of this animated series, Jem and a magician named Astral become involved with a rival band who are taking advantage of a rich widow by telling her that the ghost of Houdini has returned. There is an escape from a straitjacket and the episode finishes with the Water Torture Cell.

HOUDINI (1998)

This "TNT Original" cable movie stars Jonathon Schaech as Houdini, Stacy Edwards as Bess, and Mark Ruffalo as Theo. It is the first of the Houdini movies to actually deal with the magician's egotism and he is far less likable or endearing than in other depictions. The movie gives an accurate picture of how Houdini and Bess met and shows the young Ehrich Weiss making his deathbed promise to his father to look after his mother. Escapes are well-presented, the film looks good and the performances are excellent. It was nominated for three Emmys and won one.

THE SIMPSONS (2011)

In the episode "The Great Simpsina," Lisa learns magic from The Great Raymondo who, she finds out, had been given the Milk-Can Escape by Harry Houdini himself. Having learned how to perform the escape, she passes it to illusionist Cregg Demon by mistake. He performs it, claiming to have been given its secret by Harry Houdini but he becomes trapped inside the milk-can and is in danger of drowning. When Lisa tries to save him, she is confronted by the magicians Ricky Jay,

David Copperfield, and Penn & Teller, who reveal that they had substituted Houdini's milk-can with a fake one as they want Demon to fail so that he will be eliminated from the competition he is in. Demon quits magic and Lisa performs a magic act with The Great Raymondo.

HOUDINI (2014)

The two-part miniseries, *Houdini*, made for the History Channel, stars Oscar-winner Adrien Brody as Harry Houdini. The first episode follows the life of the great magician from Appleton through his discovery of Robert-Houdin, his meeting with Bess, his adventures on the vaudeville circuit and his performances for royalty and celebrities. Houdini is recruited by MI5 to spy on the Kaiser in Berlin in the run-up to the First World War. The second shows Harry devising ever-greater illusions, trying to communicate with his dead mother, and then the phase of his life in which he exposed fake mediums. The fatal punch is delivered as it actually happened.

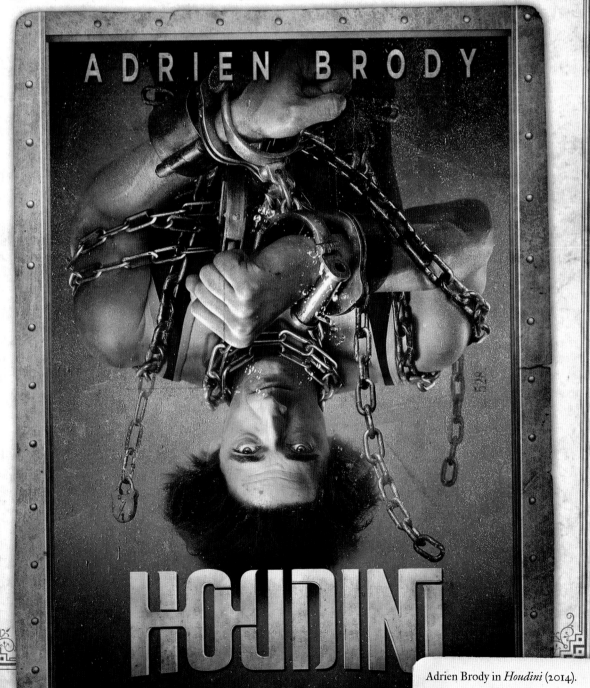

Adrien Brody in *Houdini* (2014).

Stephen Mangan (left) as Doyle and Michael Weston as Houdini in *Houdini & Doyle* (2016).

HOUDINI & DOYLE (2016)

In this 10-episode British-Canadian-American production, Harry Houdini, played by Michael Weston, and Sir Arthur Conan Doyle played by Stephen Mangan, turn investigators. Houdini is a rational skeptic and Doyle is a believer in the paranormal and each case they investigate features them arguing from their own specific points of view. The series was cancelled after just one season.

TIMELESS (2017)

Houdini made an appearance in the television series *Timeless,* in an episode entitled "The World's Columbian Exposition." Set during the 1893 Chicago World's Fair, Michael Drayer plays a fearless, resourceful and heroic Houdini. Lyova Beckwitt plays Dash.

⋄ HOUDINI DOCUMENTARIES

THE TRUTH ABOUT HOUDINI (1971)

Also known as *The Magic of Houdini,* this BBC documentary is well worth watching.

IN SEARCH OF HOUDINI'S SECRETS (1981)

In his popular series *In Search of ...,* *Star Trek* actor Leonard Nimoy investigated things such as Bigfoot, the Loch Ness Monster, and UFOs. In November 1981, he investigated Houdini. Interestingly, there was talk in the early 1990s of Nimoy and William Shatner—Captain Kirk in *Star* Trek—joining forces in a play in which Nimoy was to play Sherlock Holmes and Shatner was to portray Harry Houdini.

THE GREATEST: HOUDINI (1999)

The fourth episode of the series *The Greatest* featured Harry Houdini. It includes interviews with magicians Penn & Teller, Dorothy Young—onstage assistant to Houdini from 1925 – 26 —and husband and wife illusionists, The Pendragons. The film includes some Houdini footage and there are re-enactments of his illusions.

HOUDINI: UNLOCKING THE MYSTERY (2005)

Magician Lance Burton explores the life of Houdini through his most prized possessions including The Chinese Water Torture Cell, the Milk-Can, his straitjackets and handcuffs, and his lock-picks. A great-nephew of Houdini is interviewed as is the last surviving member of his magic troupe.

THE MAGIC OF HOUDINI (2014)

Alan Davies, comedian and star of BBC's hugely popular *Jonathan Creek*, presents this ITV documentary, traveling to various Houdini locations in Britain and the United States. He talks with, among others, Roger Dreyer, owner of the Houdini Museum of New York, magician David Copperfield, and Houdini biographer Ruth Brandon.

HARRY HOUDINI: MAGIC AMONG THE SPIRITS (2015)

This documentary, made by Tom Wyrsch, and originally titled *The Annual Harry Houdini Séances*, tells of how Houdini became involved with spiritualism, how he died and the arrangement with Bess to try to reach her from beyond the grave. It follows the development of the annual Houdini séances that were held every year on the anniversary of his death from 1964 until 2002.

HOUDINI IN GAMING

In *Houdini*—"the world's first 40-challenge escape game"—the player is encouraged to think like the great man himself. The game contains a small Houdini body and legs and small props to use to try to make escapes, including ropes, a lock, and rings.

PurelyGames have produced several Houdini online games. *Harry Houdini* recreates his world tour of 1924 but in the game, the Twins Blavatsky and their Seven Fold Soul are trying to kill the great escaper. In *The Temple of the Serpent*, you can help Harry escape from booby traps, scorpions and a lot more, while *Jail Escape* encourages you to use your wits to solve a series of clues that will enable you to escape from a prison cell.

If you really want to try your skills on a real lock, the Houdini Puzzle Lock Game gives you the opportunity. You have to find the trick to opening the lock and there are two different lock games for you to choose from.

Houdini-Opoly is a board game for 2-6 players. As you go around the board you learn about the life of the great magician. You can't escape the fun!

There are plenty more Houdini accessories that can be purchased for both children and adults. You can buy Houdini handcuffs to escape from, Houdini brainteasers, Houdini playing cards, and even a Houdini straitjacket for a few hundred dollars.

HOUDINI VIDEO AND COMPUTER GAMES

What must have been the very first Houdini video game was *Houdini Escape* by ALA Software, for use with the Commodore 64 which was one of the first computer gaming systems. Interestingly, the blurb on the back of the box references "Henry" Houdini.

There are several computer games that trade on the reputation of Harry Houdini. In the thrilling Hidden Object Puzzle Adventure game, *The Great Unknown: Houdini's Castle*, while you are enjoying your honeymoon your plane crashes on an uncharted island where your husband/wife is kidnapped by a madman. In order to save him/her, you have to pass sinister tests and solve the mysteries of Houdini's Castle. En route, you will uncover Houdini's secret past and learn all about the brilliant apprentice that saved his life.

In *Midnight Mysteries: Haunted Houdini* you are approached by the spirit of Bess Houdini who seeks to reunite with her famous partner. As you investigate Harry's life you uncover bitter rivalries such as the one he enjoyed with Sir Arthur Conan Doyle and his rival Thurston the Magician. You can solve puzzles and discover Houdini's secret connection with a secret society.

FURTHER READING

This biography of Harry Houdini is designed to be an informative and entertaining introductory text. There are many more academic publications available should the reader wish to delve more deeply. Publications that were especially useful during the preparation of this book are listed below, and contemporary newspaper and magazine articles are cited at the point where they appear within the text.

Bell, Don *The Man Who Killed Houdini*. Montreal, Véhicule Press, 2004.

Brandon, Ruth, *The Life and Many Deaths of Harry Houdini*. London, Pan Books, 1993.

Cannell, J.C., *The Secrets of Houdini*. London, Hutchinson & Co., 1931.

Christopher, Milbourne, *Mediums, Mystics and the Occult*. New York, Thomas Y. Crowell Co., 1975.

Culliton, Patrick, *Houdini Unlocked*. Two volume box set: *The Tao of Houdini* and *The Secret Confessions of Houdini*. Los Angeles, Kieran Press, 1997.

Culliton, Patrick, *Houdini: The Key*. Los Angeles, Kieran Press, 2010.

Ernst, Bernard M.L., *Houdini and Conan Doyle: The Story of a Strange Friendship*. New York, Albert & Charles Boni, Inc., 1932.

Fleischman, Sid, *Escape!: The Story of the Great Houdini*. New York, Collins, 2006.

Gibson, Walter B., *Houdini's Escapes and Magic*. Blue Ribbon Books, Inc., 1930 (also released in two separate volumes: *Houdini's Magic* and *Houdini's Escapes*).

Gibson, Walter B. & Young, Morris N., *Houdini's Fabulous Magic*. New York, Chilton, 1960.

Haldeman-Julius, Marcet, "An Interview with Harry Houdini." Girard, Kansas, *Haldeman-Julius Monthly* Vol. 2.5 October, 1925.

Hilgert, Ronald J., *Houdini Comes to America*. Appleton, WI, The Houdini Historical Center, 1996.

Houdini, Harry, *A Magician Among the Spirits*. Cambridge, Cambridge University Press, republished 2011.

Houdini, Harry, *The Right Way to Do Wrong: A Unique Selection of Writings by History's Greatest Escape Artist*. Brooklyn, Melville House, republished 2012.

Kalush, William and Sloman, Larry, *The Secret Life of Houdini: The Making of America's First Superhero*. New York, Simon & Schuster, 2006.

Magico Magazine "The Houdini Birth Research Committee's Report." Reprint of report by The Society of American Magicians (SAM), 1972.

Polidoro, Massimo, *Final Séance: The Strange Friendship Between Houdini and Conan Doyle*. New York, Prometheus Books, 2001.

Rapaport, Brooke Kamin, *Houdini: Art and Magic*. New York, Jewish Museum, 2010.

Rauscher, William V., *The Houdini Code Mystery: A Spirit Secret Solved*. Magic Words, 2000.

Rinn, Joseph F., *Sixty Years of Psychical Research*. New York, Truth Seeker Co., 1950.

Sandford, Christopher, *Houdini and Conan Doyle*. London, Duckworth, 2011.

Shatner, William & Tobias, Michael, *Believe*. New York, Berkeley Books, 1992.

Silverman, Kenneth, *Houdini!!!: The Career of Ehrich Weiss: American Self-Liberator, Europe's Eclipsing Sensation, World's Handcuff King and Prison Breaker*. London, Harper Collins, 1996.

Solomon, Matthew, *Disappearing Tricks: Silent Film, Houdini, and the New Magic of the Twentieth Century*. Chicago, University of Illinois Press, 2010.

Spraggett, Allen, with Rauscher, William V., *Arthur Ford: The Man Who Talked with the Dead*. New York, New American Library, 1973.

Weltman, Manny, *Houdini: Escape into Legend, The Early Years: 1862–1900*. Los Angeles, Finders Seekers Enterprises, 1993.

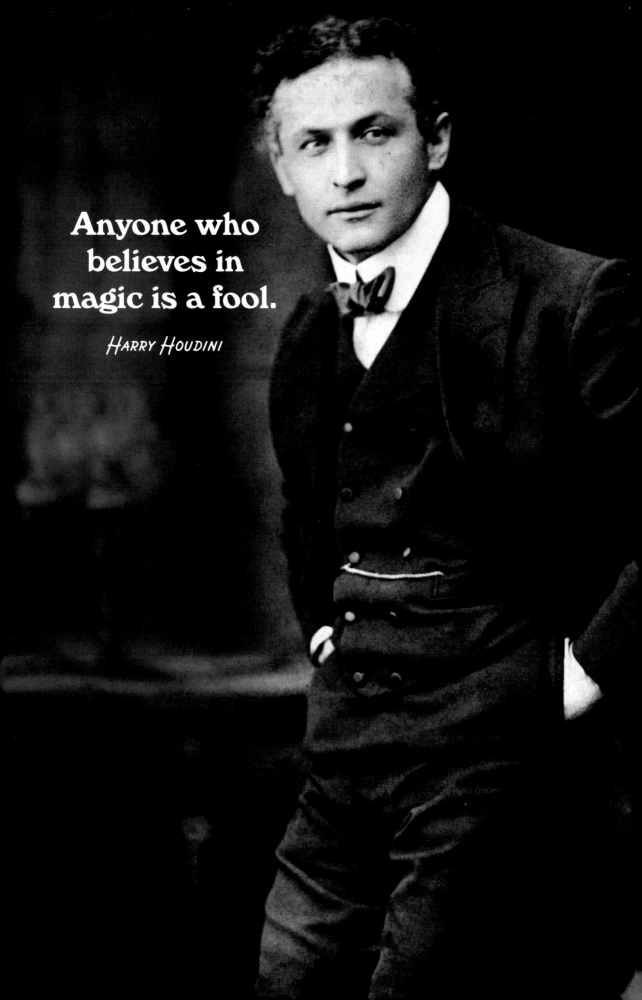

Anyone who
believes in
magic is a fool.

Harry Houdini

Harry Houdini lies on top of a plane's wing in a scene from *The Grim Game* (1919).

Index

Page numbers in italic denote an illustration

Inspiring | Educating | Creating | Entertaining

Brimming with creative inspiration, how-to projects, and useful information to enrich your everyday life, Quarto Knows is a favorite destination for those pursuing their interests and passions. Visit our site and dig deeper with our books into your area of interest: Quarto Creates, Quarto Cooks, Quarto Homes, Quarto Lives, Quarto Drives, Quarto Explores, Quarto Gifts, or Quarto Kids.

Picture Credits

Many of the images in this book are from the public archives of the Rare Book and Special Collections Division (RBSCD) of the Library of Congress, Washington D.C. (loc. gov). The publishers are also grateful to the Official Houdini website known as Wild About Harry (wildabouthoudini.com). The images listed below are all in the public domain unless otherwise stated.

Cover: Shutterstock / iStock / loc.gov / The Tatler / Everett Collection Historical / Sidney H. Radner Collection / Granger Historical Picture Archive / LaPine Studios, Seattle, WA / Lithograph 1895 The Print Collector / McManus-Young Collection / The Protected Art Archive / Alamy.

Part titles: Darkened Studio / Alamy.

Internal images: 1 Darkened Studio / 2 Sidney H. Radner Collection / 4 LaPine Studios, Seattle, WA, 1915 / 6 McManus-Young Collection / loc.gov / 7 Hear Houdini tour poster / Affiliated Bureaus 1920/ 8 Everett Collection Inc / Alamy / 11 RBSCD 1907 / loc.gov / 12 Appleton Public Library / 13 Harvard Theater Collection, Houghton Library, Harvard University / 15 the-magic-detective.com / travsd.wordpress.com / 16 Lithographie von Adolf Dauthage 1855 / 18 loc.gov 1890 / 19 The Print Collector / Alamy / 22 loc.gov 1895 / 23 Lithograph 1895 / The Print Collector / Alamy / 24 RBSCD 1907 / loc.gov / 26 Magic-at-the-contemporary-jewish-museum / 28 gypsy-rose-lee 1940 / 29 wild-about-houdini.com / 30 the-magic-detective.com / 31 The Tatler 1903 / Lordprice Collection / Alamy / 33 Strobridge Lithographing Co. 1894 / loc.gov / 35 original-daguerreotype / narrative.ly / 37 lithographic-poster 1895 / loc.gov / 38 Apic /Getty Images / 40 World History Archive / Alamy / 43 RBSCD 1900 / loc.gov / 44 wild-about-houdini.com / 46 The Protected Art Archive / Alamy / 47 Everett Collection Inc / Alamy / 49 anonymous-old-photograph-1911 / 51 The Old and the New Magic 1906 / Henry Ridgely Evans / 53 RBSCD 1905 / loc.gov / 54 El Ático De La Magia / ferranrizo / 57 Russell-Morgan Print / New York Public Library Digital Collection / 60 Studio Atelier J. Zier, Liepsig 1902 / 63 RBSCD 1900 / loc.gov / 65 Royal Collection RCIN Sergey Levitsky 1894 / 68 Ian Dagnall Computing / Alamy Stock Photo / 69 RBSCD 1903 / loc.gov / 70 Everett Collection Inc / Alamy / 72 The Tatler March 23,1904 / 73 London's Daily Illustrated Mirror 1904 / 74 RBSCD 1907 / loc.gov / 75 Theater Magazine Company, Nickolas Muray, July1928 / 77 natedsanders.com / 78 piperhoudini.com / 80 Everett Collection Inc / Alamy / 82 Granger Historical Picture Archive / Alamy / 83 The Strobridge Litho Co. Cincinnati, Howard K. Elcock 1914 / 85 lithographic-poster 1908 / 87 FPG / Getty Images / 89 Bettmann / Getty Images / 90 Ian Dagnall Computing / Alamy / 92 State Library of New South Wales 1910 / 97 RBSCD / loc.gov / 98 Granger Historical Picture Archive / Alamy / 101 RBSCD / loc.gov / 102 Everett Collection Historical / Alamy / 105 X3A / Alamy / 107 Everett Collection Historical / Alamy / 108 Fort Wayne Journal Gazette, Sept 3, 1914 / 110 McManus-Young Collection / loc.gov / 113 White House Photo 1913 / loc.gov / 114 Pittsburgh Sun, Nov. 6, 1916 / 117 Bain News Service 1915 / 118 Félix Nadar 1864 / 120 RBSCD / loc.gov / 121 James E. Purdy, Boston 1905 / 123 B.A. Rolfe Productions 1919 / 125 Paramount Pictures legendary collection of Charles A. Dyas / 127 Motion Picture Classic 1920 / 129 Paramount Artcraft Pictures Motion Picture News Mar-Jun 1920 / 130 Houdini Picture Corporation 1921 / 131 Houdini Picture Corporation / Getty Images Archive Photos / Stringer / 132 Granger Historical Picture Archive / Alamy / 135 Toronto Public Library / 137 Davenports 1870 / loc.gov / 138 RBSCD / loc.gov / 139 Granger Historical Picture Archive / Alamy / 140 The Marsden Archive / Alamy / 141 Albert von Schrenck-Notzing 1912 / 142 arthurcdoyle.files / 145 Chronicle / Alamy / 148 prairieghosts.com / 149 Chronicle / Alamy / 151 Chronicle / Alamy 152 New York Post Archives 1939 / Getty Images / 154 Mary Evans Picture Library / Alamy / 157 Everett Collection Historical / Alamy / 159 Fenham Publishing / Chicago Tribune / 163 Granger Historical Picture Archive / Alamy / 164 Library of Congress / Corbis / VCG via Getty Images / 168 Everett Collection Inc / Alamy / 169 New York Daily News Archive / Getty / 172 psychic-truth.info / 173 Everett Collection Historical / Alamy / 174 support.bl.uk / 177 Dynamite Entertainment / © Carlos Furuzono 2014 / 179 Everett Collection Inc. / Alamy / 181 AF archive / Alamy / 182 Fox Image Collection / Getty / 185 Ian Dagnall Computing / Alamy / 186 John Springer Collection / Corbis Historical / Getty